NEIGHBORHOOD SERVICES

NEIGHBORHOOD SERVICES

Making Big Cities Work

JOHN MUDD

YALE UNIVERSITY PRESS
New Haven and London

Published with assistance from
the Lewis Stern Memorial Fund.

Designed by Christopher Harris
and set in Times Roman type
by The Saybrook Press, Old Saybrook, Connecticut.
Printed in the United States of America by
BookCrafters, Inc., Chelsea, Michigan.

Library of Congress Cataloging in Publication Data

Mudd, John, 1939–
  Neighborhood Services

  Includes index.
  1. Neighborhood government—New York (N.Y.)
  2. Decentralization in government—New York (N.Y.)
  3. New York (N.Y.)—Politics and government—1951–
  4. Municipal services—New York (N.Y.) 1. Title.
  JS1228.M83   1984   352′.000473′097471   84-20975
  ISBN 0-300-02657-9 (alk. paper)

The paper in this book meets the guidelines for permanence
and durability of the Committee on Production Guidelines
for Book Longevity of the Council on Library Resources.

10 9 8 7 6 5 4 3 2 1

To LUCIA, PETER, WILLIE, and ANNA

CONTENTS

PREFACE   ix
PROLOGUE   xiii
1. INTRODUCTION TO THE "RAT PROBLEM"   1
    Reorganization and Organizational Process   2
    Coordination and Responsiveness   6
    Why the Problems? Some Causes and Consequences   13
2. CITY GOVERNMENT IN THE COMMUNITY:
        STRATEGIES OF THE PAST   23
    Strengthening Central Management   26
    Citizen Participation   32
    Multiservice Centers and Colocation   52
    Mayoral Outreach Programs: Neighborhood City Halls and
        Urban Action Task Forces   57
3. PLANNING THE NEW PROGRAM   65
    The Shift to Administrative Decentralization   65
    What Decentralized Administration Means   70
    The Politics of Planning to Decentralize   92
4. THE DISTRICT MANAGER CABINETS   102
    The Cabinets Meet   102
    Common Coordination Projects   108
    Community Projects: Flexibility and Responsiveness   120
    ONG: The Central Role in Decentralization   143
    Institutionalizing District Manager Cabinets   150
5. THE IMPACT OF DISTRICT CABINETS   157
    Lessons of the Experiment   158
    The Coordination Problem   166
    Decentralized Management   177
    Neighborhood Responsiveness   184

6. EPILOGUE   190
    Land Use   193
    Geographic Budgeting   197
    Coterminality and Management Decentralization   203
    Service Planning and Coordination   209
    Options for the Future   214
    The Prospects for Decentralized Management   219
INDEX   223

PREFACE

This book examines why and how New York City developed a new administrative system of district manager cabinets to improve the coordination and responsiveness of public services in the city's neighborhoods. The initial model was designed during Mayor John Lindsay's second administration in the early 1970s. Combined with an expanded system of community advisory boards, the district managers and cabinets were incorporated into the city charter in 1975. Together they form the basis of a unique strategy for strengthening the institutions of city government in the local communities of a big city.

The New York experience illustrates how the organization of government affects the operation of government. It reveals the structured sources of the many day-to-day, nitty-gritty problems that aggravate and frustrate citizens, civil servants, and elected officials alike. Moreover, a case study of the district manager cabinets is relevant not only to New York and other big cities. The problems of coordinating the operations of specialized public agencies in geographic communities are common to federal, state, and large county governments as well. The issue of coordination has been pushed aside in recent years by debates over domestic budget cuts and the new New Federalism. But throughout this period, the underlying structure of specialized public programs has been preserved essentially intact, and the problems of coordination among them remain. This study attempts to capture the lessons from one major organizational reform so that we can learn from them before our next round of efforts to improve coordination.

The district manager cabinet system attracted a great deal of attention by independent researchers during its early years. This assessment, however, is presented not only by a participant but by one who bore responsibility for a good part of the design and implementation of the original demonstration project. From 1970 to 1974, I served as deputy and then director of the mayor's Office of Neighborhood Government (ONG), which planned and managed the new program. This can enrich the insights, but the tension between prior advocacy and current objectivity is present for both the reader and the writer.

In such a venture, one accumulates more debts than it is possible to acknowledge. Perhaps too easy to forget is the obvious fact that none of this experience would have been possible without support for the initial project from John Lindsay and others in his administration. Special gratitude goes to Lew Feldstein, the first director of ONG, a colleague and friend whose verve has been an inspiration and whose advice has been thoughtful through the years. To the district managers and ONG central staff and to the many extraordinary civil servants who worked on the cabinets, my admiration and thanks. Many consented to be interviewed and quoted in this book. A fellowship at the Woodrow Wilson International Center for Scholars in the State and Local Government Program enabled me to start writing the first sections of the study, and a grant from the Kettering Foundation helped extend my stay at the center. Jeffrey Mayer, administrator of the program, showed enormous patience and skill in going through multiple drafts of materials and provided extremely helpful substantive and editorial advice. Many others read and commented on the work at various stages: Manuel Carballo, Herbert Kaufman, and James Q. Wilson all shared their thoughts; James Fesler not only took the time to give detailed comments but, more important to a writer in process, he communicated understanding, encouragement, and support for the endeavor, even though he had no personal stake in it. Others in this long enterprise have given different kinds of help. Marian Wright Edelman at the Children's Defense Fund let me use space for reflection and writing. David Grossman and Bruce Gombos at The Nova Institute provided not only a desk but also their perceptions based on many years of work with New York City agencies and communities. For generous efforts to give me some feeling for writing clear English, my thanks to Bill Herman. And finally, there is my family—my mother and father, who taught me the value of committed intellectual and social action, and my wife and children, who through too many years have borne the brunt of my struggle to complete this book with quiet confidence and remarkable resilience. I dedicate it to them.

PROLOGUE

■ Next to a playground in the Bronx, trash blows around the street for days where, following standard operating procedure, the parks maintenance crew left it to be picked up by the Sanitation Department. The local parks foreman has never met or talked with the sanitation superintendent who works in the same district.

■ A civic leader in southern Queens phones the local police precinct asking that barricades be placed around a gaping hole in a nearby vacant lot where children play. She is told it is a Highways Department problem. The community relations officer there says the danger is the Board of Education's responsibility, since a school used to occupy the site. The Board of Education reports that a new school has been built several blocks away and the land has reverted to the Department of Real Estate. Real Estate checks and finds that the demolition contractor for the old school was responsible for closing a sewer drain at the bottom of the hole, the contract for the job ran out six months ago, and the department does not have the equipment to deal with it.

■ A three-year-old in Brooklyn is discovered to have lead poisoning. She is kept in a hospital for six months at a cost of $125 per day (in 1972), because the Housing Department's Emergency Repair Program has not completed de-leading a wall of the family's apartment (a $500 job) as authorized by the Health Department.

■ A Traffic Department engineer in central Brooklyn gets a call about cars blocking the streets around a storefront drug program that he had never been informed would open.

■ The volunteer chairman of the local community advisory board in Queens protests that neither schools nor sewers will be available when a public housing project is completed and that no preparations have been made to handle the additional garbage, traffic flow, and recreation needs of the new residents.

■ A Neighborhood Police Team sector commander is continually harangued by local homeowners in a small area of the north Bronx. They complain that the Sanitation Department's street sweepers always drive down the middle of the road without touching the mess in the gutters, because commuters from outside the city jam their block with parked cars every morning before catching the subway. The sergeant diligently files a report, which goes through police supervisory channels over to the Sanitation Department, where the problem is referred back down the chain of command to the district superintendent in the community. He in turn requests a ban on parking in the area between 8 A.M. and 9 A.M., when his mechanical street sweeper cleans adjacent blocks that have parking meters. The recommendation goes back up through the sanitation hierarchy and is duly forwarded to the Traffic Department. Traffic sends out an investigator who turns down the suggestion because the department has never approved such a ban on a nonmetered street.

■ The assistant general parks manager responsible for maintaining recreation facilities throughout the eastern third of the Bronx complains that "they" have built a skating rink he cannot freeze and a swimming pool he cannot drain. The "they" in this case are the planners and contract officers in the central office of his own department. The sixty-four-step administrative process required to complete park construction does not provide for consultation about the design of a new project with the maintenance officers on the spot.

■ Exhausted after participating in four consecutive evening meetings of the police precinct council, the antipoverty corporation board, the comprehensive health planning committee, and the community board, a civic leader in central Brooklyn throws up her hands in exasperation. She has just learned that the Highways Department is going to repave a street in her neighborhood unnecessarily. At the same time, the Traffic Department refuses to install the stoplight that her homeowners' association has been requesting for over a year because of "insufficient funds."

■ An apartment building newly renovated with a Housing Department subsidy rapidly deteriorates as a number of large welfare families with drug and alcohol problems move in. The Departments of Housing and Social Services have no system for providing counseling and other professional support for concentrations of welfare recipients in rehabilitated buildings.

Life in the big city—citizens being shuffled and bureaucrats passing each other in the dark. These examples all come from New York, but they could easily be found in any other large urban area across the country.

1
INTRODUCTION
TO THE "RAT PROBLEM"

Those who have their eyes on the stars are likely to trip over the cracks in the sidewalks. I for one, would be satisfied with getting the cracks in the sidewalks fixed.

—*Paul Haney, City Councilman*[1]

In 1972, New York City initiated an experiment with district manager cabinets designed to improve the coordination and responsiveness of municipal service delivery in urban neighborhoods. These cabinets were composed of the local field officers from fifteen major operating agencies (the police precinct commander, the sanitation district superintendent, the general parks foreman, the district health officer, and so forth) who worked under the direction of a district manager appointed by the mayor. The strategy was designed and overseen by the mayor's newly formed Office of Neighborhood Government (ONG).[2]

Like many cities, New York had implemented a variety of other organizational reforms during the previous two decades. It had strengthened executive management (superagencies, PPBS bud-

---

1. Paul Haney, "Comment and Dissent," in a report of the Greater Rochester Intergovernmental Panel, *Two-Tiered Government in Monroe County, New York* (Washington, D.C.: National Academy of Public Administration, June 1975), p. 17.

2. The original plan appears in John V. Lindsay, *Program for the Decentralized Administration of Municipal Services in New York City* (New York: Office of the Mayor, December 1971).

geting systems, productivity programs); increased citizen participation (community action and model cities programs, neighborhood advisory councils, community school boards); colocated several programs in a single physical facility (multiservice centers); and created mayoral complaint centers (neighborhood city halls, urban action task forces).

The district manager cabinets shared with many of these approaches the premise that there were institutionalized gaps in the existing service delivery system that did not simply call for new programs but required changes in the organizational structure of the system itself. On the one hand, gaps existed among the increasingly specialized but interrelated administrative agencies *(the coordination problem)*, and on the other, between the actions of these agencies and the preferences of those served *(the responsiveness problem)*. The district manager cabinet approach differed from the other reforms in its strategic focus on decentralizing the internal administrative structure and the operations of existing city bureaucracies responsible for delivering safety, sanitation, social, health, housing, and other services in order to begin to solve these problems.

Reorganization and Organizational Process

The organization of government administration institutionalizes certain capabilities, values, and interests—and deinstitutionalizes others. It affects which policies are formulated and how they are implemented. That "organization matters" in such a wide range of issues—from the viability of democratic institutions to the use of chemical warfare in Vietnam, from the treatment of a young drug addict in Massachusetts to the repair of a leaky fire hydrant causing potholes in New York City—makes the study of reorganization important.[3]

3. The quotation is from Graham Allison and Peter Szanton, *Remaking Foreign Policy* (New York: Basic Books, 1976), p. 14. See also Herbert Kaufman, "Administrative Decentralization and Political Power," *Public Administration Review* 29 (January–February 1969); *The Children's Puzzle* (Boston: Institute for Governmental Studies, University of Massachusetts, February 1977); and Sidney Jones (district manager in Bushwick, New York City), in an interview with the author on 14 January 1975.

Over the past few decades there has been a great deal of energy devoted, and diverted, to structural innovation throughout the federal system. Surveys have identified more than four thousand substate districts spawned under a score of national programs. There have been five new federal departments and analogous "superagencies" in many states and local governments, multistate regional commissions, city-county mergers and other metropolitan reforms, a proliferation of new systems for citizen or community participation, and block grant program consolidations.[4]

CONFLICTING THEORIES

Many of these reforms were intended in part to improve the coordination and responsiveness of public services. But despite, or perhaps because of, this variety, profoundly conflicting theories and recommendations about the need, direction, and impact of organizational change continue to exist. To some, reorganization should simplify and consolidate similar administrative functions under central direction and perfect hierarchic bureaucracy.[5] Others argue for the benefits of duplication, bureaucratic competition, overlappng jurisdictions, and fragmentation of authority.[6] Some assert that coordination requires central direction and the creation of intermediary institutions from the top to the bottom of the federal system.[7]

4. Many of these developments are traced and described by the Advisory Commission on Intergovernmental Relations in *Substate Regionalism and the Federal System,* vol. 1: *Regional Decision Making* (Washington, D.C.: U.S. Government Printing Office, October 1973), and *Improving Federal Grants Management* (Washington, D.C.: U.S. Government Printing Office, February 1977).

5. Luther Gulick, "Notes on the Theory of Organization," *Papers on the Science of Administration,* ed. Luther Gulick and L. Urwick (New York: Institute of Public Administration, 1937); for a more recent example, see Jack Knott and Aaron Wildavsky, "Jimmy Carter's Theory of Governing," *The Wilson Quarterly* 1 (Winter 1977).

6. See Martin Landau, "Redundancy, Rationality, and the Problem of Duplication and Overlap," *Public Administration Review* 29 (July–August 1969); William A. Niskanen, *Bureaucracy: Servant or Master?* (London: Institute of Economic Affairs, 1973); and Vincent Ostrom, *The Intellectual Crisis in American Public Administration* (University, Ala.: University of Alabama Press, 1973).

7. James L. Sundquist, *Making Federalism Work* (Washington, D.C.: Brookings Institution, 1969).

Others believe that the problems of coordination can generally be resolved through voluntary negotiation, bargaining, and mutual adjustment among the affected specialized units.[8] Systems of coordination have been viewed as a crucial impetus for promoting institutional reform; conversely, they have been criticized as fundamentally conservative, tending to reaffirm the existing bureaucratic environment.[9] Critics warn the many who invest energy and expectations in structural reform that the significant problems of coordination are not susceptible to organizational solutions but rather derive from a lack of consensus on policy that is itself rooted in the unresolved political conflicts of our pluralistic society.[10]

Among the many reasons for the absence of consensus on government organization, or reorganization, theory are the general lack of reliable evidence, the difficulty of comparing the evidence that does exist, and a pervasive and almost perverse inattention to the existing organization of the bureaucracies whose activities the reforms are designed to change. Most surprising is this widespread failure to give sufficient attention to organizational process—the internal structures, routines, and repertoires of established bureaucracies—in analyzing and designing government reorganization.[11] The vast preponderance of public resources will continue to be filtered through existing administrative units, whether they be local police departments or federal cabinet departments. Policies will be formulated in and will be implemented, distorted, or frustrated by these institutions. Yet it is precisely with respect to the inner workings of these agencies—the bureaus in the bureaucracy, the systems of field administration, the environment of the street-level civil servant—that analysis and understanding are least adequate. This is all the

8. Charles E. Lindblom, *The Intelligence of Democracy* (New York: Free Press, 1965).

9. For the former position, see Peter Marris and Martin Rein, *Dilemmas of Social Reform* (New York: Atherton Press, 1967); for the latter, see Roland L. Warren, Stephen M. Rose, and Ann F. Bergunder, *The Structure of Urban Reform* (Lexington, Mass.: D. C. Heath, 1974).

10. Martha Derthick, *Between State and Nation* (Washington, D.C.: Brookings Institution, 1974).

11. See the "organizational process paradigm" in Graham Allison, *Essence of Decision* (Boston: Little, Brown, 1971), pp. 78–96.

more remarkable in that the importance of these factors is neither a new nor a mysterious idea. Political scientists have written about the islands of institutional power in cities, the bureaucratic cultures that color the styles of public employees, and the traditional "iron-triangle" alliance between the permanent bureaucracy, legislative committees, and special interest groups.[12] Against this richness of perception, many a reorganization plan or theory seems thin indeed.

Two new but very different circumstances provoke us to expand our understanding of the potential impact of government organization. First, public administration orthodoxy—grouping agencies by major purposes, the absence of overlap and duplication, a clear chain of command, limited span of control—offers little guidance in facing the organizational issues inherent in dealing with complex social needs, which require horizontal rather than hierarchical concepts of management.[13] Practical application of past dogma has tended to assume away the problems of coordination across major program units.[14] Yet many of the most pressing political concerns (like community economic development, neighborhood preservation, or strengthening the family) almost inevitably require coordination among large, functionally specialized agencies.[15] There is at present no consensus on alternatives to traditional administrative principles that could give direction to current action. In this limbo, an attempt to provide concrete evidence about the strengths and weaknesses of different strategies, at least in one big city, could be instructive.

Second, the traditional forum for articulating needs and adapting general policies to the particular concerns of citizens in their

12. See Wallace Sayre and Herbert Kaufman, *Governing New York City* (reprint, New York: Norton, 1965); James Q. Wilson, *Varieties of Police Behavior* (Cambridge: Harvard University Press, 1968); Michael Lipsky, *Street-Level Bureaucracy* (New York: Russell Sage Foundation, 1980); and Hugh Heclo, *A Government of Strangers* (Washington, D.C.: Brookings Institution, 1977).

13. Harold Seidman, *Politics, Position, and Power,* 2d ed. (New York: Oxford University Press, 1975), p. 311.

14. See the description of Governor Rockefeller's reorganization of the New York State administration in Basil J. F. Mott, *Anatomy of a Coordinating Council* (Pittsburgh: University of Pittsburgh Press, 1968), pp. 145–47.

15. See Charles L. Schultze, *The Politics and Economics of Public Spending* (Washington, D.C.: Brookings Institution, 1968), pp. 130–32.

communities—the political party—continues to decline in its ability to perform these roles effectively.[16] Again, there is no clear alternative to replace or supplement it. Where great blocks of voters are political independents or new participants from disadvantaged minorities, where one of the largest groups of activists in public affairs is the "communalists," who are deeply involved in the civic concerns of their communities but not in partisan politics, what institutional systems can provide citizens with effective access to and legitimate influence over the actions of government?[17] Because New York implemented a variety of plans for increasing citizen participation, its experience may be instructive on this score as well.

Americans entered the last period of great expansion in the role of government during the 1960s with relatively great faith in their "political competence" to influence elected representatives but much less confidence in their position as "subjects" to be treated responsively by the agencies of government. Indeed it is precisely in this arena of "administrative competence" (or administrative democracy) that many problems increasingly lie.[18]

Coordination and Responsiveness

Certainly there are many complaints about the lack of coordination and the unresponsiveness of government. But these terms are so loose that it is not clear whether the critics are talking about the same thing (in any technical sense), or that what they refer to is really a problem of coordination or responsiveness and not some other issue, like unclear or conflicting policies, inadequate resources, or uncertain knowledge about how to solve the matter at

16. Norman H. Nie, Sidney Verba, and John R. Petrocik, *The Changing American Voter* (Cambridge: Harvard University Press, 1976), p. 356.

17. For a profile and description of communalists see Sidney Verba and Norman H. Nie, *Participation in America* (New York: Harper and Row, 1972), pp. 76–80. In their analysis, communalists compose 20 percent of the population; the rest are political "campaigners" (20 percent), "voting specialists" (21 percent), "parochial participants" (4 percent), "inactives" (22 percent), and "complete activists" (11 percent).

18. Gabriel A. Almond and Sidney Verba, *The Civic Culture* (Princeton, N.J.: Princeton University Press, 1963), p. 218.

hand. Is government unresponsive if it does not put a cop on every beat? Or make people feel safe on the streets at night? Or provide bilingual education? Is government uncoordinated if freedom of movement for welfare clients leads to neighborhood protests and blockbusting in an area rehabilitated with public funds?

It is difficult to define coordination and responsiveness precisely, and even more difficult to measure what they mean in practice. But in a situation where analysts differ so profoundly—where it is possible for some to identify the need for institutional coordination as a central problem while others call for increased fragmentation and overlap in government—it is important to try. This section attempts to clarify what is meant by coordination and responsiveness of services in urban neighborhoods and to marshal the often indirect evidence that suggests whether these concepts identify real problems or merely reflect a lot of confused and irrelevant debate.

COORDINATION

Coordination in public administration tends to be an insider's concern. It implies both a process and a goal. As an objective, coordination means that the actions of two or more agents of government are consistent and mutually reinforcing, without unintended conflict or duplication.[19] Deficiencies in achieving this harmonious state of affairs can occur vertically, between different layers of government, or horizontally, within or among separate agencies at the same level. Coordination can involve planning sequential steps over time, or simultaneous operations, or both.[20] Its targets can be defined by socioeconomic group (the poor, minorities), problem (alcoholism, vandalism), function (primary health care, housing rehabilitation), objective (building strong families, economic development), or any other "natural" grouping that seems appropriate.[21] This study focuses on interagency coordination in geographic communities. However, it should be recognized that some

19. With some modification, this definition essentially follows the one suggested in Sundquist, *Making Federalism Work,* p. 18.
20. See Martin Rein, *Social Policy* (New York: Random House, 1970), p. 106.
21. See *Integration of Human Services in HEW,* publication no. SRS 73−02012 (Washington, D.C.: Department of Health, Education, and Welfare, 1973), p. 13. The study was prepared for HEW by Marshall Kaplan, Gans, and Kahn, and The Research Group, Inc.

competition among these different concerns is inevitable. Giving special weight to any single consideration, such as area, in coordinating services may conflict with the requirements for improving coordination from other vantage points, such as social grouping or functional programs.

Even with these conceptual refinements, the costs and benefits of coordination are difficult to measure. Attaching numbers to deficiencies in "mutually reinforcing action" is not easy, although surely something is amiss when a child abuse agency attempts to reduce the number of cases referred to the courts while the police are increasing such referrals.[22] Perhaps for this reason, evidence about the extent and nature of the coordination problem is long on illustrative example and short on systematic data. In Boston, members of the Mayor's Office categorize the frustration of trying to obtain joint action by separate agencies on even the simplest, most immediate service issue as "the rat problem." If a rat is found in an apartment, it is a housing inspection responsibility; if it runs into a restaurant, the health department has jurisdiction; if it goes outside and dies in an alley, public works takes over.[23] More complex undertakings compound the confusion.[24]

In human services, the lack of coordination can be particularly inefficient and burdensome. A high proportion of health and welfare clients have multiple problems (pregnant teenage dropouts, for example) that require varied, simultaneous, and sequential attention. Analysts have placed this figure at more than 85 percent.[25] Yet studies estimate the odds that an individual in need will get to a single service as only four in ten, and the likelihood of a successful referral to a second agency as one in five at best.[26] Thus, apart from

22. Rein, *Social Policy*, p. 48.

23. Interview with the director and staff, Office of Public Service, 6 February 1975.

24. The classic study of the difficulty in mounting a federally sponsored economic development and minority employment program is found in Jeffrey L. Pressman and Aaron B. Wildavsky, *Implementation* (Berkeley and Los Angeles: University of California Press, 1973).

25. Sheila B. Kamerman and Alfred J. Kahn, *Social Services in the United States* (Philadelphia: Temple University Press, 1976), p. 441.

26. A summary of these studies, on Lancaster (Pennsylvania), Los Angeles, Boston, and Macon County (Illinois), is found in "Interim Report of the FY 1973

any questions about the quality of services provided, only a tiny fraction of the recipients in the multibillion-dollar social welfare system even come in contact with the appropriate agencies, despite the evidence that attempting to deal with their problems in isolation has little positive long-term impact. Should a given client or family manage to reach the many separate agencies, their queries would very likely loose a flock of outreach, intake, treatment, and follow-up caseworkers and counselors, often performing similar functions but without any connection to each other. Perhaps such duplication and competition can be effective; usually it is ineffective and confusing.[27]

One of the only attempts to determine the extent of the need for coordination among a wide range of agencies in the neighborhoods of a big city was carried out in connection with the district manager cabinet experiment in New York.[28] Over one hundred district officers from twelve departments operating in ten different communities were interviewed. Virtually all said that they shared operating responsibilities and needed assistance from at least one other agency; most needed cooperation from at least five others. They reported "intense interdependence" (many areas of overlapping responsibility) with only one or two other agencies, but most stated that cooperation from different departments "had a substantial effect on the total performance of their own office."[29]

Services Integration R&D Task Force," (Department of Health, Education, and Welfare, Washington, D.C., Mimeographed), p. 3.

27. See the description of fourteen caseworkers counseling one family in Richard Severo, "The System Fails, and an Abused Child Dies," *New York Times* 6 September 1977, p. 37.

28. This research was sponsored by the Bureau of Applied Social Research at Columbia University under a grant from the National Science Foundation.

29. John M. Boyle, "Local Operating Officials' Responses to the Experiment: Service Integration, Agency-Community Relations, and Overall Attitudes," in Allen H. Barton et al., *Decentralizing City Government* (Lexington, Mass.: D. C. Heath, 1977), pp. 155–56. By the same author also see "Reorganization Reconsidered: An Empirical Approach to the Departmentalization Problem," *Public Administration Review* 39 (September–October 1979): 458–65. If anything, this research sample probably understates the perception of interdependence because it excluded ten of the fifteen regular participants in the cabinets, including some of the more active representatives from Parks, Recreation, Highways, Water Resources, Traffic, and City Planning.

Assuming that local officers perceive the need for coordination, do they act on their perceptions, and is the existing institutional environment adequate to promote the desired cooperation? From their statements, the answer to both questions would be no. A former welfare center director in South Brooklyn reported:

I've been in this district with the department for about five or six years. . . .I did know the police captain because of mutual business whenever we had sit-ins or something. But I never knew anybody else. I knew vaguely that they must exist somewhere, but if there was any question with sanitation or any other agency, we just had no channel [of communication].[30]

The channels which were supposed to exist often turned out to be triplicate forms that more often than not led to the circular file or some other dead end. A general parks foreman in charge of maintaining recreation facilities for an area with almost two hundred thousand residents in the north Bronx commented: "As a front-line supervisor, you never met the others. It was either by phone or letter—very impersonal. And you couldn't get your problems through." For example, to get cooperation from the police in dealing with kids destroying property, "we used vandalism reports and these were easy to ignore."[31] Of all city agencies, the police are likely to have the most extensive daily contact with the public and are frequently approached with requests for information and services beyond their immediate safety responsibilities. Yet except on certain common and urgent issues like broken traffic lights, there is little joint effort to transfer problems to the agencies that have the formal responsibility, if not always the resources, for solving them. A police precinct commander in central Brooklyn offered this explanation: "Individually men are in competition for salaries, position, and everything else . . . [and] that individual competition continues right into the agencies. So generally they aren't looking to do anything to assist us, and neither are we looking at anything particular to assist them."[32]

30. Glen Barrett, interview,15 January 1975.
31. Frank Roseti, interview, 17 January 1975.
32. Adam Butcher, interview, 15 January 1975.

Most of this evidence of a coordination problem is random and subjective. But the information gathered from New York does demonstrate one rarely recognized fact. The front-line field officers, the bureaucrats who are often made scapegoats for failures in city services, are caught in a situation where they recognize their interdependence with others but find it difficult to communicate, sort out responsibilities, or develop mutually supportive operations with their peers in other agencies or with neighborhood leaders.[33] Complaints by local "generalist" officials—the elected mayors and legislators or their top managers—about their inability to control and coordinate the "specialists" nominally under their command have been much more widely reported.[34]

RESPONSIVENESS

The issue of responsiveness raises questions that touch the fundamental values of democratic society—who can, and does, bring effective influence to bear over public institutions in our system of representative government? Responsiveness in subdistricts of big cities is defined here to mean that the actions of government corresponds with the preferences of the public and community leaders on matters of local concern—within the legal, technological, and resource constraints of the larger political system. This definition intentionally rules out the major issues of policy and equity in the distribution of public resources, which must be resolved at higher political levels, and of performance, where our knowledge about how to perform is inadequate. It directs attention to a lower level series of issues. Most obvious are the mundane questions about which parks are maintained, which local streets are repaired, how available recreation or police patrol resources are used, how often refuse in residential or commercial areas is picked up, whether existing health and social services should give more attention to teenagers or to the elderly, and so forth. The distinctions between

---

33. This conclusion is supported by additional interviews with field officers gathered in New York and reported in Douglas Yates, *Neighborhood Democracy* (Lexington, Mass.: D. C. Heath, 1973), pp. 132–33.

34. See Study Committee on Policy Management Assistance, *Strengthening Public Management in the Intergovernmental System* (Washington, D.C.: U.S. Government Printing Office, 1975).

local issues and those that extend beyond the neighborhood to affect other communities or the policies of higher authorities are not always easy or clear. What if changing neighborhood police patrols may displace crime to surrounding areas? Establishing a public housing project is usually a matter of city (or state, federal, judicial) policy; however, the local consequences of its design, location, impact on other neighborhood services, and so on, are matters that the community should be able to influence. Further questions about responsiveness arise in this context: how much weight are neighborhoods given within the urban political system, and is the administrative structure of government able to deal coherently with these geographic subdistricts? The little data that is available does not directly answer these questions, but it suggests that on none of these aspects of neighborhood responsiveness do big city service delivery systems score well.

That citizens think city government in New York does a terrible job in dealing with their problems is not surprising. In a poll conducted before the financial crisis of the mid-1970s, only 8 percent of the residents gave the city administration a favorable rating, while an overwhelming 89 percent ranked it only fair or poor.[35] But their feeling that the municipal administration gave even less attention to their general "neighborhood problems" than to providing police protection is surprising, given the widespread worry about safety in the streets.[36] As might be expected, people in different subdistricts of the city have different priorities for improving services.[37] But although New Yorkers on the whole had a relatively low estimate of their ability to affect government action, they felt they had more chance to influence citywide policy than to change service delivery

35. The Gallup Organization, *Attitudes of New Yorkers about Reorganizing Their City Government* (New York: State Study Commission for New York City, June 1972), p. 1. Opinions were gathered from a citywide sample of 709 respondents in late spring 1972.

36. Ibid., pp. 2—3.

37. Although differences in priority by neighborhood are widely assumed, they have rarely been demonstrated. Data that substantiate the assumption for New York are reported in Theresa F. Rogers and Nathalie S. Friedman, "The Quality of Big-City Life in 1972," in Barton et al., *Decentralizing City Government,* pp. 199 and 231.

patterns in their own neighborhoods. Only one in five people even knew about a place in the community that could help resolve their problems with government agencies.[38] Of those who had contacted a central or local city department about their most important problems (about one-third of the total), more than two-thirds were dissatisfied with the way they were handled.[39] Why should this happen? Why should the service delivery system that has evolved in big cities like New York appear confusing, hidden, distant, and unresponsive to individuals in urban neighborhoods?

Why the Problems? Some Causes and Consequences

Three interrelated trends have had a pervasive impact on the coordination and responsiveness of service delivery in urban neighborhoods: programmatic specialization in an expanding range of government services, centralization of executive authority, and the rise of new institutional forces that undercut the territorial political party without replacing its capacity to articulate local needs or adapt general policies to particular concerns. Many of these developments reflect success in implementing key parts of the municipal reform agenda for rooting out the corruption of clubhouse politicians. But the reforms have often had unintended consequences. Reinforced by other national trends, they have produced a system of functional centralization in fragmented administrative units.[40]

38. Ibid., pp. 207–08, 193.

39. Nathalie S.Friedman and Theresa F. Rogers, "Decentralization and the Public," in ibid., p. 225.

40. Among the many analyses of the nature and extent of the municipal reform movement in American cities that have informed this discussion (although their authors would not necessarily agree with my conclusions), see the overview by Edward C. Banfield and James Q. Wilson, *City Politics* (Cambridge: Harvard University Press and MIT Press, 1963), pp. 138–50. The impact of the movement in New York is summarized in Sayre and Kaufman, *Governing New York City,* pp. 725–36. Two analyses in the context of recent political developments are Norman I. Fainstein and Susan S. Fainstein, *Urban Political Movements* (Englewood Cliffs, N.J.: Prentice-Hall, 1974), pp. 14–30; and Robert K. Yin and Douglas Yates, *Street-Level Governments* (Santa Monica, Calif.: Rand Corporation, October 1974), pp. 1–20.

PROGRAM SPECIALIZATION

Program specialization in the administration of services brings with it the significant benefits of expertise and professionalism. It can also create problems. All too often, the solution to the "rat problem" has been the creation of a new "Bureau of Rat Control."[41] This focuses attention and resources on the immediate issue, but it may also have costs. A former district health officer in New York described some of the negative consequences in reflecting on his work in Central Harlem and Washington Heights:

> You've got to have bureaucracy that formalizes and standardizes. But as this bureaucracy grows and technology grows, one becomes very functional and compartmentalized, so that individual technical skills become the basis on which a bureau or an agency develops. These become the functioning subunits. However, as it is in the seventies, the functioning subunit becomes in itself too narrow, and you have overspecialization. If you have overspecialization, you can only respond to a small piece of the problem. And the problems that exist among people, the problems that exist within communities, and the problems that exist within the city, very, very rarely can be compartmentalized into one narrow area.[42]

Compartmentalization tends to diminish awareness of individuals and families with multiple problems by segmenting their needs into isolated "minor" health, housing, or social service complaints. Not only does the public have a difficult time finding its way through the specialized maze, but "nowhere throughout the whole administrative hierarchy of fifty to sixty line agencies in the city government—from the commissioners' level all the way down through the deputy commissioners, the regional directors, and out to the district representatives in the field—is there any point of

---

41. And once established, such bureaus rarely fade away, although they may be shuffled to new locations within the bureaucracy. See Herbert Kaufman, *Are Government Organizations Immortal?* (Washington, D.C.: Brookings Institution, 1976).

42. This and the quotes in the next paragraph are taken from an interview with Anthony Mustalish, 17 January 1975.

[interagency] communication, any point of ongoing program development or policy center . . . except what may occur within the Mayor's Office."

CENTRALIZATION OF EXECUTIVE AUTHORITY

A strong chief executive—a mayor in big cities and a city council and city manager in middle-sized urban areas—was the reformers' counterweight intended to provide policy control and administrative direction to the separate, specialized bureaucracies. In range of operational responsibilities and authority to appoint and dismiss top officials, concentration of power in the chief executive has gone further in New York than in most other big cities. The mayor formally controls not only the usual core departments of city government, including police, fire, sanitation, highways, traffic, housing, parks, and recreation, but many of the health and welfare services that would be county or state functions elsewhere. In addition, he directs an elaborate staff in the budget bureau, city planning department, law department, and his own office.[43]

While the mayor has increased his authority, the function of other elected officials like the borough presidents and city councilpersons has weakened. What this means is that the mayor—the elected representative farthest from daily, direct exposure to people in their communities—is the one official who has both the incentive to develop a citywide constituency among voters in their neighborhoods and formal authority over the multiple agencies which deliver city services.

INSTITUTIONAL CONSTRAINTS

To develop and implement coherent policies for subcity neighborhoods, it is necessary to know their needs and to coordinate the operations of administrative agencies within their boundaries. The traditional territorial political party, at some periods and for some groups, was able to fulfill these functions of articulation and control. With the decline of the party organization, the mayor faces a

43. Independent agencies with a special purpose have continued to play a dominant role in education, ports and airports, mass transit, public housing, and the municipal hospital system.

formidable array of institutional constraints that inhibit his capacity to translate formal power into effective action to improve coordination and responsiveness of city services in urban neighborhoods. Among the many obstacles are hierarchic distance, the civil service merit system, municipal unions, the media, and increasing intergovernmental dependence.

Hierarchic distance. The fact that the mayor is at the top and people in their communities are at the bottom (or vice versa) means there are a number of political and administrative layers between them, through which accurate communication is unlikely. The odds greatly favor ignorance and distortion of information. Elected officials are to some extent in competition with the mayor for votes and are likely to color their presentations accordingly. Bureaucrats at the middle levels, at least those who want to survive without risk, are likely to minimize or hide news, especially bad news, about their own operations. Given these circumstances, it would be reasonable to assume that the mayor knows consistently little about the needs of neighborhoods or the local impact of city service delivery. When John Lindsay became mayor of New York and faced his first volatile racial confrontation in an east Brooklyn community, he found that "communication did not exist—that we were reacting to events instead of anticipating them, and that it was only *after* trouble broke out that we became aware of what we did not know."[44]

Civil service merit system. Many constraints imposed by civil service regulations and unionization have been valuable in overcoming past abuses of power and improving the rights of workers; many have also complicated the process of increasing the coordination and responsiveness of neighborhood service delivery. In practice, the merit system not only prevents extensive political meddling with city employees but also inhibits rewarding personnel for successful management or for following the new policies of elected leaders. Salaries and promotions are predominantly based on seniority or scores on written exams, rather than performance on the job as judged by recipients, political superiors, or civil servant

44. John V. Lindsay, *The City* (New York: Norton, 1969), p. 100.

supervisors.[45] In addition, the civil service system reinforces an introverted specialization within the established bureaucracies, rather than a broader view of interrelationships among agencies. Most of the core city service departments (police, fire, sanitation, highways, parks) have "base entry" systems in which everyone, including the chief of staff, starts at the bottom and works up through the ranks. Job advancement and many intangible rewards or penalties are derived almost exclusively from a closed bureaucratic culture. "Lateral entry" of outsiders into middle- or upper-level management and transfers from one department to another are unknown if not impossible. This breeds a narrow, hierarchical orientation. As one early analyst of functional specialization wrote of the middle-level bureaucrat: "With his eyes so strongly developed for looking upward and downward, the muscles that would turn his eyes to the right and to the left tend to atrophy."[46] Problems that require wider vision inevitably suffer. The incentives for cooperation outside the closed "village" culture of each bureaucracy are minimal.[47]

More serious, the incentives for field officers to manage service delivery even within their own agencies are negligible. Middle-level managers are usually treated as "compulsory intermediaries" of questionable competence who are resistant to change—and that is what many of them become and remain, not necessarily through any fault of their own.[48] An irony of American public administration is that field supervisors are often promoted from within the specialized bureaucracies on the theory that their intimate knowledge of professional service needs will make them more effective administrators than outsiders, yet they are rarely given the authority or training to manage. Higher-ups hoard what little authority the system leaves them and expend it on inappropriately detailed deci-

45. For a heavily critical assessment, see E. S. Savas and Sigmund G. Ginsberg, "The Civil Service: A Meritless System?" *Public Interest* 32 (Summer 1973).

46. James W. Fesler, *Area and Administration* (University, Ala.: University of Alabama Press, 1949), p. 14.

47. The village analogy for the civil service bureaucracy is developed in Heclo, *A Government of Strangers*, pp. 111-12.

48. The quoted phrase is taken from Michel Crozier, *The Stalled Society* (New York: Viking, 1973), p. 170.

sions.[49] Too often, field administration becomes a matter of processing paperwork—not managing resources or being held accountable for performance. As one study of the New York system reported: "There is no point at which a worker who becomes a manager changes his perspective. . . . Managing to survive takes precedence over managing for productivity."[50]

Municipal unions. The growth of public employees' unions has significantly reinforced the shift of power away from geographic neighborhoods to large, functional interests and the central institutions of local government. The public unions realize that they operate essentially in a political rather than an economic marketplace. As one local leader stated: "We have a natural that no other union has. We can elect our employers."[51] Many unions are extremely active politically. The leader of New York's uniformed sanitation workers quietly made sure the mayor's staff saw that the files holding the thousands of address cards for current and retired members were organized not on the basis of work location but by election district and assembly district, the basic political units of the city. Politicians don't ignore this potential resource, particularly in light of the declining influence of the neighborhood clubhouse; as a former New York Democratic party county leader confessed, "I would today rather have John DeLury's sanitation men with me in an election that half the party headquarters in town."[52]

The *quid pro quo* required to secure employees' support may involve the usual bread-and-butter issues of increasing or preserving employment, wage rates, and fringe benefits. But the dynamics of collective bargaining have other important consequences for service delivery in cities. Because of their enormous impact on the budget, union negotiations are highly centralized, often in an office

49. This ethos is described for the Boston bureaucracy in Eric A. Nordlinger, *Decentralizing the City* (Cambridge: MIT Press, 1972), pp. 93–130.
50. *Improving Productivity in Municipal Agencies: A Labor-Management Approach* (New York: New York Productivity Council, October 1975), p. 23.
51. Quoted in Jack Stieber, *Public Employee Unionism* (Washington, D.C.: Brookings Institution, 1973), p. 199.
52. Edward N. Costikyan, *Behind Closed Doors* (New York: Harcourt, Brace and World, Harvest Books, 1966), p. 354.

of labor relations under the mayor, with the affected agency administrators frequently playing only a peripheral role. The line between the rights of management to set program policy and the rights of organized employees to bargain over working conditions has been blurred, and unions have forcefully stepped into questions of assignment, scheduling, staffing, technology innovation, and administrative reorganization. High-level management authority is further weakened because many field supervisors—police captains, sanitation superintendents, or parks foremen—have their own "officers'" unions or even belong to the same bargaining unit as the men they direct.[53] The clout of unions may affect not only larger political issues like the introduction of a civilian review board for the police or the decentralization of public schools, but more immediate operational questions, such as whether a building inspector can be assigned to a local storefront, whether a parks foreman can personally drive maintenance laborers to different facilities, or what functions a community social service worker will perform. Decisions on many service delivery matters important to individuals or neighborhood leaders are in this way pushed upward to the highest level of city government to be resolved in negotiation between representatives of the specialized bureaucracies and political officials who may depend more heavily on the unions than on the local party or other community organizations for election.

The media and the decline of the territorial political party. If the civil service and the municipal unions did not knock out the neighborhood clubhouse, the media dealt it a major blow. While television particularly helps undercut the local party organization by presenting candidates and incumbents, at least in the more visible citywide offices, with a powerful new means of gaining independent access to voters, it can implicitly dictate just as powerful terms of dependence.[54] As a primary method of communication between political

53. In addition to the study by Stieber noted above, see the other volumes published by The Brookings Institution in that series: Harry H. Wellington and Ralph K. Winter, Jr., *The Unions and the Cities* (1971), and David T. Stanley, *Managing Local Government under Union Pressure* (1972).

54. See David L. Rosenbloom, "The Press and the Local Candidates," in *The Role of the Mass Media in American Politics*, ed. L. John Martin, *The Annals* 427 (September 1976).

representatives and voters, the organizational and technological pressures of the media can strongly influence what mayors and their constituents know about each other and consider important—and this rarely concerns the mundane complexities of service delivery in neighborhoods. A bitter comment often heard among the City Hall staff during the Lindsay years in New York was that it took a riot or a natural catastrophe to get a television crew out of downtown Manhattan. Community residents would find out what were deemed to be significant events in their city on the six o'clock or eleven o'clock news, which more often than not would turn out to include the latest controversy at City Hall. These same reports would frequently set the next day's agenda for the mayor and his staff as well.

With this centralized orientation, the citywide media tends to downplay and divert attention from particular community concerns and local civic activity.[55] New York has a relatively extensive neighborhood press which can compensate for this centralizing influence of the media to some degree. But the sixty or so weeklies, each with an average circulation of approximately twelve thousand, cannot compete for the mayor's or the public's eyes with the citywide press and daily televised news in establishing a frame of reference for government action.[56]

Under the combined pressures of the civil service, public unions, and the media (along with the New Deal, ethnic assimilation, and the growth of the middle class), parties and party organizations have not disappeared in New York, but their prominence in neighborhoods has been vastly reduced, although it varies from county to county and district to district. Difficulties in recruiting workers, limitations on day-to-day service to constituents, and frustrations in affecting larger political bodies are great. In general, local party organizations have not maintained the vitality, acceptance, or power to function adequately as a citywide system for gathering informa-

55. Data from a national study of the declining rates of "communal activity" due to the influence of "external media" are found in Verba and Nie, *Participation in America*, p. 245.

56. For a listing of neighborhood papers with estimated circulation figures, see "Community Newspapers" (New York: City Hall Neighborhood Press Office, April 1971).

tion about neighborhood needs and translating this into action through the institutions of government.[57]

Intergovernmental dependence. State and local governments have been among the fastest growing sectors of the national economy over the past decades, in terms of both overall expenditures and employment. Much of the structure and direction for this expansion was set by the federal government through the marked increase in specialized federal programs during the days of President Johnson's Great Society. By 1973, when New York was trying to coordinate neighborhood services, it was estimated that there were approximately 550 national "main-line grants-in-aid" in an overall total of 1,200 separate programs administered by 61 federal departments, commissions, independent agencies, and councils.[58] This specialization at the federal level led to a comparable introduction of new bureaucratic units to sponsor and administer projects in the states and cities. State aid to localities was also frequently tied to specific purposes. Municipalities became increasingly dependent on this funding from higher levels of government, which on the average by the early 1970s had come to account for almost one-third of their revenues.[59] The spate of programs created in the 1960s and 1970s brought new resources and opportunities to bear on issues that had too often been avoided or neglected. They also brought a new complexity that compounded the control and coordination problems of local elected representatives. One study found these offi-

57. For example, see the descriptions of activity in a "reform" clubhouse by a former Manhattan district and county leader in Costikyan, *Behind Closed Doors,* pp. 85–93 and 289–93. The "regular" Democratic organization is able to maintain a stronger hold on some of the less visible, local council or borough candidates and has a virtual monopoly on deals to select judges. See Jack Newfield and Paul DuBrul, *The Abuse of Power* (New York: Viking, 1977), pp. 199–230.

58. William H. Kolberg, "The New Federalism: Regional Councils and Program Coordination Efforts," in *The Administration of the New Federalism,* ed. Leigh E. Grosenick (Washington, D.C.: American Society for Public Administration, September 1973), p. 51.

59. Advisory Commission on Intergovernmental Relations, *Federal-State-Local Finances: Significant Features of Fiscal Federalism* (Washington, D.C.: U.S. Government Printing Office, February 1974), p. 19.

cials "at a loss to understand the maze of program operations within their jurisdictions for which they are, none-the-less, politically accountable."[60] Program specialists, grantsmen, and special interest groups could at least penetrate their own narrow corridors of the maze. However, city mayors, legislators, and neighborhood leaders frequently felt their influence diminish as they were increasingly required to validate the decisions of the functional experts allied at each level of government.

Within big cities, the consequences of these multiple trends were far-reaching. Many of the former virtues of the institutions and values of the reformers now appeared to be defects. The civil service system and unionization protected public employees not only from the vagaries of political whim but from the need to respond to new direction. Bureaucratic efficiency came to mean red tape. Objectivity in administration led to inflexibility. Professionalism brought the benefits of expert knowledge but also a disregard for clients' judgment—a situation exacerbated in central cities by the increasing racial differences between the providers and the recipients of services. Programmatic specialization focused attention on parochial fragments of problems, rather than their interrelatedness. Centralization in the name of public good produced insensitivity to the particular needs of individuals or local communities. Too often "good government" created unresponsive administration.

Functional specialization and its undermining of geographic cohesion has for some time been noted as an emphasis and problem unique to American bureaucracy.[61] The explanation of one federal official reflected a growing concern: "We have no organizational philosophy, only a program philosophy."[62] It was increasingly in the organization, and reorganization, of government that solutions were sought.

60. Study Committee on Policy Management Assistance, *Strengthening Public Management in the Intergovernmental System*, p. viii.

61. See Michael Crozier, *The Bureaucractic Phenomenon* (Chicago: University of Chicago Press, Phoenix Books, 1964), pp. 232–36, and Robert A. Dahl and Charles E. Lindblom, *Politics, Economics, and Welfare* (New York: Harper and Row, Harper Torchbooks, 1963), p. 269.

62. Quoted in Sundquist, *Making Federalism Work*, p. 13.

2
CITY GOVERNMENT IN THE COMMUNITY: STRATEGIES OF THE PAST

A Tale of Two Burnouts

Early 1900s in New York, Boss George W. Plunkitt speaking:

What tells in holdin' your grip on your district is to go right down among the poor families and help them in the different ways they need help. I've got a regular system for this. If there's a fire in Ninth, Tenth, or Eleventh Avenue, for example, any hour of the day or night, I'm usually there with some of my election district captains as soon as the fire engines. If a family is burned out, I don't ask whether they are Republicans or Democrats, and I don't refer them to the Charity Organization Society, which would investigate their case a month or two and decide they were worthy of help about the time they are dead from starvation. I just get quarters for them, buy clothes for them if their clothes were burned up, and fix them up till they get things runnin' again. It's philanthropy, but it's good politics too—mighty good politics.[1]

Early 1970s, the "Standard Operating Procedures" of the reformed system:

For a family caught in a burnout, the Fire Department's battalion chief at the scene issues a written "notification of possible need

1. William L. Riordan, *Plunkitt of Tammany Hall* (New York: E. P. Dutton, 1963), pp. 27–28.

for temporary or permanent shelter for persons due to fire" for the occupants (and for families in adjacent water- or smoke-damaged rooms, when this is brought to his attention) and calls his dispatcher who in turn informs the central Emergency Desk at the Department of Relocation, which reports the case to their personnel in the nearest hotel or shelter that the agency uses for such cases—*if* the fire is between 9 A.M. and 5 P.M., Monday through Friday. If not, the fire dispatcher notifies the Red Cross, which places the family overnight and refers the case to relocation officials in the morning—*assuming* the family is living in a private dwelling. If the house or apartment is owned by a public agency like the New York City Housing Authority, the Department of Real Estate, or Urban Renewal, the Department of Relocation has no jurisdiction. In these cases, the Department of Social Services is responsible, *if* the family is already on public assistance or qualifies for special emergency aid. After the family is housed, it must make an appointment at the nearest Income Maintenance (Welfare) Center for an interview to apply for a "disaster relief grant" covering clothes, food, and lost furniture; arrange for children to go to schools in a new area, since the shelters are usually not in the same community; and begin to look for an apartment with the assistance of housing staff in the Departments of Relocation or Social Services.

In 1971, over thirteen hundred families were found living in squalid "welfare hotels" as a result of burnouts, evictions, and relocation due to public construction projects. The mayor established a special Hotel Task Force. To make the reformed system function, a permanent Office of Special Housing Services was created in the Human Resources Administration to help people wend their way through the maze of specialized bureaucracies.[2]

In the 1960s many new and very different organizational strategies were developed to improve the coordination and responsive-

---

2. See Diana R. Gordon, "A Hotel Is Not a Home," *City Limits*, ch. 7 (New York: Charter House, 1973), pp. 255–94. The burnout procedures for the 1970s were pieced together from telephone interviews with Robert Jorgen, Director, Office of Special Housing Services, Human Resources Administration, and Martin Press, Director, Emergency Housing Division, Department of Relocation, 27 October 1976.

ness of public services in local communities. Yet, ironically, it appears on close analysis that none of these approaches gave sufficient attention to the internal organization and reorganization of field administration in the existing service bureaucracies of city government. This failure to affect the ongoing operations of the traditional agencies in any significant way accounts for many of the problems and limitations of these reforms. It explains why planners in New York eventually turned to a new strategy of decentralized administration that led to the district manager cabinet model. But to understand the distinctive character of the new approach, it is important to understand the alternatives that had already been attempted. More than most other cities, New York tested a variety of techniques for improving services during this period. These can be grouped under four broad categories:

strengthening central management, which included the creation of "superagencies," the introduction of planning-programming-budgeting (PPB) systems, and the development of productivity programs;

citizen participation, including the federally-sponsored Community Action Programs (CAPs) and Model Cities program, neighborhood advisory councils, and the movement to achieve community control in the schools;

colocation of city service agencies in multiservice centers; and

mayoral outreach programs, including both neighborhood city halls and urban action task forces.[3]

3. In addition, New York created one of the first and largest community development corporations (CDCs) in the country. This approach is not included among the strategies discussed because the CDCs, in New York as elsewhere, focused more narrowly on economic and physical development rather than on the public service delivery system generally. See Kilvert Dun Gifford, "Neighborhood Development Corporations: The Bedford Stuyvesant Experiment," in *Agenda for a City: Issues Confronting New York,* ed. Lyle C. Fitch and Annamarie Hauck Walsh (Beverly Hills, Calif.: Sage Publications, 1970), and Robert K. Yin and Douglass Yates, *Street-Level Governments* (Santa Monica, Calif.: Rand Corporation, 1974), pp. 174–90.

The one major strategy New York did *not* develop was a computer-based information and referral system, a technique that became popular in some other areas, especially in the social service field.

Strengthening Central Management

In New York, as well as in many other cities and states, the central management strategy was reflected in efforts to consolidate the proliferation of separate service departments into larger but fewer "superagencies," the insertion of PPB systems, and the design of productivity programs. These approaches all shared an assumption that more rational *central* organization and planning would produce improvements in *local* service delivery. They consciously increased the weight of mayors or managers in contrast to specialized agencies, legislators, or neighborhood institutions. But precisely how stronger central administration would be channeled through the established bureaucratic system to have an impact on citizens and communities was rarely spelled out or analyzed. The implicit faith that this implementation process would be automatic and effective often proved unwarranted. In promoting the coordination and responsiveness of services in urban neighborhoods, these central reforms frequently had minimal or at best ambiguous success.

SUPERAGENCIES

Although the New York City Charter revision of 1963 placed all the major city service agencies under the mayor, it did little to reduce their number or rationalize their responsibilities. Over fifty separate departments and numerous commissions reported directly to City Hall. One of Mayor Lindsay's first innovations after taking office in 1965, was to consolidate some of this administrative morass into a few superagencies that theoretically could be managed more coherently and efficiently. His Task Force on Reorganization quoted a former commissioner describing health services in the city as a "many-splintered thing" that "takes its toll in human inconvenience and suffering as well as in municipal funds."[4] The familiar litany of fragmented responsibility was documented in almost every functional area. Three different departments paved the streets, four agencies operated slum rehabilitation projects, and over thirty programs scattered throughout the government provided job training

4. The Mayor's Task Force on Reorganization of New York City Government, *Report and Proposed Local Law* (New York: Institute of Public Administration, December 1966), p. 30.

and placement. Each new problem had been met with a new bureaucracy, and the residue was an apparently unmanageable melange that undercut political direction and wasted resources. The task force recommended that "the functions now performed by almost all the line departments be regrouped into ten line agencies, called 'administrations.' "[5]

In approving this approach, the mayor attempted to create at the municipal level a set of agencies analogous to federal cabinet departments. For example, the Human Resources Administration grew from a core in the old Welfare Department to assimilate a wide range of other social services including the Youth Services Agency, the Agency for Child Development, the Manpower and Career Development Agency, and the Community Development Agency (the city's administrative arm for the OEO-funded poverty program). Similarly, the Environmental Protection Administration (EPA) brought together the formerly separate units responsible for sanitation and water and air resources. Comparable consolidations were carried out in the fields of health, parks and recreation, housing, transportation, finance, and municipal services.

But consolidation into superagencies did not directly affect the field organization or operations of the component departments. Each of the former agencies maintained its separate, preexisting systems for delivering services to citizens and communities. Departmental commissioners within the same superagency were pressed into some structured communication with each other, if only to resolve competing demands for their joint administrator's support on budget and personnel questions. But at the local level, the district officers continued to work in their own segmented and isolated bureaucratic worlds. Mechanical street sweepers from the Sanitation Department were often hindered by flooding due to clogged catch basins or storm sewers. Catch basin cleaning was the responsibility of the Department of Water Resources, another component of the Environmental Protection Administration. But sanitation district superintendents in the field had no formal communication system with their counterparts in other departments of the same superagency. As local city officials, often their only re-

5. Ibid., p. 1.

course was to telephone the citywide citizen complaint number at EPA, just like any other member of the public—and then wait, along with idled drivers and equipment, to see if this produced any action. Such situations, ludicrous to an outsider, were apparent in most of the new superagencies. Parks recreation officers had only tenuous relations with parks maintenance personnel. A district health officer would not be consulted about decisions on mental health programs in his area. Youth services, manpower training, and welfare officials did not discuss plans for the same clients in the same neighborhoods.

If intra-agency cooperation even within the same superagency was difficult, inter-agency coordination among departments in different superagencies was almost nonexistent. The worlds of the functional bureaucracies were so self-contained and insulated that only rarely would a sanitation officer speak directly with a police commander or a district health official, except perhaps during a riot or some other crisis. In fact, many departments had standard operating procedures that insured that horizontal communications with other agencies would be processed "through [vertical] channels." If a local officer in one department wanted a change in operations from the field manager of another department in the same community, he was forced to take an elaborately circuitous bureaucratic path—the "up-over-and-down" route. He was to direct his initial request to his immediate supervisor, usually at the borough level, who would report it to the central staff, who would refer it to the commissioner's office, where someone would contact a counterpart in the second commissioner's office. After appropriate consultations down the second agency's chain of command, sometimes including discussions with its field personnel in the community, a policy decision would be made and dutifully transferred through the ranks in both agencies from the central offices to the boroughs, and finally out to the districts. Even day-to-day operational decisions could drain the time and attention of high-level staff if interagency action was required. A sanitation officer's request for minor changes in street parking regulations would literally trace this tortuous path. This was not only time-consuming, but so cumbersome that it usually didn't work. Most district officers gave up even before starting. The police didn't use their forms for reporting potholes or broken fire hydrants, a sanitation superintendent would not think of recommending street repairs even though he might not be able to get his equipment through an area, and a health officer would hardly be presumptuous enough to suggest changes in local housing inspection operations, even though they might directly affect the welfare of his patients.

In practice, it was extremely difficult to implement the central consolidation, much less the operational field integration, implicit in the superagency strategy. The persistence of separate bureaucratic organizations underneath the superstructure sharply limited the new units' potential for improving mayoral control or increasing the responsiveness of government to citizens in their neighborhoods. Consolidating and strengthening the administrative management of central agencies might improve the coordination of citywide policy-making, but it had little effect on the coordination of municipal service field operations in the communities. The flow of information and action between the bottom and the top of the system continued to be structured by relatively narrow functional hierarchies. The superagency itself had no organizational existence in the field. There was no district superintendent of environmental protection, no district director of human resources, and no comparable officials capable of asserting an agencywide presence at the local level in any of the new institutions. For a citizen or civic leader in the neighborhood, where reorganization did not integrate the already diffuse range of contacts with government, the superagencies might simply mean another, more distant layer of central bureaucracy to work through in order to get action.

Two organizational lessons are evident for this experience. First, superagencies that are consolidated on paper are frequently little more than an institutional façade for the old bureaucratic systems. And second, these central administrative reforms do not automatically change the way services are delivered unless they are accompanied by a reorganization of field operations in the communities where citizens live.[6]

6. Such field reorganization is rarely attempted. Florida did consolidate sixteen separate agencies into a Department of Health and Rehabilitation Services with eleven new geographic service areas covering the state. See the report of a panel of the National Academy of Public Administration, *Reorganization in Florida* (Washington, D.C.: National Academy of Public Administration, 1977); and Sheldon P. Gans and Gerald T. Horton, *Integration of Human Services: The State and Municipal Levels* (New York: Praeger, 1975).

CENTRAL STAFF ANALYSIS AND PRODUCTIVITY PROGRAMS
Many of the other common techniques for strengthening executive management tend to focus on improving staff analysis rather than changing operational administrative organization. Plans are elaborated, budget categories are regrouped, management objectives are listed, and productivity goals are specified. But more often than not, performance targets are projected for, and implementation occurs through, unchanged bureaucratic organizations. These strategies share with the superagency approach a faith in establishing central controls over public agencies, but they are generally distinguished by their emphasis on numerical measures (dollars, "inputs," "outputs") as a technique to improve service performance. Although PPB systems or productivity programs could in theory specify *neighborhood* service delivery as an analytic objective, in practice in New York City they did not. For example, subcity or district budgets might have been powerful tools for the mayor and local civic leaders, but they were never developed during this period.[7] Instead, these approaches concentrated on citywide (functional agency or special project) goals, and, from the perspective of a citizen in a community, their impact could be two-edged. This is most clearly illustrated by the way the productivity program was implemented in the city.

"Productivity" was used to describe a variety of benefits in New York: the reduction of unit cost where service output was easily measurable (increasing tons of garbage collected per truck); changes in the deployment of personnel to match the work force with the work load (shifting police patrols to high crime hours); improvements in processing procedures (speeding medical reimbursements); and the introduction of new technology ("slippery water" in fire fighting).[8] The strategy paid important dividends in increasing the citywide resources available for operations in the neighborhoods. The definition of measurable objectives gave management new leverage in negotiating with public employees' unions. In one

---

7. There has been a serious effort in recent years to develop the components of a "geographic budgeting" system for local communities in New York. See Chapter 6.

8. Edward K. Hamilton, "Productivity: The New York City Approach," *Public Administration Review* 32 (November–December 1972): 787.

case, new work standards for mechanics led to a reduction in the "down-time" rate for sanitation trucks from 38 to 11 percent, which meant that more than four hundred additional vehicles would be on the streets every day.[9]

However, productivity standards sometimes inhibited or reduced the flexibility of field managers in deciding how their resources would be used in subcity communities. For example, there were cases in which community organizations urged the cleaning and development of vacant lots that had become visible sources of neighborhood deterioration. However, the highways foremen in the field were reluctant to consider using their asphalt allocations to pave the empty land because only work on the streets was counted as fulfilling their service production targets. A second example illustrates other potential problems with productivity programs. The new central Bureau of Industrial Engineering in the Sanitation Department applied sophisticated operations analysis in designing more productive street sweeping patterns throughout the city. When the plan was introduced in Washington Heights in northern Manhattan, however, it quickly became apparent that although the routes might have optimized the use of men and equipment, they also required that a community of orthodox Jews violate a strict religious prohibition by moving their cars on Saturdays. Local sanitation field officers said they had not been sufficiently consulted in devising the proposal, and the new system had to be readjusted immediately.

In theory, these deficiencies could have been corrected. Practically, in the rush to specify hundreds of separate citywide productivity measures, the program decreased the operational flexibility and initiative of field managers. Since targets were narrowly defined in terms of specific functions, it also discouraged interagency cooperation. A later review of the productivity effort by a joint city and union council found that the tendency to concentrate on technology and measurement-counting had restricted the impact of the approach. It recommended a shift of emphasis to decentralized administration and underlined the need "to stress organiza-

9. Ibid., p. 789.

tional (management) changes, and employee motivation" in future productivity programs.[10]

As with the superagency strategy, the consequences of citywide productivity reforms for neighborhood service delivery were neither automatic nor unambiguous. In both approaches, stengthening the central institutions of city government created a capacity for improvements in decentralized field operations, but this positive potential was frequently not realized. And the possible inadequacies, diversions, or negative effects of these central reforms were often unrecognized. Implemented without complementary organizational changes, neither superagencies nor other central management strategies effectively resolved the problems of subcity service coordination and responsiveness. However, there was one major, positive, indirect effect. The introduction of superagencies, PPBS, and productivity programs in New York allowed the mayor to insert hundreds of planners, analysts, and politically accountable administrators into the governmental system of the city. They were more flexible, commited to reform, and responsive to new direction than the traditional bureaucrats. Their presence provided the mayor with a source of leverage over the older departments that would prove extremely important in pressing new policies for improving neighborhood service delivery against bureaucratic inertia or resistance.

Citizen Participation

Citizen participation in big-city neighborhoods is a strategy of political decentralization. It involves broadening the distribution of influence through nontraditional forms of representation to include people in smaller geographic areas or specific beneficiary groups in the planning and operation of government programs.[11] Such a

10. *Improving Productivity in Municipal Agencies* (New York: New York City Productivity Council, October 1975), p. 10.

11. For definitions of political participation and decentralization, see and compare Alan A. Altshuler, *Community Control* (Indianapolis: Pegasus, 1970), p. 64; and Annamarie H. Walsh, "What Price Decentralization in New York," *City Almanac* 7 (June 1972): 7.

transfer of rights and powers can take a variety of forms, from a simple requirement for local hearings to a grant of full governmental control. It implies, at a minimum, creating ground rules that establish a new basis for *negotiation* between citizens in their communities and the public agencies that affect them.[12] In the big-city service delivery system, the participatory strategy was frequently perceived as asserting the wishes of minority and poor citizens and neighborhoods exclusively. It often threatened elected legislators, confronted mayors, and challenged both the professional values and the institutional existence of the specialized bureaucracies.

In the years following the initial federal CAP mandate for "maximum feasible participation" in 1964, the approach developed in many directions, both nationally and locally. On the one hand, federal policy rapidly weakened its requirements for citizen participation and reintroduced legal provisions insuring that ultimate control over public programs would lie with mayors and legislators— as in the case of Model Cities. Simultaneously, though, some form of nontraditional public involvement became a seemingly obligatory part of almost every domestic grant program. No complete catalogue of specialized federal requirements exists, but even partial listings reveal hundreds of different statutes and regulations governing participation in a score of agencies.[13] By the early 1970s 65 percent of all cities and counties with populations over twenty-five thousand reported the presence of some (usually weak) advisory committee system for specific services.[14] On a more ideological plane, the "power-to-the-people" logic of the participatory strategy led to a number of proposals for full-scale neighborhood

12. See Michel Crozier, *The Stalled Society* (New York: The Viking Press, 1973), pp. 73–74.

13. See *Citizen Participation* (Washington, D.C.: Community Services Administration, 1978), and Advisory Commission on Intergovernmental Relations, *Citizen Participation in the American Federal System* (Washington, D.C.: U.S. Government Printing Office, 1980). For an attempt to sort out the multiple participatory policies just in the Department of Health, Education, and Welfare, see *Ties that bind . . .* (Seattle, Wash.: U.S. Department of Health, Education, and Welfare, Region X, 1976), pp. 48–52.

14. Advisory Commission on Intergovernmental Relations, *The New Grass Roots Government?* (Washington, D.C.: U.S. Government Printing Office, 1972), pp. 9–10.

government or community control.[15] In practice, this degree of political decentralization was seriously tested in only five or so big cities, and there solely for the school system.[16] Increasingly common, however, were local initiatives to establish formal neighborhood advisory councils, which have been developed in more than thirty cities and counties.[17]

New York City had extensive experience with all the major participatory strategies—Community Action and Model Cities programs, school decentralization, and neighborhood advisory boards. They all encouraged attention to a smaller scale of government operation but differed in their scope, changes in political power, and organizational impact. Both Community Action and Model Cities explicitly attempted to improve the coordination and responsiveness of all public programs in urban neighborhoods. They varied in the tactical balance of authority among citizen representatives, chief executives, and existing agencies. In contrast, school decentralization focused on a single bureaucracy. More than any of the other participatory approaches, it offered insight into the premise that the assertion of power by program beneficiaries would improve the responsiveness of services—but it avoided the coordination issue. The purposes of neighborhood councils in improving service delivery were broad, but their powers were weak. They tested the assumption that communicating citizen concerns to government more effectively would increase the responsiveness of bureaucratic action.

While the citizen participation strategy concentrated on building

15. See Milton Kotler, *Neighborhood Government* (Indianapolis: Bobbs-Merrill, 1969); The Committee for Economic Development, *Reshaping Government in Metropolitan Areas* (New York: Committee for Economic Development, February 1970); Altshuler, *Community Control;* Joseph F. Zimmerman, *The Federated City: Community Control in Large Cities* (New York: St. Martin's Press, 1972); Edward N. Costikyan and Maxwell Lehman, *Re-Structuring the Government of New York City* (New York: State Study Commission for New York City, 1972); and Howard Hallman, *Neighborhood Government in a Metropolitan Setting* (Beverly Hills, Calif.: Sage Publications, 1974).

16. See George R. La Noue and Bruce L. R. Smith, *The Politics of School Decentralization* (Lexington, Mass.: D. C. Heath, 1973).

17. For the most complete description of these efforts, see Howard Hallman, *The Organization and Operation of Neighborhood Councils* (New York: Praeger, 1977).

community organizations to shift political power and improve communication between neighborhoods (or program beneficiaries) and public bureaucracies, it neglected a parallel restructuring of the organizational environment for the professional specialists in the established administrative agencies. Often as the participatory strategy played itself out in practice, more attention was devoted to organizing communities to express their needs than to reorganizing the administrative bureaucracies so that government could respond to these newly voiced concerns. Political decentralization took place alongside continued administrative centralization—an organizational formula that frequently produced conflict, frustration, and disillusionment on all sides. One community leader said: "They're killing us with participation. What we need is for someone in government to pay attention to us."[18]

Yet despite frequent frustration and conflict, the persistence of the citizen participation strategy in its many forms reveals the public's pervasive and continuing concern about fundamental strains in its relationship to government. The traditional institutions of representative democracy no longer seem adequate for their essential tasks of articulating community needs or controlling bureaucratic actions. With the expanding scope and intensity of government activities, the gap between the "sweeping" decisions of elected officials and the "intimate" impact of administrative agencies on people's lives has increased.[19] The vote may be the most powerful democratic technique for holding leaders accountable and making them responsive, but it is a "blunt instrument" that communicates little specific information about people's preferences or problems.[20] To articulate public concerns and adapt general policies to concrete circumstances, the institutional infrastructure of urban neighborhoods needs to be strengthened. This implies both more developed *civic* and *administrative* organizations in the com-

18. Testimony at the Ward Three Public Hearing, Task Force on Advisory Neighborhood Councils, Chevy Chase Community Center, Washington, D.C., 21 April 1975.

19. Herbert Kaufman, "Administrative Decentralization and Political Power," *Public Administration Review* 39 (January–February 1969): 5.

20. Sidney Verba and Norman H. Nie, *Participation in America* (New York: Harper and Row, 1972), p. 326.

munity. Historically, underdevelopment on all fronts—in voting, communal activity, and governmental administrative capacity— appears greatest in poor, minority areas. But the gaps between citizens and government are systemic and affect all races and economic groups in big cities. Citizen participation strategies did develop new neighborhood institutions. But neither the Community Action and Model Cities programs nor the neighborhood advisory councils adequately resolved the problems of service coordination and responsiveness in urban communities.

COMMUNITY ACTION IN URBAN NEIGHBORHOODS

The Community Action Program, sponsored by the Office of Economic Opportunity, introduced new organizations into the institutional environment of city government. They were designed to empower residents of poor neighborhoods to negotiate with established political officials and administrative bureaucracies so that together they could comprehensively improve the subcity service delivery system. By the late 1960s, over a thousand new Community Action Agencies (CAAs) had been created throughout the country. Generally, leadership of the local entities was gradually vested in a political troika with roughly equal representation by the poor, public officials, and private civic groups. In practice, the participatory aspects of the CAP strategy stressed the development of new community-based organizations. The service delivery strategy emphasized program innovation and coordination.

Under Mayor Lindsay, the Community Action Program in New York was implemented through an elaborate structure that eventually included a central Council Against Poverty and twenty-six local community corporations, each with its own elected board of directors covering a designated poverty area of the city.[21] In total, the system included almost one-half of the city's neighborhoods and spent about $40 million annually on its directly funded operations.

Despite their federal mandate to act as the preeminent coordinators of all public and private antipoverty activities in their areas, the community corporations in New York rapidly came to serve as

21. The approach was laid out in the "Sviridoff Report," *Developing New York City's Human Resources* (New York: Institute of Public Administration, June 1966).

special-purpose supplements to the established bureaucracies, which continued to dominate the service delivery system. For example, safety might be an overriding concern, but instead of working with the Police Department to redeploy existing patrolmen, the CAP agency (or its delegate) would independently operate a new escort service in the community. Head Start projects would spring up under local sponsorship, but neither the educational innovations nor the organized involvement of parents would extend to the public school system. In some cases, cooperative programs with city agencies might be generated, for example, in tenant education and housing inspection, or in setting up programs to employ neighborhood youths in recreation and after-school programs. But the CAP agencies rarely moved beyond the coordination of individual projects to a more systematic interaction with the traditional departments of government. The "insular nature" of the poverty program in New York was "its greatest problem," in the judgment of one who helped design the original structure.[22] This conclusion was corroborated by a later study prepared for the State Charter Revision Commission, which noted:

> The conduct of New York City's community action program reveals the conviction of its officials that control over program operations is critical if there is to be an impact on the lives of the poor. The Council [Against Poverty] and corporations have thereby insulated these operations from the city's other major agencies and institutions, and as a result have over time grown more and more isolated from them and their activities.[23]

What happened in New York was not that different from events in many other parts of the country. As one early analyst wrote in summarizing a survey of programs in twenty-seven localities:

> None of the community action agencies that we observed were anywhere near the center of the power structures of their com-

22. James A. Krauskopf, "New York City's Anti-Poverty Program," *City Almanac* 7 (December 1972): 11.
23. State Charter Revision Commission for New York City, *The Community Action Experience* (New York: State Charter Revision Commission for New York City, November 1973), p. 43.

munities. A few appeared to be at the edge, awaiting acceptance, and doing their best to conduct themselves inoffensively in the meantime. But most of them either had no evident desire to join the club, or they have been black-balled already. Inevitably, then, in their community-wide planning, mobilizing, and coordination functions—which depended on acceptance, in lieu of power—they were defeated.[24]

He concluded: "The CAAs have become, essentially, one more in the array of operating institutions in their communities, which in the first instance, they were conceived to coordinate."[25] Their successes "have not been as coordinators. They have been, rather, as inducers of innovation and constructive change."[26] Ten years later, the National Advisory Council on Economic Opportunity came to a similar judgment:

> For the most part, rather than coordinating previously established services, CAAs concentrated on supplementing existing delivery systems and on programs that filled unmet needs, such as Head Start, nutrition for the poor, legal aid, and training for employment, homemaking and other practical skills.[27]

The CAP agencies were neither given, nor did they earn, the sources of power in money, political backing, independent constituency, or general acceptance that would have enabled them to become effective coordinators. There was a fundamental conflict between the advocacy role of the poverty corporations on the one side, and the service coordination goal on the other. It would have required extraordinary leadership to maintain a creative balance between these two pressures, and this was usually not forthcoming.

24. James Sundquist, *Making Federalism Work* (Washington, D.C.: Brookings Institution, 1969), p. 74.
25. James Sundquist, "Co-ordinating the War on Poverty," *Annals* 385 (September 1969): 46.
26. Sundquist, *Making Federalism Work*, p. 47.
27. National Advisory Council on Economic Opportunity, *Tenth Report* (Washington, D.C.: National Advisory Council on Economic Opportunity, 31 March 1978), p. 47.

In practice, after an initial period of conflict with the established political and administrative authorities, the choice for CAP agencies often came down to isolated independence or almost total assimilation into the existing system. One state official told a researcher baldly that "the coordinating reach of the CAAs extends only as far as their money extends."[28] The CAPs could buy some cooperation for the few programs their funds could finance, but they achieved little beyond those relatively narrow limits. The traditional bureaucracies remained defensive and hostile, protecting their prerogatives and preserving their institutional independence. Once a political accommodation had been achieved, many mayors allowed the CAP agencies to operate their federally funded projects, but in isolation from the core of traditional city government. In effect, the community corporations were given direct control over a tiny piece of the governmental pie but were reduced to weak, often ignored advocates for change with respect to the established bureaucracies. Although estimates of municipal expenditures in subcity districts are difficult to determine, it is unlikely that a typical community corporation controlled more than a small fraction of the total resources managed by municipal agencies in the same area. For example, the South Bronx community corporation in New York had an annual budget of approximately $1 million. A study of seven city agencies estimated that they spent $190 million in the same area per year.[29]

If CAP funds were too small to buy institutional rather than project coordination in the neighborhoods, the only alternative routes to that goal would have been for the mayor to order agencies to cooperate in integrating their services or for the CAPs to develop a powerful, independent political constituency to force such action. Neither possibility was realized. Initially, mayors were more likely to view the new institutions as competitors than as trusted agents. Gradually, another role became apparent. The CAPs served as buffers in deflecting community protest from the mayor's doorstep, instead of providing strategic leverage to change the operations of

28. Sundquist, *Making Federalism Work*, p. 47.
29. See *Municipal Expenditures By Neighborhood* (New York: New York City Administrator's Office, 1972), p. 71.

government bureaucracies. As a training ground for leaders from poor and minority communities to enter the traditional electoral and administrative systems, CAPs were often successful, but this function did not translate into a mobilized constituency for themselves as institutions. Typically in New York during this period, elections for representation of community corporations drew less than 3 percent of their area's voters.[30] This minimal turnout both undercut their legitimacy with the established bureaucracies and signaled their political weakness to elected officials. As a political entity, the CAPs became yet another organized interest fighting for recognition in an already crowded city.

The most debilitating political blow to the CAP system in New York and many other big cities came with the federal decision to implement the Model Cities program through a separate organizational structure. Just two years after the inception of the poverty corporations, when many of them were finally resolving their internal and external conflicts, a new institution was inserted in their midst to do much the same job. Instead of building on the OEO participatory system, the next influx of federal funds was apparently delivered into the hands of the mayors and used to create a rival institution in their communities. The short-term confrontations and failures of the Community Action experience had convinced both politicians and planners that the mobilization and coordination of resources to overcome neighborhood poverty required a better balance between central executive leadership and decentralized citizen involvement.

THE MODEL CITIES MODEL

In contrast to the OEO requirement for the creation of new Community Action organizations at the local level, the Model Cities legislation specifically provided that its programs would be mounted through a City Demonstration Agency responsible to mayors and

---

30. From 1967–69, there were a total of 47 elections in New York. Turnouts varied from 1 to 8 percent with most in the 2- to 4-percent range. In 1970, despite more elaborate planning and provision for voting over two days, participation averaged only 2.5 percent throughout the city. See *The Community Action Experience*, pp. 31–34.

municipal legislators. Partly this was a response to the political furor caused by the independent CAPs that made Congress and HUD determined "to return the genie of citizen power to the bottle from which it had escaped in a few cities";[31] partly it was an effort to give the mayors sufficient incentive and leverage to bring about the coordination among city, state, and federal agencies that had not been achieved in the urban poverty programs. Residents would have "access" or "influence" rather than control over the new structure. This combination of *decentralized citizen participation in planning* with *central mayoral control over administration* was the new formula for improving the coordination and responsiveness of city bureaucracies.

According to this model, community representatives would spell out policy and, with federal money and mayoral backing, the existing agencies of government would implement the programs. Such a structure would remove citizen participants from the direct operational responsibilities that tended to absorb energy and divert attention from planning and coordination. The coordinator would no longer be one among the many service agencies it was designed to coordinate. The Model Cities model projected a subtle balance of interests and powers on paper; in practice, however, Model Cities became another separate, supplemental program that dissipated much of its impact on the existing service delivery system. The bureaucratic dynamics of this process were revealing.

Amid considerable tension, New York designated three different areas as targets for Model Cities funds. Each eventually selected a Local Policy Committee representing community residents and nominated candidates for the position of neighborhood director, who was then appointed by the mayor. When program implementation lagged seriously by 1970, Mayor Lindsay issued an executive order raising Model Cities to superagency status under a strong administrator. The New York model for decentralized citizen planning and centralized administration was in place.[32]

---

31. Sherry Arnstein, "A Ladder of Participation," *Journal of the American Institute of Planners* 35 (July 1969): 220.

32. The stages of development are described in State Charter Revision Commission for New York City, *Report on Model Cities* (New York: State Charter Revision Commission for New York City, December 1973).

Despite the mayoral dominance that in theory would insure program coordination, bureaucratic fragmentation continued and even increased at the point of service delivery in the communities. The mayor specified that neighborhood directors would be responsible for "coordinating *existing* programs operating in the Model Cities areas"—but this did not occur.[33] More than the CAP managers, the local Model Cities directors had the resources and, in a few programmatic areas, the authority to require cooperation and coordination from other city operating departments. However, this formal legitimacy was limited to physical planning and construction projects that were also funded by HUD—approving new and rehabilitated housing, or the demolition of unsafe buildings, for example. It did not extend to day-to-day city service delivery issues.

In the pressure to spend funds rapidly, the existing city agencies created special administrative divisions within their bureaucratic systems to implement the Model Cities projects. This served the constructive purpose of enabling top administrators to follow progress carefully and hold subordinates accountable. It also insured that the Model Cities efforts would be segregated from normal departmental operations; by the same token, it reduced, if it did not eliminate, the impact of the new programs on standard agency practices. For example, when Model Cities funded a supplemental sanitation program to clean alleyways and vacant lots—off-street work that was illegal for regular city employees—a new Model Cities program office was established within the Department of Sanitation. Similarly, when the neighborhood policy committees approved a Community Service Officer (CSO) program to provide safety services supplementing the normal uniformed police patrols in the Model Neighborhoods, a new section was established within the Police Department. These new divisions created relatively self-contained administrative structures paralleling the normal bureaucratic chain of command. But this meant that at the point where such services were delivered in the communities, the existing commanding officer of a department had very little, if anything, to do with the implementation of the new Model Cities program components operating in the same district.

33. Ibid., p. 68 (emphasis added).

Even minimal service coordination was hindered by the creation of these parallel Model Cities bureaucracies. For example, a police precinct commander in the South Bronx revealed that he had assigned a number of his uniformed officers to local schools where there had been a series of violent incidents. Not only were his patrolmen inadequately trained to deal with the conflicts that arose among elementary school children, but this kept a number of men off the streets, where they were supposed to be. The Model Cities neighborhood director asked why some of the sixty CSOs financed with federal funds and administered through the Police Department could not be used in the schools. The precinct commander immediately agreed with the suggestion but said he had nothing to do with managing the CSOs in the area. He could assign his normal allocation of patrolmen there and that was all. The CSOs working within his precinct were responsible to a separate Model Cities command at Police headquarters.

To some outside observers, the consequences of such as organizational arrangement might appear trivial. After all, the cops and the CSOs were within the same department and their commanders were ultimately accountable to the same boss. But in practice, commonsense assumptions about coordination through central control break down when confronted with the realities of bureaucratic behavior, as the school safety example shows. The insularity of bureaus within the same agency is often as extreme as the more expected isolation of major departments from each other.[34] In the implementation of the Model Cities program in New York, the specialized structure of field operations overwhelmed the theories of coordination through vertical administration.

Although Model Cities had much more extensive funding than the OEO-sponsored Community Action Programs to buy services and cooperation, its resources still constituted only a small fraction of the total city investment in any given area. In New York, each of the Model Neighborhoods had a supplemental budget of approximately $20 million per year. Using the South Bronx area as the basis

34. The similarity between interbureau and interdepartmental coordination problems at the federal level is discussed in James W. Fesler, *Area and Administration*, (University, Ala.: University of Alabama Press, 1949). pp. 84–86.

for comparison, roughly half this allocation was devoted to physical rehabilitation or construction, leaving $10 million for safety, sanitation, drug, day-care, and other service programs. Even this amount represented less than 5 percent of the estimated annual city expenditure for services in the area. To the extent that the Model Cities programs, like the CAPs, were isolated in their own functional and bureaucratic worlds, they lost the chance to affect 95 percent of the ongoing service delivery system operating in their communities. The failure of this second federally inspired institutional innovation to coordinate the delivery of all public services in designated communities was not an isolated experience dependent on an environment unique to New York. The same inadequacies were apparent to analysts of similar programs in many other cities.[35]

NEIGHBORHOOD COUNCILS
Neighborhood councils, by one definition, are "broad-based organizations of residents from geographic subareas of a city or county . . . which have some kind of official or quasi-official relationship with local government."[36] They come in many shapes and sizes, from formal charter-mandated entities to informally recognized civic associations. In general, their role is advisory, and they have not provoked the power struggles of the Community Action or community control movement. Their purpose is to deal comprehensively with problems and plans for geographic neighborhoods as wholes, instead of focusing on specific programs in education, housing, transportation, and so forth. Neighborhood councils represent a moderate form of political decentralization in which local activists can articulate community interests to government, but in most cases, government itself has done little to restructure its established administrative agencies in order to respond consistently or coherently to these concerns.

New York has one of the oldest officially sanctioned neighborhood advisory council systems but many other cities have instituted

35. See the study of eight different areas in George J. Washnis, *Community Development Strategies* (New York: Praeger, 1974), pp. 11–12.
36. Hallman, *The Organization and Operation of Neighborhood Councils*, p. 4.

similar approaches in recent years.[37] The history of the approach in New York goes back to recommendations for the creation of local planning districts by the Citizens' Union in 1947.[38] During the 1950s, a number of councils were informally established in Manhattan. Finally, in 1963, the revised charter mandated the creation of community districts that "shall coincide, so far as feasible, with the historic communities from which the city has developed and shall be suitable as districts to be used for the planning of community life within the city."[39] For each of the sixty-two districts that were eventually designated in 1968, the appropriate borough president was authorized to appoint a community planning board of up to fifty members to advise him primarily on land use and capital construction issues. In 1969, Local Law number 39 changed the name of these local bodies to "community boards." The seemingly minor omission of "planning" from the title reflected an effort to expand their mandate beyond the initial focus on physical projects to include any matters affecting "the district's welfare and orderly development."[40]

Because the mayor had no responsibility for selecting members, the community boards were politically isolated within the city administration and mostly dependent on the leverage they could acquire through their borough president's votes on the Board of Estimate. Membership usually represented the old-line civic organizations—taxpayers' or homeowners' associations and the like—and did not reflect the recent, often poor and minority immigrants who had entered the communities within the last decade. The latter had not yet developed the kind of stable organizational base from which community board members were most often selected. Many of these newer groups felt that the boards themselves were

37. Ibid., pp. 5–15, contains a brief description of neighborhood council status and structure in thirty cities and counties throughout the country.

38. The details of this early history are traced by Marsha S. Bruhn, "Decentralizing Citizen Participation in the Planning Process: A Study of the Community Boards in Staten Island" (Master's thesis, Virginia Polytechnic Institute and State University, May 1974), pp. 36–46.

39. New York City Charter, Section 83.

40. *Local Laws for the City of New York for the Year 1969*, No. 39.

backwaters, and their first points of entry into the governmental system were institutions like the community corporations, Model Cities, or the schools, which appeared to offer direct access to jobs and power. The boards did not have a broad public constituency. Typically, only about 20 percent of the people in a community were even aware of their existence.[41] The boards tended to be defensive in their orientation. They generally took little initiative except in mobilizing their forces to block changes sponsored by government. Only a rare few were anxious to foster new public programs in their districts. After surveying six boards in operation, one observer described the effect of this outlook:

> In general, the activity pattern of the boards is one of protracted debate and grievance-articulation punctuated by an occasional burst of protest; . . . boards become lightning rods for community opposition to government initiatives. Since the role of the boards is reactive, it is not surprising that they operate as semi-institutionalized critics of government.[42]

Gradually, in the early 1970s, a number of community boards began to play a more constructive role in promoting a dialogue between agency administrators and subcity neighborhoods. In specific projects, like developing a marine transfer station for sanitation refuse, tunneling for new water lines, removing outmoded elevated train superstructures, or planning major street reconstructions, they were closely consulted and helped smooth the way for community acceptance of inevitable disruptions. For city administrators, this often meant tough bargaining, but it had advantages. In evaluating local concerns, a government agency could work through one organization as the only legally constituted, communitywide, representative institution, rather than creating an ad hoc consultation process to deal with scores of separate civic groups.

---

41. Nathalie S. Friedman and Theresa F. Rogers, "Decentralization and the Public," in Allen H. Barton et al., *Decentralizing City Government* (Lexington, Mass.: D. C. Heath, 1977), p. 228.

42. Douglas Yates, *Neighborhood Democracy* (Lexington, Mass.: D. C. Heath, 1973), p. 40.

The quality and level of board activities often varied with the support provided by each borough president. In general during this period, boards in Manhattan and the Bronx were encouraged to assume greater responsibility, while in Brooklyn, Queens, and Staten Island they were kept on a tighter rein.

Increasingly, however, as community board members attempted to play a more substantial role, defects in the organization of this neighborhood advisory council system were revealed. Commenting on the change of title in 1969, a board chairman in Queens stated: "They have dropped 'Planning' probably for a very simple reason; nobody really cares about planning in Queens. They care about services."[43] But it was precisely in their relation to the service delivery departments of government where the greatest failure of the structure lay. With a history of involvement in "planning" and no institutionalized mechanism to deal consistently with operating agencies in their neighborhoods, the boards tended to retreat from service questions or, if they attempted to enter the fray, rapidly became frustrated with their inability to obtain adequate attention or response. With no officially designated contacts in the bureaucracies at the local level, each of the sixty-two boards would try to communicate with headquarters offices in "the City," as residents of New York boroughs refer to downtown Manhattan. In the process, they found that "letters to agencies go unanswered; telephone calls are not returned; requests for agency representatives to appear at board meetings are ignored."[44] The most comprehensive study of the community board experience highlighted this defect in their organizational structure:

Minimal involvement of Community Boards with service delivery, including inadequate relations with service deliverers, has been their most glaring deficiency. . . . Citizen bodies at the local level must have strong ties with other power centers—the City's service and overhead agencies in particular. If isolated, the ability of local citizen bodies to effectively participate in decision-making will be minimal. As community advocates, they may

43. Bruhn, "Decentralizing Citizen Participation," p. 70.
44. Ibid., p. 77.

achieve some degree of leverage over those modest functions delegated to their exclusive jurisdiction. But, for the bulk of City services . . . local citizen bodies run the risk of being ignored or cut off without formal ties to other units of government. Such linkages must be mandated and enforced.[45]

Analysts of neighborhood advisory councils in other cities have also noted their negligible impact on the local service delivery system, when not accompanied by either significant political authority or a reorganized administrative system.[46]

SCHOOL DECENTRALIZATION AND THE COMMUNITY
CONTROL MOVEMENT
The demand for community control in the New York City school system set the political tone for subsequent decentralization efforts. In contrast to Community Action or Model Cities programs, where citizen involvement was focused on a broad range of supplemental projects, the community control advocates confronted the largest single entrenched bureaucracy in New York, which at that time had a budget of $2 billion and over sixty thousand teachers represented by the biggest union local in the country. The struggle rapidly escalated into a blatant racial contest for power over jobs that traumatized the school system and threatened to rend the political fabric of the city.

   The immediate events surrounding the controversy began unfolding in the summer of 1967 when the Board of Education recognized three "demonstration districts" to encourage community involvement in local schools.[47] All the projects were in poor, minority areas, and each received planning grants from the Ford Foundation. Local "Governing Boards" were elected and quickly

45. State Charter Revision Commission for New York City, *Community Boards* (New York: State Charter Revision Commission for New York City, May 1974), pp. 10–12.
    46. See Hallman, *The Organization and Operation of Neighborhood Councils,* pp. 90–93.
    47. For a brief history of community control in New York, see Norman I. Fainstein and Susan S. Fainstein, *Urban Political Movements* (Englewood Cliffs, N.J.: Prentice-Hall, 1974), pp. 36–40.

became embroiled in disputes over the selection of school personnel. During the fall of 1968, the United Federation of Teachers called three citywide strikes to protest the "transfer" (or illegal "firing") of teachers in Ocean Hill–Brownsville. The entire public school system was closed to almost all students for nearly three months, from early September until mid-November. In 1969, the state legislature approved the School Decentralization Act, in which, as one study concluded, the representatives finally "joined together to pass a bill that would still the conflict and prevent a cataclysm in New York City."[48]

The legislation that emerged from this confrontation provided a structure that retained an appointed central Board of Education with a strong new chancellor and created thirty-one decentralized districts, each with a community school board elected through complex proportional representation procedures. The powers of the local boards were essentially confined to the selection of a community school superintendent and the allocation of supplemental federal program funds. Authority over the hiring, firing, tenure, and promotion of teachers and principals was hemmed in by tight legislative, civil service, and collective bargaining restrictions. With budgets set centrally and many educational policy questions such as class size determined in the union contract, the community school boards and their superintendents had little leverage over the system.

The short-term impact of school decentralization on both the quality of education and community participation was disappointing to many. First, citizen involvement in voting was generally low. Turnouts in the initial community school board elections during the late 1960s and early 1970s ranged from 9 to 14 percent citywide.[49] Elections are not definitive indices of participation, but most observers have commented that even on a day-to-day basis the level of public involvement in the schools did not increase dramatically.

48. State Charter Revision Commission for New York City, *School Decentralization in New York City* (New York: State Charter Revision Commission for New York City, June 1974), p. 34.

49. Statistics on these early voting rates are reported in *School Decentralization in New York City*, pp. 68–69. For comparably low turnouts in later elections, see the *New York Times*, 2 May 1980, p. D17.

What changed was the intensity of participation and the opening of the system to new leadership.[50]

Second, local elections proved to be a highly uncertain strategy for increasing community power. Although ethnic minorities did achieve greater representation in the school boards than in traditional political institutions like the city council, the district boards were dominated by the organized citywide interests of the parochial schools and the teachers' union. In 1970, the typical public school board member was described as "a white, male Catholic, professionally trained, who had lived in his district for about nine years and had two children in parochial school."[51] In 1973, candidates supported by the United Federation of Teachers won 156 of 288 positions, and a majority in 21 of the (by then) 32 districts.[52]

Third, power in a local school board was not readily translatable into improved education for children. In general, the evidence revealed little change in what happened in the classrooms; the educational reforms that did occur had no clear relationship to decentralization; and, ironically, some of the most important new programmatic policies were a result of central initiatives.[53]

The long-range impact of school decentralization is more far-reaching than this early history would suggest. But one substantive lesson from the experience in the early 1970s was that the single-minded focus on power that permeated the first years of the community control movement produced much less programmatic change than its proponents had anticipated. The political lesson of the community control movement in New York was even cruder. Despite the new institutions and leadership nurtured through the CAP and Model Cities programs, minority neighborhoods did not have sufficient power to succeed in a direct confrontation with major bureaucratic interests. No elected officials could remain immune to this political fact of life. To many observers at the time, Mayor Lindsay's strong backing for school decentralization seemed

50. La Noue and Smith, *The Politics of School Decentralization*, p. 229.

51. Mario Fantini and Marilyn Gittell, *Decentralization* (New York: Praeger, 1973), p. 49.

52. *School Decentralization in New York City*, p. 73.

53. La Noue and Smith, *The Politics of School Decentralization*, p. 215.

almost to cost him reelection in 1969. Combined with his earlier defeat in attempting to create a Civilian Complaint Review Board outside the Police Department, this insured that community control was dead as a major strategy for reforming core city services in the neighborhoods.

CONSEQUENCES OF THE CITIZEN PARTICIPATION STRATEGY
The variety of participatory systems spawned by the multiple national and local efforts to increase public involvement had the effect of fragmenting citizens' energies in urban neighborhoods. Functional specialization in administration led to functional specialization in citizen participation and diverted attention away from the issues of the geographic community viewed as an interrelated whole. Even those institutions designed to promote a neighborhood perspective, like CAP or Model Cities, rapidly became simply one more special-purpose addition to the existing organizational environment. Neighborhood councils were intended to play a broader role, but they often had little influence or public recognition.

The fragmentation of participation was extreme in New York. In a poor area of the city, it was not unusual to find, in addition to a CAP, Model Cities program, community board, and local school board, separate specialized citizen advisory committees dealing with comprehensive health planning, a municipal hospital, mental health, ghetto medicine, urban renewal, a multiservice center, Head Start, day-care programs, and a police precinct community council. While this multiplicity of organizations offered an extraordinary opportunity for widespread participation in community service, it also created problems. Experience had demonstrated that in most subcity communities there were only a small number of civic activists, perhaps 50 to 100 in a district of 150,000 people, who were willing to give the time and energy to become sufficiently knowledgeable about local programs to serve intelligently and creatively on such advisory committees. In the process of extending the number of opportunities for participation, unreal demands had been placed on the community leadership for continuous involvement. People complained that they were out at meetings every night of the week and still did not have the time or the structured opportunity to deal with communitywide concerns. Although very nearly the same set of individuals was active in each of the different organizations, no single institution was viewed by both the residents and the city administration as the legitimate representative of the area. A citizen participation strategy that maximized the functional channels for participation exhausted the energy of local leaders, splintered their focus, and made it impossible to deal with either the interrelationships between services or the comprehensive concerns of the community as a whole. This participatory fragmentation reinforced the ability of the functional bureaucracies (and the locally elected politicians) to preserve their own autonomy. Members of one among ten or twenty organizations "representing" an area could much more easily be manipulated, co-opted, or ignored than could a single entity speaking with the full weight of the community behind it.

As a component of government programs directed primarily toward the poor and ethnic minorities, the citizen participation strategy contributed to developing and strengthening a constituency for these groups. In a society that continues to respond to organized interests such a result could promote greater equity. But the repeated lesson of the participatory experience in CAP, Model Cities, school decentralization, and neighborhood councils has been that organization to articulate interests is insufficient; it must be accompanied by either a significant grant of power to the participants or a reorganization of government administration, if its impact is not to be blunted by the established bureaucracies. Citizen participation produced program innovation, developed new leadership, and encouraged a focus on urban subcommunities as objects of government attention. But with a political base primarily in poor and minority areas, the participatory strategy had neither the power nor the organizational design to penetrate deeply into the operations of the service delivery system in big city neighborhoods. And the more extreme experiences with community control in New York frightened powerful groups of citizens into opposing any significant extension of political decentralization in this form.

Multiservice Centers and Colocation

Multiservice centers represent another distinctive strategy for improving government performance in big city communities. Its distinguishing characteristic is colocation—placing a number of public (and private) agencies under one roof. This approach usually includes a broad range of social and health services but typically has little to do with traditional municipal departments like police or sanitation. It may involve citizen participation in giving advice or controlling center operations, but this is not essential and often does not occur in practice.[54] The concept of the multiservice center assumes that physical proximity will improve both the accessibility and the coordination of the services delivered. In practice, while locating a new facility in a particular part of town may increase the quantity and availability of programs for those in the area, experience indicates that other administrative reforms are necessary to attack the coordination problem with any degree of success. The walls that insulate bureaucracies from each other are organizational, not physical.

Federal support for neighborhood multiservice centers was authorized in the Housing Act of 1965 and received impetus from the highest level one year later, when President Johnson called for the creation of "one-stop" centers in every ghetto neighborhood.[55] Funds to match such a national commitment were never authorized. Less than two hundred multiservice centers eventually obtained federal financing under this program. Local initiatives increased this number, and surveys have found that about 20 percent of the cities and counties with populations over twenty-five thousand operated multiservice centers in the early 1970s.[56] These ranged from multimillion dollar operations in some big cities to relatively modest recreation and youth programs in rural areas, but they all apparently suffered from similar organizational defects.

Nationally, the Department of Housing and Urban Development

54. In one survey, citizen boards were present in only one-third of the "multiservice programs," a category that included neighborhood centers and other strategies. See Yin and Yates, *Street-Level Governments*, pp. 145–46.

55. For a brief background of the neighborhood service center programs, see Howard Hallman, *Neighborhood Control of Public Programs* (New York: Praeger, 1970), p. 158.

56. *The New Grass Roots Government?*, pp. 9–10. See also Judith E. Grollman, "The Decentralization of Municipal Services," *Urban Data Service* vol. 3 (Washington, D.C.: International City Management Association, February 1971), p. 2.

(HUD) was made the "convener" for a joint effort by five federal agencies to implement the multiservice center program. HUD could provide funds only for the development of a physical facility; OEO was supposed to contribute "core" administrative support; and HEW and Labor would finance specific services through their normal categorical programs. Even though the federal guidelines for the neighborhood service centers called for coordination of the various service components, fragmentation at the federal level made this extremely difficult to carry out. Without central control over service operations funds, HUD did not have much leverage, and its regional staff in the field complained about the lack of cooperation from other departments.[57] Locally, the sponsorship of multiservice centers was generally left to specialized social service or community development departments. Big city mayors did not view the approach as a basis for promoting governmentwide program coordination and were not required by the funding agencies to play an active role.[58] Without their involvement as a counterweight to the usual institutional jealousies of the municipal bureaucracies, improvement in coordination was unlikely.

In New York, the city designated Hunts Point in the South Bronx as the test site for the first of what it was hoped would be a number of multiservice centers in poverty areas spread throughout the four largest boroughs. Eventually, a major new facility was constructed for a multi-million-dollar program concentrating on health and social services. The additional federal funds substantially increased the quantity of human services available in one of the poorest neighborhoods in the city. An independent citizen board determined which programs would be developed, and new opportunities for paraprofessional employment were opened. On the negative side, the center had a volatile history with numerous allegations of fiscal improprieties and patronage that had more to do with the

---

57. See *Neighborhood Facilities: A Study of Operating Facilities*, Community Development Evaluation Series no. 1 (Washington, D.C.: Department of Housing and Urban Development, December 1971), p. 35.

58. In a survey carried out during 1973, HUD found that for 186 operating centers, not one application came from a Mayor's office. See "Findings" (unpublished HUD report on neighborhood facilities, mimeograph), p. 14.

growth of a new political leadership in the Puerto Rican community of New York than with the generic problems of urban decentralization. However, the Hunts Point center also revealed the limitations of establishing a supplemental service delivery program that had no organizational mechanism to affect the established city agencies continuing to function in the same area. Analogous to the Community Action and Model Cities experiences, the result was the addition of new services whose ultimate impact on the community was marginal compared to the ongoing operations of the city administration. Although there were some attempts to develop cooperative ventures with the Departments of Health and Social Services, these did not lead to extensive coordination with the district health center or the welfare center in the same neighborhood. Attempts by the Hunts Point leaders to involve city agencies were "viewed as additional requests for services, rather than a way of reorganizing how those services should be delivered."[59]

The dynamics of the situation in New York all worked against creating an areawide service delivery system. City and federal officials allowed the center to become an experiment in community control, rather than a test of program coordination. Neither the political clique that dominated the local board nor the city agencies were much interested in cooperation. As one observer put it, "mistrust was rampant on both sides."[60] This was understandable, given the center director's coordination strategy. It was, he told a federal evaluator: "Give us all the money and let us provide everything for the area."[61] Neither politically (because of its community control identification), financially (because it required large supplemental funding), nor organizationally (because of the jealousies with operating agencies) did the Hunts Point center represent a viable strategy for promoting neighborhood service coordination.

Despite the political idiosyncracies of the New York multiservice

59. Eloise Hirsch, "Multi-Service Centers" (unpublished notes for the study of decentralization sponsored by the Association of the Bar of the City of New York), p. 16.

60. Ibid., p.11.

61. Quoted in Abt Associates, *A Study of the Neighborhood Center Pilot Program*, vol. 2: *An Evaluation of the Thirteen Neighborhood Service Programs* (Cambridge, Mass.: Abt Associates, September 1969), p. 608.

center history, its organizational experience was typical. Colocation may facilitate service coordination, but it does not insure it, either for those services directly operated in the same facility or those related programs implemented by other public agencies in the same area. The most extensive investigation of the first federally funded centers flatly concluded: "Interagency and intergovernmental coordination did not materialize."[62] Similar points are made in most analyses of colocated multiservice centers. Generally, they concentrated on the direct delivery of additional services to individual clients; the integrative clout of their new funds did not cover a very broad spectrum of programs; there was little communication or coordination among agencies either internally or externally; and there was confusion and competition among departments that started at the federal level and extended down through the local sponsors into each center.[63] Attempts at producing coordination through colocation without additional organizational reforms did not have much success in overcoming the insularity of the traditional bureaucracies. As one study noted:

The simple idea that people who work close to each other work better is not true. It is like saying that apartment dwellers will be closer friends than those living in detached housing. . . . The commonality of housing and location must also be accompanied by a managerial system that is integrated with the process of service delivery.[64]

62. Ibid., vol. 1: *Summary and Recommendations,* p. iv.
63. See *Integration of Human Services in HEW,* publication no. SRS 73-02012 (Washington, D.C.: Department of Health, Education and Welfare, 1973), p. 164; Hallman, *Neighborhood Control of Public Programs,* p. 159; Abt Associates, *Study* vol. 2, pp. 106, 155, 161; Oakland Task Force, *An Analysis of Federal Decision-Making and Impact* (San Francisco: Federal Executive Board, August 1968), pp. 122-28; Richard E. Walton, *A Study of the Federal Management System for the Neighborhood Center Pilot Program: Final Report* (Washington, D.C.: NTL-Institute for Applied Behavioral Sciences, October 1968), pp. 6-33; and Sheila B. Kamerman and Alfred J. Kahn, *Social Services in the United States* (Philadelphia: Temple University Press, 1976), p. 451.
64. John DeWitt, *Managing the Human Service "System,"* Project Share, Human Services Monograph Series No. 4 (Washington, D.C.: Department of Health, Education, and Welfare, August 1977), p. 21.

Proximity may breed lots of things, but improved coordination and responsiveness are not necessarily two of them.

The vastly different roles and powers of the directors in multiservice centers indicate whether such a strategy will lead simply to the *decentralized delivery* of services or whether it can be the basis for the *decentralized management* of the service delivery system in a geographic community. Generally, there are three types of center directors. First is the "housekeeper" responsible for allocating office space, maintaining the facility, and, perhaps, supervising receptionists or information and referral staff. The second is the "center coordinator" who integrates those programs directly operating from the center itself. The third is the "area manager" with the authority and responsibility for coordinating all public service agencies operating in a subdistrict of the city or county. Experience indicates that there is no automatic progression through these stages from decentralized service delivery to decentralized service management. Even where a system of multipurpose centers is conceived as the institutional foundation for neighborhood or regional service coordination, practice often does not develop beyond improving the availability of specialized programs for the public. Without a reorganization of local administration under strong chief executive leadership, the center directors are prone to function, as one confided to an interviewer, "like a garbage can"— responsible for all the problems that no one else wants to touch but unable to promote service coordination systematically. In general, mayors in big cities were relatively isolated from the agencies sponsoring the multiservice center strategy. They were more likely to try to establish a direct link to communities through institutions immediately under their control—neighborhood city halls and urban action task forces.

Mayoral Outreach Programs: Neighborhood City Halls and Urban Action Task Forces

Mayoral outreach strategies gained some national notice during the mid-1960s when newly elected Mayors John Lindsay and Kevin White established neighborhood city halls in New York and Boston. Eventually, nearly twenty other cities mounted similar efforts.[65] The approach was developed in response to a number of organizational problems that emerged as big city leaders faced the threat of riots in minority areas: the lack of communication between city hall and local neighborhoods, the absence of coordination among municipal departments, the inaccessibility of many services, and the inadequacy of citizen complaint systems. Many mayors found they could not trust the traditional executive agencies to keep them informed about the reality of service delivery problems or the new tensions rising in ethnic communities. The concern was heightened by the realization that in racial confrontations, the city officials forced to deal directly with local crises were precisely those perceived with great suspicion by the black and Spanish-speaking poor—the police. The isolation of city bureaucracies from each other meant that patrolmen and their local commanders were "compelled to deal with ghetto residents angered over dirty streets, dilapidated housing, unfair commercial practices or inferior schools—grievances which they had neither the responsibility for creating nor the authority to redress."[66] In such situations, a mayor would want better contact with community leaders, improved control over government officials on the spot, and a method for handling problems before they escalated into crises. All of these concerns pointed to the need for direct outreach from the mayor and his immediate staff into the neighborhoods.

Structurally, neighborhood city halls were a system of complaint centers physically located in subcity communities and administered by mayors' offices. In scope, they were comprehensive, with a mandate to work on all service delivery problems affecting an area. In scale, they focused mayoral attention on the unique issues affecting subcity districts. Politically, they were often viewed with suspicion, particularly by elected city council members who feared the local offices as extensions of the mayor's influence onto their turf. Organizationally, other than stationing some direct service staff in neighborhoods, the little city halls had no major impact on the internal structure of the established agencies. This last point is rarely understood.

65. See Grollman, "The Decentralization of Municipal Services," p. 1. and *The New Grass Roots Government?*, pp. 9–10.

66. *Report of the National Advisory Commission on Civil Disorders* (Washington, D.C.: U.S. Government Printing Office, 1968), p. 77.

Conventional wisdom has mistakenly seen the approach as "another form of administrative decentralization" or a strategy "to decentralize a number of city services on a communitywide basis."[67] There are surface aspects of these mayoral outposts that do represent weak forms of decentralization: local access to information and referral assistance, convenience in filling out government applications, and a direct channel of communication from neighborhoods to chief executives. But more significantly, the little city hall system was an organizational strategy for centralizing power by increasing the mayor's capacity to control the traditional line departments. As one observer in Boston put it: "For the first time since the political machine, there is an organization to set priorities outside the bureaucracies."[68] The mayoral outreach strategy increased the capacity of city government to deal with ad hoc citizen complaints. Fully developed, it provided an alternative source of information to chief executives that could influence central plans and policies for subcity communities. But without complementary changes in the structure of the established administrative agencies, it did not systematically improve the coordination and responsiveness of the service delivery system in urban neighborhoods.

Building on his experience with a storefront campaign operation in the 1965 election, Mayor John Lindsay proposed creating neighborhood city halls in a number of poverty areas. His recommendation was quickly blocked on political grounds. The Democrat-dominated City Council and Board of Estimate would not approve funds for an independent, Republican mayor to develop institutions that could provide the neighborhood base for a new political machine. Determined to proceed, Lindsay raised private financing for six neighborhood city halls. Subsequently, he obtained public budgetary support for a similar, but less expensive neighborhood outreach program—the Urban Action Task Force. By the summer of 1967, local task forces were operating in over twenty poor communities. For each area, a high-level city official (usually a department commissioner) served as the task force chairman, in addition to his other responsibilities, and one or two "neighborhood aides"

67. See Hallman, *Neighborhood Government in a Metropolitan Setting*, p. 104, and Washnis, *Community Development Strategies*, p. 320.
68. David Rosenbloom, interview, 6 February 1975.

were hired to provide information and process complaints in local storefronts. Prior to the 1969 election, when the mayor began to realize his political vulnerability in white-ethnic and middle-income communities, the task forces were extended into many new areas. Ultimately, the system was established in over fifty of the city's sixty-two planning districts.

The Urban Action Task Force structure demonstrated a number of expected and unexpected strengths. It helped the city administration begin to sort out priorities among the multiple service delivery problems from a community perspective. It provided insight into the competence and constituencies of different neighborhood leaders. In each community, task force chairmen would hold a monthly public meeting that was normally attended by the heads of twenty-five to fifty civic associations. Combined with the ongoing work of the task force aides in the area, these activities generated a level of intelligence about subcity communities that was not available through the bureaucracies or the political system. This understanding enabled the mayor to move quickly in calming racial conflicts at a time when incidents in many other cities touched off destructive rioting.[69] The task forces provided an elaborate information and complaint processing network through which individuals could receive support in making the city bureaucracies respond to their particular problems. The vast preponderance of such activity concerned immediate service issues: missed garbage pickups, unfilled potholes, backed-up storm sewers, lack of heat or hot water, demands for new traffic signals, and so forth. By 1970, the system was handling approximately 350,000 complaints per year.[70] In addition, each of the local task forces was usually involved in one or two more ambitious projects—the rehabilitation of a park; the development of drug, senior citizens', or infants' day-care programs; better street lighting or safety in neighborhood commercial

---

69. A revealing personal account of the early Urban Action Task Force operations that focuses on their usefulness in crisis situations, rather than their relevance to the systemic service delivery problems at issue in this study, is found in Barry Gotterher, *The Mayor's Man* (New York: Doubleday, 1975).

70. John A. Kaiser, *Citizen Feedback* (New York: City of New York Office of Administration, April 1971), p. 20.

areas. During summer months, the task forces sponsored hundreds of bus trips and coordinated a variety of other local recreation programs including mobile vans that brought films, puppet shows, and sports events into the neighborhoods. With the Operation Better Block program, it encouraged the formation of almost five hundred new block associations in poor and transitional areas throughout the city and provided continuing assistance to the thousands of existing tenant and homeowner organizations in arranging cleanups, social events, and a wide range of special projects.

In addition to these direct local initiatives, the task forces had an indirect impact by pulling high-level departmental commissioners out of their downtown offices and into the communities, where they would be exposed to citizens' feelings about the operations of municipal service agencies. This independent, if subjective, reporting system enabled the city administration to spot many problems before they would normally have come to the surface through the traditional bureaucracies. Such information often gave some life to the mayor's cabinet meetings; the typical presentations of steady improvement by agency commissioners would be challenged by other commissioners speaking from their concrete experience with the failures and frustrations of service delivery in specific neighborhoods. The nagging problems of parks maintenance, the precipitous disruption of sanitation service in a specific area, and the complex question of welfare housing in middle-class communities were all first highlighted for the mayor by city officials speaking at cabinet meetings but in their capacity as task force chairmen. Whether the city government had the commitment, resources, or institutional capability to act on this information was, obviously, another question.

The organizational strengths of the Urban Task Force approach were also a source of weakness. In effect, the strategy institutionalized a system of logrolling between the heads of agencies that reinforced an inefficient and ineffective centralization in the city administration. Complaints received in the field were transmitted to special liaison officers downtown in each commissioner's office to be resolved on an ad hoc basis. One task force chairman, who also happened to be the commissioner of highways, might call the commissioner of traffic to request the installation of a stoplight that had become an emotional issue in his community. The traffic commissioner was more likely to respond favorably if he knew that at a later date he could return the call to expedite a street repaving job in his task force area. Such favor trading could produce a few rapid rewards for lucky communities, but it was inefficient in bucking too many minor problems up to the highest levels of government; it was ineffective because commissioners and their central staffs rapidly became overloaded with requests; and it diverted energy into treating the effects rather than preventing the causes of service delivery problems. The mayor's executive assistant for neighborhood government analyzed this self-destructive side of the system:

> First of all it forced all decision making, even on the smallest local crisis, up to the top of the administration, so that we had administrators of super-agencies dealing with the pothole problem. . . . Second, it confirmed the present practices of the agencies. It was as if the system was a $9 billion dollar machine trundling down the road . . . and it was spewing out behind it all these screw-ups. And running along as fast as they could behind it were our various offices, task forces, and city halls, catching these things as quickly as they could before they hit the ground and broke and caused a riot or a problem. No mayor ever used his office to get alongside the machine and tinker with the mechanism.[71]

As a strategy to improve service delivery in urban neighborhoods, the task forces became essentially a band-aid operation that depended on an "executive ax" approach to public administration. A former staff worker described the nature of its limitations:

> We would sit as troubleshooters in the Mayor's office, and when we would find a problem, we would call the commissioner or the deputy commissioner or the mayoral assistant who would help us bulldoze our way through until, finally, the word filtered down to the local guys. What happened . . . was that when the bulldozer operators were gone, there was nothing left.[72]

71. Lewis Feldstein, quoted in "Command Decentralization (A)," (Boston: Harvard Business School, Intercollegiate Case Clearing House, 1972), p. 5.

72. Martha Thompson, quoted in Bryant Mason, "Getting Heads Together in New York," *New York Sunday News,* 23 September 1973, p. 67.

Experience with the Urban Action Task Forces revealed not only their own inadequacies but deeper structural problems in the organization of the subcity service delivery system. Attempts to deal with the day-to-day problems of citizens highlighted two interrelated issues: the overcentralization of field administration and the lack of coordination among specialized departments. Many of the most nagging community concerns required action by more than one city agency. For example, sanitation workers needed help from the police in enforcing parking regulations in order to sweep the streets; the police needed cooperation from health and housing inspectors to try to close down illegal bottle clubs. Yet because of the vertical organization of the bureaucracies, there was no mechanism to encourage consistent horizontal coordination of services among multiple agencies in the community. The issue was not simply communication. Even when the task force staff brought local representatives of the relevant agencies together to work on a problem, this was not effective. The district officers charged with supervising agency field operations did not have (or felt they did not have) the authority to coordinate their activities with other agencies in the same area. After the frustration of one group session, a mayoral assistant commented: "These guys can't even commit themselves to tie their shoes, let alone deal with a community problem."[73]

Without a systematic attempt to decentralize increased operational responsibility to the city officials administering service delivery in the community, the mayoral outreach strategy continued to be limited by the organizational constraints of the traditional central bureaucracies in its attempts to improve the coordination and responsiveness of neighborhood service delivery. The history of little city halls in other cities like Boston strikingly confirms these conclusions about the strengths and weaknesses of the approach.[74]

Experiences with Urban Action Task Forces and little city halls pointed in similar directions. The mayoral outreach strategy provided a valuable independent source of information about neighborhoods for chief executives. This intelligence was useful both in

73. Lewis Feldstein, quoted in "Command Decentralization (A)," p. 12.

74. For a perceptive analysis of Boston's little city halls in their early days, see Eric Nordlinger, *Decentralizing the City* (Cambridge, Mass.: MIT Press, 1972).

spotting crises and in asserting mayoral control over the traditional agencies. Citizens often appreciated the improved access to city government. But there were serious limitations to both the complaint referral systems and the use of central authority in modifying local service operations. Simply placing a mayoral representative in the community did not materially improve the coordination or responsiveness of the neighborhood service delivery system. Eliciting constructive involvement from the existing field officers in the established bureaucracies who directly supervised the actual delivery of services appeared to be a critical gap in the approach. The new administrative decentralization strategy looked to supply this missing element.

3
PLANNING THE NEW PROGRAM

We are faced by a choice of adjusting area to function or adjusting function to area. To avoid being immobilized on the horns of this dilemma, we are forced to develop practical compromises. This task is not an academic exercise, for it is the ordinary citizens, you and I, whose ox is being gored.

—James Fesler[1]

The Shift to Administrative Decentralization

When Mayor Lindsay formed the Office of Neighborhood Government (ONG) at the beginning of his second term in 1970, and a spokesman said that it would be the "year of the neighborhoods," no one knew precisely what this meant. The extensive commitment and energy devoted to earlier organizational innovations, from superagencies to little city halls, had not resolved either the coordination problem or the responsiveness problem in the delivery of municipal services to subcity communities. The source of both predicaments was seen in the proliferation of specialized bureaucracies, and the solutions centered primarily on the assertion of political control by the mayor from the top of the administrative hierarchies or by citizens from the bottom. However, analysis of past approaches began to pinpoint the need for engaging the established agencies, and especially the field managers who supervised

1. James W. Fesler, *Area and Administration* (University, Ala.: University of Alabama Press, 1949), p. 15

service delivery operations, in the process of change. But there were no readily recognized practical or theoretical models for doing this.

In spite of the weakened momentum behind citizen participation, it was difficult to move beyond this strategy to develop new organizational designs for neighborhoods in the New York of the early 1970s. Even with the ominous history of the struggle for community control in the schools, the political debate continued to revolve around variations of the participatory approach. As the first significant ONG initiative in mid-1970, Mayor Lindsay released *A Plan for Neighborhood Government* to stimulate discussion of the decentralization issue.[2] Over the next two years four borough presidents and one state assemblyman issued similar proposals.[3] With minor variations, all recommended marginally increased neighborhood participation through a reconstituted system of community boards. During this same period, the Association of the Bar in New York sponsored an elaborate study and a conference examining more far-reaching decentralization proposals, and the State Study (Scott) Commission published the most radical plan, calling for the creation of full-scale neighborhood government in the city.[4]

No popular political consensus emerged from this barrage of decentralization proposals. Early in the process, members of the ONG staff met separately with hundreds of community civic organizations in lengthy evening sessions to test their reactions to the mayor's plans. The report on these consultations found "strong

2. Mayor John V. Lindsay, *A Plan for Neighborhood Government for New York City* (New York: Office of the Mayor, June 1970).

3. See Borough of the Bronx, Robert Abrams, President, *A Plan for Borough and Neighborhood Government in New York City,* October 1972; Andrew Stein, State Assemblyman, *Government for New York's Communities,* September 1971; Hon. Percy E. Sutton, President, Borough of Manhattan, *A Plan for Localized Government for New York City,* February 1972; Queens Borough President Donald R. Manes, *A Program for Restructuring of New York City Government,* February 1972; and Sebastian Leone, "Remarks of Borough President Sebastian Leone at Public Hearing of the Scott Commission," Borough Hall, Brooklyn, 24 February 1972.

4. See Walter G. Farr, Jr., Lance Liebman, and Jeffrey S. Wood, *Decentralizing City Government* (New York: Praeger, 1972); and Edward N. Costikyan and Maxwell Lehman, *Re-Structuring the Government of New York City* (New York: New York State Study Commission for New York City, March 1972).

support throughout the City for the concept of neighborhood government" but concluded "we do not believe that any amount of city-wide discussion will surface a city-wide consensus."[5] People differed deeply on how neighborhood representatives should be selected (election, appointment, ex officio), what their powers should be (advice, control), and over which functions (budget, personnel, police, recreation, and so on).

The spring of 1971 brought a major shift in ONG strategy. Continued concentration on political decentralization and citizen participation appeared to lead to either emotional disputes or public uncertainty. Experience with the Urban Action Task Forces suggested potential movement in a very different direction—toward a focus on the internal reorganization of the existing executive agencies. Increased national attention to the problem of "services integration" and the availability of federal funds to support local experimentation critically reinforced ONG's development of a new approach in New York. Improving the responsiveness and coordination of a comprehensive range of services at the community level remained the goals, but the strategy changed from political decentralization to administrative decentralization.[6] Instead of drawing citizens together to exert communal power against the bureaucracies, the field officers of all the major traditional agencies would be brought together to coordinate their operations in the community—through a district service cabinet. To provide flexibility, these field supervisors would need increased power over service operations in their districts—which would require internal administrative decentralization within the existing bureaucracies. And local coordination of the specialized agencies would require authoritative direc-

5. Lewis M. Feldstein, "Report to the Mayor on Consultations," (New York: Office of Neighborhood Government, December 1970), pp. 1, 5.

6. Sid Gardner, who had worked on designing services integration projects at HEW, and Bill Josephson, long a thoughtful adviser to many in New York City and other governments, both played crucial roles as consultants during this period, helping ONG rethink its approach and giving important credibility to its new direction of focusing on decentralized administration. The background to the services integration strategy and the proposed Allied Services Act of 1972 is described by the secretary of HEW who did most to promote it, in Elliot Richardson, *The Creative Balance* (New York: Holt, Rinehart, and Winston, 1976), pp. 181–83.

tion from the chief executive, transmitted through district managers appointed by the mayor. In theory, the district manager cabinets would be more effective than past approaches in improving both the coordination and responsiveness of the service delivery system at the subcity level. Coordination would occur through the encouragement and self-interest of the district officers in the local cabinets. Responsiveness would increase because civic leaders could have access to influence (although no control over) a new service institution in the community.

In planning the program, New York was breaking new ground. The many unanswered questions covered the full gamut of issues, from the specific details of implementation to the viability or advisability of the overall strategy. Administrative decentralization in government had not received a great deal of attention from scholars or activists, and multipurpose administrative decentralization had received even less. As a concept, "areal" administration had been discussed, when at all, primarily at the national, state, or metropolitan levels.[7] Until the flurry of concern provoked by the New York experiment, there were only a few proposals for creating a subcity level of municipal administration, and no experience with it.[8]

7. For the classic statement of the tension between area and function in public administration, see Fesler, *Area and Administration.* He has attempted to keep the areal perspective alive in later writings, including "Approaches to the Understanding of Decentralization," *Journal of Politics* 27 (1965); "Departmental and Interdepartmental Field Administration" (prepared for the President's [Heineman] Task Force on Government Organization, March 1967); and "The Basic Theoretical Question: How to Relate Area and Function," in *The Administration of the New Federalism,* ed. Leigh E. Grosenick (Washington, D.C.: American Society for Public Administration, September 1973). In addition, Arthur Maas convened a faculty seminar at Harvard to study the "areal division of power," and one set of papers was published in Arthur Maas, ed., *Area and Power,* (Glencoe, Ill.: Free Press, 1959).

8. One early recommendation was a brief note by Clarence E. Ridley and Orin F. Nolting, "Taking City Government Back to the People," *Public Management* 21 (April 1939). The Citizens Union in New York briefly outlined a subcity service management system to complement their goal of promoting neighborhood-based planning in "The Citizens Union Program for Community Planning," *Searchlight* 37 (July 1947). A more probing idiosyncratic presentation is in Jane Jacobs, *The Death and Life of Great American Cities* (New York: Vintage, 1961). One of the few studies

Looking almost exclusively at studies of single federal departments, public administration analysts had traditionally expressed a number of fears about the potential consequences of decentralizing administrative authority. It could lead to the distortion of central policies, inequity in the treatment of recipients, favoritism, or outright corruption. In addition, decentralized officials might gradually "go native." They could become parochial advocates for their areas and, instead of promoting greater efficiency in adapting existing central resources to local needs, might exert pressure for ever-larger budgets. Even if the approach were theoretically sound, there was a serious question whether lower-level field officials would have the managerial competence to handle the job. And finally, pressing bureaucrats to deal directly with neighborhood leaders or citizens might be counterproductive. Faced with challenge and conflict, field officers might retreat into even more rigid bureaucratic routines as a defense against the feared onslaught by the public.[9]

However, the strongest critique of New York's administrative decentralization experiment came from proponents of neighborhood government. From their perspective, the district manager cabinets dealt with "cosmetics, not substance" in failing to delegate new political power to citizens in their communities.[10] Rather than supporting the momentum toward decentralization, the system would add to bureaucratic power and create "another obstacle" to

---

of administrative decentralization in cities is Herbert Kaufman, "The New York City Health Centers" in *State and Local Government: A Case Book*, ed. Edwin A. Bock (University, Ala.: University of Alabama Press, 1963). This covered only a single agency and still stands almost alone in the published literature on the subject.

9. See David Bicknell Truman, *Administrative Decentralization* (Chicago: University of Chicago Press, 1940); Herbert Kaufman, *The Forest Ranger* (reprint, Baltimore: Johns Hopkins University Press, 1967); Herbert Kaufman, "Administrative Decentralization and Political Power," *Public Administration Review* 29 (January–February 1969); Annamarie H. Walsh, "What Price Decentralization in New York," *City Almanac* 7 (June 1972); and Michael Lipsky, "Street Level Bureaucracy," in *Neighborhood Control in the 1970s*, ed. George Frederickson (New York: Chandler, 1973).

10. Costikyan and Lehman, *Re-Structuring the Government of New York City*, p. 9.

political decentralization.[11] Or, more subtly, though administrative decentralization might produce benefits, it would be "inherently unstable."[12] The pressures on top political managers of being accountable for everything in the eyes of the public would inevitably lead them to recentralize control over local operations, unless there were legal requirements backed by a political constituency to defend decentralization.

Despite the rhetorical sting in many of these criticisms, there was little realistic possibility of implementing the neighborhood government approach. In constrast, neighborhood administration appeared to present a strategic opportunity, and ONG began the task of fleshing out the details of the model.

What Decentralized Administration Means

The mayor's eight-part plan was deceptively staightforward: (1) select neighborhood districts; (2) revise existing field operations boundaries to conform with each other in the designated communities; (3) decentralize administrative authority to district officers representing all service agencies; (4) establish district cabinets; (5) appoint district managers; (6) station central planning and budget bureau staff in each community; (7) develop districtwide management information systems; and (8) prepare neighborhood budgets.[13] But in crucial elements, this strategy camouflaged both practical complexity and theoretical uncertainty. What was a district (neighborhood, community) in a modern big city? What did administrative decentralization of the executive agencies involve? What were the powers and duties of the mayorally appointed district managers?

WHAT IS A NEIGHBORHOOD DISTRICT?
The Office of Neighborhood Government decided to use New York's existing Community Planning Districts (CPDs), which had

11. Ibid., p. 133.
12. Farr et al., *Decentralizing City Government*, p. 10. Costikyan and Lehman also make this point in *Re-Structuring the Government of New York City*, p. 116.
13. John V. Lindsay, *Program for the Decentralized Administration of Municipal Services in New York City Communities* (New York: Office of the Mayor, December 1971).

an average population of 125,000, as the basic geographic units for the proposed program. There was no single set of commonly accepted neighborhood, political, or administrative boundaries in the city, but the CPDs presented an adequate compromise between areas small enough to encourage increased participation and responsiveness, yet large enough to support a level of decentralized service management that would be meaningful to the residents. One political philosopher articulated these countervailing pressures some years ago:

> The larger and more inclusive a unit, the more its government can regulate aspects of the environment that its citizens want to regulate. . . . Conversely, the smaller the unit, the greater the opportunity for citizens to participate in decisions of their government. . . . Thus, for most citizens, participation in very large units becomes minimal and in very small units it becomes trivial.[14]

New York, like all big urban areas, was subdivided into vastly different scales of activity—from the city as a whole down through five boroughs, about thirty city council (and school) districts, sixty CPDs (and sanitation garages), over three hundred named historic neighborhoods, to many thousands of street blocks. The decision where to cut into this layered structure of the city to select the geographic scale of subdistricts was not insignificant, administratively or politically. It could effectively determine which interests would be heard with what weight, and who would respond at what cost.

There is no demonstrably "right" size for community districts in modern big cities. Without self-evident boundaries, how should they be defined: by population? by objective socioeconomic measures of need, homogeneity, or heterogeneity? by historic name, or current custom? by natural or man-made physical barriers, commercial centers, or transportation routes? by social or political units? by efficiency in service operations? or by some combination

---

14. Robert A. Dahl, "The City in the Future of Democracy," *American Political Science Review* 61 (December 1967): 960.

of these and other factors?[15] In attacking the problem, most analysts balance four criteria: cohesion of civic organization, economies of scale, political weight, and administrative simplicity. Unfortunately, there is little concrete evidence about the implications of these often conflicting concerns. No one knows precisely the upper limits beyond which the loss of social interaction prevents a meaningful political community. And, although seemingly susceptible to more rigorous analysis, the data on the optimum scale for producing public services are hardly more definitive. One judgment of the size for a viable "civil community" places its outer limits between 20,000 and 250,000 people.[16] Similarly, a survey of service delivery costs found neither economies nor diseconomies of scale in areas with populations from 25,000 to 250,000.[17] Such ranges are extremely broad. Applied to a city like New York, the upper limit would establish about thirty subdistricts, while the smaller would imply well over three hundred. To insure that areas are big enough to have political clout in the city as a whole and that their number does not overwhelm the channels of communication, many planners argue for fewer units. They suggest a sliding scale by which the larger the urban area, the larger the subdistrict. A Boston or a Baltimore might be able to support communities in the 30,000 to 50,000 range, but in the largest cities the minimum would rise to 100,000 and the maximum to 250,000.[18]

In contrast, ONG's analysis of geographic scale stressed the critical need for compatibility between the proposed communities

15. For the difficulty of defining and locating stable neighborhoods in big cities, see Suzanne Keller, *The Urban Neighborhood* (New York: Random House, 1968). The most revealing account of the complexity in specifying new subcity district boundaries is found in The Boston Urban Services Project, Harvard Law School, *Political and Administrative Decentralization of Municipal Government in Boston* (Cambridge, Mass.: Boston Urban Services Project, June 1969).

16. Daniel Elazar, "Community Self-Government and the Crisis of American Politics," *Ethics* 81 (January 1971): 95.

17. Advisory Commission on Intergovernmental Relations, "Size Can Make a Difference," *Information Bulletin* N. 70−8, 16 September 1970, p. 2.

18. See Alan A. Altshuler, *Community Control* (Indianapolis: Pegasus, 1970), pp. 130−31; Jacobs, *The Death and Life of Great American Cities*, pp. 424−25; and Howard Hallman, *Neighborhood Government in a Metropolitan Setting* (Beverly Hills, Calif.: Sage Publications, 1974), p. 174.

and the size of the administrative field districts in the operating agencies. The proponents of neighborhood government who dominated the discussion of the subcity community tended to overemphasize social, historical, or political definitions of neighborhood and underestimate the importance of bureaucratic organization. Implicitly, and sometimes explicitly, they assumed that without demonstrable economies of scale for many city services, the administrative system could adapt to politically designated subcommunities almost cost-free. Yet established field organizations not only involve immobile capital assets like police stations or community health centers, but also define an existing level of field management. Although less visible than physical facilities, the internal administrative organization of government bureaucracies has its own institutional permanence. In ONG's view, to map citizen attitudes or neighborhood civic associations and not make a comparable analysis of the local police, sanitation, health, or welfare field operations' systems was to neglect a crucial aspect of reality in defining subcity communities. The reorganization of established field units to match new neighborhood districts involves high costs, not only in relocating buildings and equipment but also in revising field supervision, reallocating personnel, redesigning communications systems, and so forth. Yet structuring community participation on one scale and the administration of services on another (often larger) scale would predictably reduce the influence of the civic subcommunities on the service delivery system.

The fact that many city agencies had field districts at approximately the same scale as the existing community planning districts was a critical argument in ONG's selection of them as the basis for the administrative decentralization program.[19] At that time, there were sixty-two CPDs covering New York. The Police Department maintained seventy-four precincts for uniformed patrols, Sanitation used fifty-eight districts for garbage collection, and Parks

19. Ironically, the criteria for designating CPDs explicitly *excluded* any serious consideration of existing service administration boundaries. See Barney Rabinow, "Community Districts in New York City" (New York: Department of City Planning, n.d.).

Maintenance had forty-five regular field offices with a number of additional special districts for recreation, pools, and golf courses.[20] None of their boundaries matched, but at least there was an existing level of command within the departments that operated in areas roughly comparable in size to the CPDs. The supervising officers in each service district could be designated to represent their departments on the decentralized cabinets without a major reorganization in the internal structure of the established bureaucracies. From the citizen's perspective, although areas encompassing 125,000 residents could hardly be viewed as intimate neighborhoods, there was a growing tradition of civic action through the community boards at that level. In addition, the CPDs did *not* conform to council or other electoral districts. This meant that the traditional political organizations would not be in a position to dominate community participation in the new approach.

The decision to use community planning districts was not without serious problems. The overlap between the existing field boundaries of the agencies and the CPDs was often grotesque. It was not unusual to find two police precincts and two sanitation districts for one area, and in the worst cases there were four or five field districts from each of these agencies covering parts of a single community. Realigning the boundaries to create a common set of service districts for all agencies in a CPD would be complex and costly. Moreover, many departments operated on a much larger scale. There were, for example, only twenty-two district health centers, nineteen city hospitals, and forty welfare centers. Housing code enforcement and rent control inspectors were supervised from the borough level. Traffic had one borough office but managed the rest of the city from its headquarters building in Queens. Devising administratively decentralized field systems for each of these agencies to coordinate their service operations in district manager cabinets at the CPD level raised many difficult organizational issues.

20. McKinsey and Company, *The Impact of Coterminal Service Districts on the Delivery of Municipal Services* (New York: State Charter Revision Commission for New York City, November 1973), Exhibit 1, pp. 3:6–7.

ADMINISTRATIVE DECENTRALIZATION
AND AREAL ADMINISTRATION

Administrative decentralization was the most complex and problematic aspect of the New York strategy. As applied in the district manager program, it was to some extent a misnomer. By definition, administrative decentralization means the delegation of authority from superior to subordinate levels within the same organizational hierarchy. ONG's objective could more accurately be described as areal administration—the creation of relatively self-contained field units managed by district officers from all major municipal agencies operating at the same geographic scale in subcity communities. Administrative decentralization and areal administration are critically interdependent, but they can have vastly different organizational implications. The former assumes an existing bureaucratic hierarchy that can be decentralized; the latter may require developing new hierarchies to administer field operations.

The problem of areal administration was not simply that bureaucratic superiors would hoard power, although this was frequently the case, but that power was often splintered among many functional specialists with multiple lines of authority controlling the actual delivery of services in the communities. District administration implied that these separate lines of activity could be concentrated through field officers at the CPD level. Some service functions (refuse collection) were sufficiently broadly defined to justify decentralization within the existing bureaucratic specialty. But not every specialty (venereal disease control) could have a management presence in the district. To take bureaucratic units administering operations from a single headquarters (traffic) or a few large areas (employment training) and expand their field systems to sixty-two CPDs would have been prohibitively costly and inefficient. That fact forced some hard, and threatening, choices. Narrow functions could be consolidated into larger units with integrated management in the district. Or central specialists could share control over local service operations with existing or new district officials. In either case, the specialists would lose autonomy over the delivery of their particular services, and they could be expected to resist. Overcoming this opposition would require the assertion of authority by their "generalist" superiors in the bureaucracy before decentralization could occur to the generalists in the districts. This conflict between the functional specialist and the generalist both in the center and in the field was, and is, the classic problem of areal administration.[21] Analysis in this tradition suggested that the degree of specialization in any bureaucracy would to a great extent determine the difficulty of decentralizing effective administrative authority to the district level.[22] ONG's experience confirmed this thesis, but it also revealed how political pressures, professional traditions, and economies of scale compounded the problem.

When ONG began its operational planning, there were no comprehensive models of decentralized areal administration in big cities to follow. Without definitive guidance, there was no alternative but to carry out an agency-by-agency analysis of the city's administrative structure. Although the mayor's plan mentioned a process to "transfer specific powers and responsibilities now vested in central commands to the local agency officers," no one knew precisely what these "powers" should or could be in practice.[23] From its experience, ONG initially stressed increased district-level authority and responsibility in the management of day-to-day operations, interagency coordination, and community relations. Gradually, the local role in the more sensitive areas of planning, budgeting, and personnel decisions would be enlarged as well. The reorganization of the New York Police Department represented a possible model of what administrative decentralization in a big city bureaucracy could mean.

"COMMAND DECENTRALIZATION": THE POLICE MODEL

Paralleling ONG's planning efforts, the police commissioner had taken the lead in initiating a process of "command decentraliza-

21. See Fesler, *Area and Administration*, especially pp. 65–86. For a restatement of these issues in the New York context, see Stanely J. Heginbotham and Robin Maas, *Between Community and City Bureaucracy*, pt. 2: *Responses of City Agencies to the Experiment* (New York: Bureau of Applied Social Research, Columbia University, February 1973), pp. 4–14.

22. See Kaufman, "The New York City Health Centers."

23. Lindsay, *Program for the Decentralized Administration of Municipal Services*, p. 5.

tion" within his department. He wanted to "move away from the rule-book mentality and the attitude that a commander could be judged on the basis of not rocking the boat and simply damping the fires in his precinct."[24] Over an extended period, this new style led to far-reaching changes in the pattern of police field administration.[25] Concretely, it meant that precinct commanders were given increased flexibility in assigning the uniformed forces in their districts and were authorized to shift a portion of their men to plainclothes "anticrime" patrols. In addition to the existing community relations officer, a "planning sergeant" was attached to the precinct to analyze crime patterns and develop new strategies for allocating the existing manpower. An "administrative lieutenant" was designated to release the commanding officer from paperwork so that he could spend more time managing operations and dealing directly with community leaders. A new system of "command discipline" which put more responsibility on precinct commanders for controlling corruption was instituted, and this was later supplemented with a small internal investigations staff in the field. Some of the detectives who had operated in separate, specialized divisions were placed under the control of the precinct. In return for this increased authority, the definition of responsibilities was changed. No longer was it sufficient to fulfill the detailed, and often peripheral, items on the civil service "job specs." Commanders would be held accountable for the crime rate and the level of corruption in their precincts.[26]

24. Patrick V. Murphy, interview, 30 October 1974.

25. The reforms described here combine steps taken both under Commissioner Murphy and his successor, Donald Cawley. The department never issued a comprehensive decentralization plan. The most detailed description of the early administrative changes is found in Elwyn C. Lee, "Management Decentralization: New York City Police Department" (New Haven: Yale University, Institution for Social and Policy Studies, November 1972).

26. The department also developed Neighborhood Police Teams in a number of areas. Structurally, the approach extended administrative decentralization below the precinct level to give additional command responsibilities to the "sector" sergeants. This experiment received more public attention than the changes in the role of the precinct commander. See, for example, Lawrence W. Sherman, Catherine H. Milton, and Thomas V. Kelly, *Team Policing* (Washington, D.C.: Police Foundation, 1973), pp. 28–33.

The Office of Neighborhood Government viewed the police command decentralization strategy as a model for strengthening the authority and responsibility of field officers in other agencies. Yet the Police Department was in many ways atypical of city bureaucracies. With over thirty thousand employees at that time, it was the largest department under the mayor. The agency had a comparatively homogeneous, dominant function, strong central management, an established geographic delivery system, experienced field officers at the local level, and a large, relatively stable allocation of resources in each district. No other agency could match all these conditions.

DECENTRALIZATION PLANS FOR CITY AGENCIES
Area and function: the organizational balance. What was the "organization" that would be decentralized? The ONG program eventually included all the major service units under the mayor—six superagencies (the administrations for Environmental Protection; Housing and Development; Human Resources; Health Services; Parks, Recreation, and Cultural Affairs; and Transportation), two departments (Police and Fire), and one overhead agency (City Planning)—but not education, which operated under an independent board.[27] It was apparent that creating a direct replica of the mayor's citywide cabinet at the district level would be impossible. None of the superagencies had consolidated the field operations of its constituent departments. For example, specific services in the Environmental Protection Administration continued to be delivered through the old Departments of Sanitation, Water Resources, and Air Resources. Similar organizational realities existed in each of the other superagencies. Parks had two bureaucratically separate delivery systems; Transportation had two; Health and Housing each had four; and Human Resources had five. To develop integrated field systems in every superagency was beyond ONG's substantive competence or political capacity. But this meant that in-

---

27. In addition to education, the program did not officially include mass transit (another independent, special-purpose agency), employment services (state), or social security (federal), although representatives from these agencies did participate in cabinets in some areas.

stead of a relatively manageable district cabinet composed of representatives from nine agencies, ONG was faced with the possible chore of decentralizing and coordinating almost twenty-five organizational units (see Table 1).

On first analysis, there appeared to be a relatively clear dichotomy between bureaucracies that administered services through geographically based field districts in the community and those organized around functionally based professional specialties without such territorially decentralized delivery systems. In the older agencies responsible for relatively homogenous citywide activities in safety, refuse collection, parks, and highways, there were police precinct commanders, sanitation superintendents, parks foremen, and highways foremen already established in districts roughly comparable to the areas projected for the cabinets. In these cases, the Police decentralization model for delegating power down the line in the existing hierarchy appeared directly applicable. Thus, for example, the commissioner of sanitation authorized the district superintendents who participated in the cabinets "to rearrange, reschedule, or reroute your normal complement of men and equipment, on your own initiative, to meet either specific requests for services . . . or more permanent district needs. This may include collection routing and schedules; changes in broom routings, etc."[28]

In contrast, agencies dealing with the recently expanding concerns of local government in housing, health, and social welfare were split into more narrowly organized specialties. Resources tended to be targeted to selected geographic areas or client groups, administrative units were more centralized, and services were channeled through a bewildering variety of city and private organizations. At that time, for example, the Human Resources Administration (HRA) was organized into five divisions that delivered certain mandated social services and income maintenance payments in forty welfare centers, youth services in thirty separate districts, manpower training programs in eleven regions, community action

28. Herbert Elish, Memorandum to District Superintendents, Districts 9, 28, 37, 38, 40, 41, 42, "Powers of District Superintendents in Areas Designated by Mayor's Office of Neighborhood Government for Aministrative Decentralization," 10 April 1972.

Table 1. District Service Cabinet: Composition by Agency/Department

Agency	Constituent Delivery System	District Cabinet Representation
Addiction Services Agency	Residential/Ambulatory Contracts	Borough Director (ASA)
Environmental Protection Administration	Sanitation Water Resources Air Resources	District Superintendent (Sanitation) Borough Engineer (Water)
Fire Department	Bureau of Fire	Battalion Chief (Fire)
Housing and Development Administration	Rent and Housing Maintenance Development Buildings Relocation	Area Housing Director (HDA)
Human Resources Administration	Social Services/Income Maintenance Youth Services Manpower Training Community Development Child Development	Human Resources District Director (HRA) District Director (Youth) District Director (Community Services)
Health Services Administration	Health Mental Health (Hospitals Corporation) (Comprehensive Health Planning)	District Health Officer (Health)
Police Department	Patrol Services Bureau Detectives Bureau	Precinct Commander (Police Patrol)
Parks, Recreation, and Cultural Affairs Administration	Maintenance and Operations Recreation	General Parks Foreman (M&O) Assistant Supervisor (Recreation)
Transportation Administration	Highways Traffic	District Foreman (Highways) Borough Engineer (Traffic)
City Planning Department	Borough Planning Offices	Borough Director (Planning)

programs in twenty-six designated poverty areas, and an agency for child development that contracted with private sponsors to operate hundreds of local day-care centers. There was no district-level official in any of these components consistently present throughout the city.

The planners at ONG judged that the district manager would be overwhelmed attempting to coordinate so many diverse service systems and supported the HRA administrator in establishing a new field official with authority to represent all of these social welfare departments on the cabinet. Thus the position of "human resources district director" was created. This would give the superagency itself an organizational presence in the field for the first time. But the crucial question was what authority the HRA administrator could wrest from his theoretically subordinate departmental commissioners to give to the new district officers. Would they control or even "sign off" on day-care contracts, assign homemakers, approve youth service centers, or determine employment training priorities? The answer was no. The institutional and interest group resistance to the transfer of power to a new official outside the existing hierarchies was not overcome. Instead of providing for an authoritative field manager, the job description only established a weak coordinator to "convene meetings" of local officials from all HRA constituent agencies, "foster cooperation and working relationships," "review and comment" on proposed programs, and "assess and evaluate overall progress"—a litany of the weakest words in the bureaucrat's lexicon.[29] Such "decentralization" did not change the existing service delivery systems in the field, and there was concern that without stronger central backing the new position would simply be a façade behind which the old baronies would continue to operate. ONG saw the introduction of the new field officer as the first step in reorienting the agency toward an areal basis of organization, but the details of this evolutionary process remained largely unexamined and undefined. Until the HRA district directors could assert their influence, the district managers often included representatives from some of the existing specialized departments directly on their

29. Human Resources Administration, "Human Resources District Directors," ERPP Notice no. 3, 22 February 1972.

cabinets in order to be able to coordinate service projects in the communities.

An analogous area coordinator strategy was initially applied to housing and health services. New "area housing directors" were appointed in the Housing and Development Administration to pull together interdepartmental inspection and rehabilitation activities in selected neighborhood preservation districts. A "neighborhood health services manager" was projected in the Health Services Administration (HSA) to coordinate local operations of the city's health and mental health departments as well as the semiautonomous hospitals and comprehensive health planning agencies.[30] But in the health field, these paper plans were soon forgotten: there was a prior problem. One of the HSA constituents, the Department of Health, maintained a relatively elaborate, geographically based delivery system in twenty-two district health centers spread throughout the city. However, the district health officer in each facility could not even control or coordinate his own department's activities in his area. Specialization within the department revealed how professionalism compounded the complexity of areal decentralization.

Professionalism and the autonomy of the specialist. Professional norms and traditions could markedly increase the expected bureaucratic resistance of functional specialists to decentralized control by generalist field officers.[31] This issue was presented most starkly in the Department of Health, although the tension between police detectives and uniformed patrol commanders was similar. Historically, the medical profession had given greatest status to the specialist and relatively little recognition to the general practitioner or public health administrator. In the Health Department, this tradition reinforced and sustained dominant power in nearly a score of narrowly organized central bureaus (infectious disease control, venereal disease control, child health, maternity services, and so

30. For a description of these roles, see Heginbotham and Maas, *Responses of City Agencies,* pp. 53–69.

31. An elaboration of this argument based on the New York experience is found in Geraldine Alpert, *Professional Values and Bureaucratic Behavior* (New York: Bureau of Applied Social Research, Columbia University, September 1974).

forth). The district health officers were little more than caretakers in the local health centers, where a series of separate services was delivered to the public. Bureau directors at headquarters controlled the budgets and staffing and even set the hours for the specialized clinics in each district. There had been numerous attempts to increase the health officers' power since the first district was established in 1915. Most were based on some "dual supervision" formula that tried to split authority between the "technical" (specialist) and the "administrative" (area) officials. But none successfully cracked the professional prerogatives, and the operational control, of the central bureaus.[32]

During the ONG experiment, a new health commissioner and his deputy again tackled the problem of strengthening district administration. Instead of another effort to balance area and function, they made a major commitment to assert the dominance of central and geographic authority within the organization. A series of executive orders cut the "line" of authority between the bureaus and their operating personnel in the field. The central specialists became "staff" advisors who would set standards and evaluate performance; they would not directly administer services. In effect, the commissioner first centralized authority by withdrawing it from the bureau chiefs into his own hands and then decentralized it through a new chain of command flowing from his office into the districts. This decentralization strategy was further complicated, however, by the simultaneous attempt to introduce "lay" management into the department. Day-to-day operating authority for all local clinical services was delegated to new "district health managers." While in theory these officials reported to the existing district health officers, in fact they had an independent line of responsibility to the first deputy commissioner downtown. Decentralization in this case involved not only a shift of power from technical specialists to field generalists, but from medical professionals to nonmedical managers. This development would markedly compound the tensions in implementing the new approach.[33]

32. This history is traced in Kaufman, "The New York City Health Centers."
33. See Anthony C. Mustalish, Gary Eidsvold, and Lloyd F. Novick, "Decentralization in the New York City Department of Health: Reorganization of a Public Health Agency," *American Journal of Public Health* 66 (1976): 1149–54.

Economies of scale and operational dependence. Economies of scale in producing public goods are usually associated with centralization. Sewage treatment and waste disposal plants are common examples where the reduction of unit cost in larger facilities has led to citywide (or areawide) administration. But for ONG, it became important to distinguish between services whose product was inevitably shared throughout broad benefit areas (fluoridated water), and those whose production was divisible into separate local units. For example, in the Highways Department, street repaving for the entire city was controlled centrally, and the asphalt was spread by two giant machines. But because the product could be applied in discrete amounts for different communities, the highways district foreman could be delegated the authority to decide which local streets would be repaved within the resources allotted to his area. In such cases, the economy of large-scale production could be made consistent with decentralized decision-making by field officers.

On close examination, every service function was in reality a bundle of interdependent subfunctions, and economies of scale often dictated that some of the specialized activities would be controlled by bureaucratic units above the district level. Thus, no district officer managed a fully self-contained organization, but the degree of operational dependence for specialized support from others within the same agency varied dramatically. Even in the largest departments like Police, a precinct commander was dependent on central bureaus for local operational assistance, whether in dealing with snipers or directing traffic. But with two to four hundred patrolmen under him, these limitations were marginal in relation to the core responsibility for safety and the maintenance of order. In contrast, the general parks foreman's normal complement of laborers and equipment could only perform crude maintenance and cleanup work in local recreational facilities. For many common jobs, like fixing a drinking fountain, he was dependent on the borough shop crews for plumbers, carpenters, masons, and ironworkers. Operational difficulties arose because the district officer had no idea either what overall amount of assistance he could count on during a given year or when any particular job would receive attention. He merely reported problems on a "work order," and that was his last involvement in the process. The large backlog in completing jobs meant that crews might eventually be sent to repair park benches when a broken basketball backboard had become the pressing concern of the community—a situation that occurred all too often. Typically, the approval of equipment or construction contracts presented an equivalent problem where central decisions impinged on local operations in many agencies.

Several administrative techniques could be used to strengthen the role of district officers in planning and scheduling these "outside" specialists: prorating resources for each area, setting local priorities, holding formal consultations between the district and higher levels, or simply improving the flow of information about future actions from central to district offices. The Parks Department, for example, gave the general foremen authority to set priorities among the outstanding work orders for their districts and instructed the borough shops to make assignments according to these locally devised plans, which would be jointly reviewed every month.[34]

UNRESOLVED PROBLEMS IN DECENTRALIZED ADMINISTRATION
In the process of planning for administrative decentralization with the agencies, ONG uncovered a number of problems that were left dangling.

Scale of administration. Some departments (Water Resources, Traffic, Addiction Services, City Planning) had to be represented in the cabinet by borough officials—the lowest level in their existing field systems. Their functions were too distinct to merge with others, even under the artifice of a designated area coordinator, and there was neither the need nor the funding to add new layers of local administration. Only in the case of the Traffic Department did ONG later successfully support additional borough engineer positions to decentralize responsibilities previously handled at headquarters. Borough officers would work with a few experimental cabinets but could not cover every area if the system of district administration were extended to all sixty-two community districts.

34. James H. Linden, Memorandum to All Park Managers, "Neighborhood Government," 13 January 1972.

Resources and authority. Decentralized administration depended not only on the formal delegation of authority but on the resources necessary to use it effectively. Power without the means to act would be meaningless. Leaders in the Recreation Department were anxious to increase the decision-making discretion of their field officers. Yet with only four hundred personnel citywide, their capacity to be responsive to concerns from the community or other agencies was drastically limited. The problem in recreation was not the decentralization of authority; it was money.

Resource instability. For some departments, an underlying issue in strengthening field management was less the availability of resources than the stability of their assignment to district officers. One economy of scale in large municipal agencies was that men and equipment could be shifted from one area to another to cover either long-term changes or temporary special needs. In the Sanitation Department, "attachments" and "detachments" of men and equipment occurred on a daily basis. (It was called "flying" in the Police Department.) Such practices could provide critical assistance to areas in trouble, but they could also inhibit operational planning and penalize efficient management. A sanitation district superintendent could not develop a rational plan to assign men and equipment to collection routes if he did not know what men and equipment he would have available. Nor would such a system give an individual superintendent much incentive to manage efficiently. For example, if he had only 10 percent of his trucks "down," compared to 30 percent in the next district, the borough superintendent would very likely shift his equipment to the less effective superintendent.

Ideally, administrative decentralization should have been able to preserve the gains in efficiency for the field officers who won them. But permanent assignments meant either providing additional resources or incurring the hostility of other district officers who would feel that the experimental areas were not doing their fair share. Neither ONG nor the agencies developed consistent techniques to resolve this apparent conflict between the efficiency of shifting men and equipment to optimize resource use citywide and the disincentive to improving performance that this system could produce for individual district officers.

Layers of supervision. In each of the large departments—Police, Sanitation, Parks, Highways—the position of the division, zone, or borough supervisors was particularly sensitive. Decentralized administration implied a trend toward strengthening the power of the district and the headquarters staff at the expense of these bureaucrats in the middle. Instead of being in the line of command, they would increasingly be viewed as monitors, evaluators, or sources of technical assistance to the district officers in the field. Ultimately, some of their positions might become superfluous. These implications produced the worst combination of pressures, since the middle-level supervisors sensed the long-term threat but continued to wield extensive operational control in the short term. Field commanders were placed in an extremely difficult position. If a district officer offended his borough supervisor by exercising his newly decentralized powers, he might find his operations subtly undercut next week, or next year. There was no carrot to induce cooperation from the middle-level managers; only the stick of central orders forced them to comply with the new program.

Incentives. Bureaucracies traditionally offer few incentives for field officers to take initiative or cooperate with outsiders in other agencies. Why should they put effort into the district manager cabinets? There were no salary increases attached to participation in the experiment, and ONG did not mount an extensive training program to provide new skills or motivation. Agency representatives might receive an initial boost from increased recognition by the Mayor's Office or their own commissioners, but such inducements were minor ones. The only major incentive for district officers to assist in the new program was that the district manager cabinets could prove helpful to them in doing their own jobs.

In summary, ONG's plans for administrative decentralization produced a pragmatic patchwork. The designs were strongest in the older, geographically based municipal agencies and weakest in the newer, more specialized housing and human services. The formal decentralization guidelines only scratched the surface of institutionalized bureaucratic power. Generally, they did not crack through the existing lines of functional specialization or begin to deal with the role of the districts in budget and personnel administration. But the plans did set a new tone for change in each of the agencies and in the city government as a whole. They established ground rules within which the district managers could encourage a different style of bureaucratic action on the day-to-day service delivery problems in the communities.

THE ROLE OF THE DISTRICT MANAGER

The district manager was crucial to the success of ONG's plan, yet his role was extraordinarily delicate to define. If administrative decentralization created the potential for innovative action among the members of the district cabinet, the district manager was the catalyst who would stimulate the district officers to use their new authority to improve services. The creation of a central Office of Neighborhood Government in the Mayor's Office was viewed as the chief executive's normal prerogative to organize his own staff. But the introduction of a full-time mayoral representative at the community level was certain to arouse the fears of elected officials, bureaucrats, and neighborhood activists. Would he be a partisan political agent, interrupt the chain of command in the agencies, assume the function of civic organizations—or not?

The district manager implicit in the ONG proposal was an "integrator," not a subcity manager with extensive formal powers.[35] Some writers on decentralization have assumed, and others have insisted, that an areal official would require "line" authority over local agency operations in order to coordinate community services effectively.[36] In New York, there was little substantive argument, and no political possibility, for such a course of action. No mayor who wanted to continue to govern would authorize district manag-

---

35. For the concept of the integrator in private business corporations, see Paul R. Lawrence and Jay W. Lorsch, "New Management Job: The Integrator," *Harvard Business Review* 45 (November–December 1967). The full study that served as the basis for this article is found in Lawrence and Lorsch, *Organization and Environment* (Boston: Division of Research, Graduate School of Business Administration, Harvard University, 1967).

36. For example, see Guy Black, "The Decentralization of Urban Government: A Systems Approach" (Washington, D.C.: Program of Policy Studies in Science and Technology, George Washington University, August 1968), p. 16, and George J. Washnis, *Community Development Strategies* (New York: Praeger, 1974), p. 406.

ers to overrule a police commissioner and give direct orders to police precinct commanders.

Other analysts have suggested an inverse relationship between the scope of responsibility and the degree of authority appropriate for areal officials. The narrower and more coherent the range of activities, the more likely that a district official could constructively exercise operational control. In contrast, a generalist involved with a broader spectrum of government actions could not be expected to have the knowledge or expertise to make binding decisions affecting a variety of specialized functions.[37] By this line of reasoning, the comprehensiveness of the New York program implied relatively weak formal authority for the mayor's administrator in the community. But in ONG's strategy, this formal weakness did not mean passivity. The district managers were intended to be aggressive intermediaries—between city agencies, agencies and citizens, field officers and central administrators, and, finally, neighborhoods and the mayor. They would not only facilitate voluntary cooperation in these different environments but would identify unmet problems or opportunities and stimulate the action to deal with them. Within the local cabinets, the managers would motivate, assist, and prod the district officers to improve the coordination and responsiveness of their service operations in the community.

While the positive conception of the district manager's role remained relatively vague, there was a greater awareness of what it should *not* be. The manager was not to be a community relations buffer fending off pressures from citizens so that the agencies could continue to operate in the same old ways. Through administrative decentralization, the field officers themselves would assume increased responsibility for dealing directly with neighborhood leaders. Similarly, the manager was not to be a complaint processor or ombudsman picking up the pieces after the agencies had made mistakes. Rather, the goal was to lay the groundwork for systemic changes in city service delivery patterns to prevent problems in the first place. The manager was also not to be a single-

37. Fesler, *Area and Administration*, p. 89. By the same author, see the analogous comparison between the proposed roles for different federal regional officials in "Departmental and Interdepartmental Field Administration," pp. 14–28.

minded community advocate pressing the claims of his neighbor-hood constituents for additional central resources. His mandate was to close the gap between local preferences and agency actions within the existing citywide allocations. And finally, the manager was not to be a partisan political operator. His responsibility was to improve services generally, not to manipulate public resources for patronage, allegiance, or votes in the fashion of the traditional clubhouse machine.

The district managers had minimal power to meet their complex responsibilities. The basis for their authority and influence within the administration lay primarily in their direct appointment by the mayor. Each was the designated agent of the chief executive who "coordinates and expedites the work of local agency district com-manders in a particular community."[38] But this mayoral mantel clothed the managers more with symbolic than with hard bureau-cratic powers. On paper, they could only "convene" and "preside over" the district cabinet, "receive reports upon request from district officers . . . within obvious limits of time and propriety," "desig-nate a 'lead agency' to review a specific neighborhood problem and present a solution," and "review and comment" on new agency policies "prior to their implementation in the district."[39] The dis-trict managers were not given any operational authority over ser-vice delivery, and the field officers on the cabinets were specifically told that the established chain of command in their agencies would not be affected by the program.

The authority and reward system for cabinet members continued to lie in their separate bureaucratic hierarchies. Recognizing this reality, ONG insisted that each district manager be interviewed and approved by individual agency administrators or commissioners before his appointment. Thus, when a manager appeared at the cabinet, he came with the imprimatur not only of the mayor but of each district officer's bureaucratic boss. Implicitly, this conveyed the message that although the district manager did not have direct

38. "District Manager: General Statement of Duties and Responsibilities" (ONG files, n.d.).

39. "District Manager: Examples of Typical Tasks" and "Proposed Class Specifica-tions: Project Manager (Office of Neighborhood Government)" (ONG files, n.d.).

authority, he had access to the highest levels of the administration. Local issues and problems could be bucked upstairs. Cabinet participants would know that they did not have to take orders from a district manager, but they would also know that he could go over their heads in any dispute—and not many would want to test the limits of this power.

The district managers had other potential sources of influence. The position was budgeted at a salary of $22,500 to $27,500, or about the level of deputy commissioners in the central agencies during the early 1970s, and higher than most cabinet officers at that time. Money being the conventional measure of status, this sum signaled the managers' intended weight in the system. It was much higher than the pay scale for the earlier neighborhood city hall directors and enabled ONG to recruit more competent and experienced people. Each district manager was budgeted for a small staff, usually three assistants and a secretary, and an office with meeting space, telephones, typewriters, and access to copying equipment. These were limited but tangible resources. Almost without exception, none of the agency field officers had staff who could do the planning or follow-up on special projects outside their daily routines. Many neighborhood civic associations had a similar need for assistance. The manager could provide the missing support for new activities. And finally, the district managers would increasingly become an important source of information. Occupying a unique position between the city administration and the community, they would know more about agency operations and neighborhood concerns than anyone else inside or outside of the government. This could become a progressively more valuable asset, earning credibility and influence on all sides.

In contrast to most neighborhood decentralization strategies, the first district managers were required not to be residents of the areas in which they worked. ONG was determined to suppress the specter of community control in the eyes of the agency officers and their unions and to prevent the manager from being particularly identified with any faction in the community. Such a requirement also helped assuage the predictable fears of local elected officials that the position would be used as a stepping-stone for an aspiring political competitor. On the other hand, as outsiders the managers had the delicate task of establishing themselves in the civic life of the community to mobilize a constituency for their work.

As integrators, the district managers had to gain their influence through personal skill and professional competence, not "positional power."[40] The role called for people with unusual capabilities: knowledge of city government, demonstrated initiative in program development, the ability to deal with different kinds of service bureaucracies and bureaucrats ranging from commissioners to front-line civil servants, a facility for working with citizens and civic organizations in diverse local neighborhoods—and the capacity to handle frustration. Since so much of the experiment's success or failure would depend on their performance, the program's planners spent a great deal of time searching for candidates. Given the unique new emphasis on internal administrative coordination, ONG looked for professionals experienced in municipal government and sensitive to the constraints, rules, and regulations inherent in large public bureaucracies, but not inclined to be trapped by them. The ideal candidate was a creative, entrepreneurial bureaucrat. All the initial district managers were recruited from within the city administration, but they came from the newer, rather than the traditional, civil service agencies. Only after the program was established in a number of areas did ONG risk hiring some experienced civic leaders and allowing them to work in their own communities.

The district manager cabinet experiment involved a complex reorientation of the entire administrative arm of government. The political dynamics that led to the acceptance of this strategy are revealing.

The Politics of Planning to Decentralize

In 1969, the experience with school decentralization almost lost John Lindsay his bid for reelection. Yet barely a year into a second term, he backed a major new program to decentralize the administration of city services. Why? The stake and involvement of the Mayor, agency administrators, local legislators, and community

---

40. See Paul R. Lawrence and Jay W. Lorsch, "Differentiation and Integration in Complex Organizations," *Administrative Science Quarterly* 12 (June 1967): 34–37.

leaders in this approach were very different from earlier decentralization efforts.

THE MAYOR

Multiagency action demanded the active support of the chief executive and his top staff. Experience with Community Action and Model Cities programs had shown that responsibility for interdepartmental coordination could not be delegated to one of the operating bureaucracies that were to be coordinated. But decentralized administration seemed to embroil the Mayor's Office in complex organizational questions usually handled independently by the specialists in each department according to the requirements of their separate service functions.

The district manager cabinet strategy solved a political dilemma for a mayor caught between the commitment to strengthen neighborhoods and the dangers of citizen participation. It finessed the albatross of political decentralization. The plan for areal administration maintained the mayor in a position of leadership on government decentralization without conjuring up fears of community control. It also dovetailed with the managerial image that Lindsay was cultivating to overcome the deep-seated public skepticism about his effectiveness as an administrator. Ironically, during this period in the early 1970s, the major external pressure for political decentralization came from the Republican-initiated State Study Commission for New York City, the so-called Scott Commission. Its first published report attacked the overcentralization of municipal administration under a strong mayor and called for the creation of thirty or so locally elected neighborhood governments.[41] Given the intensifying Lindsay-Rockefeller feud, the mayor could easily view the work of the Commission as an attempt to embarrass him on his own turf (and threaten his budding presidential ambitions).[42]

---

41. See Costikyan and Lehman, *Re-Structuring the Government of New York City.*

42. Some analysts saw the neighborhood government proposal as a Republican party strategy to breach the Democratic dominance of the city. Even if they couldn't capture the mayoralty, the Republicans could consistently win a few smaller districts and splinter the unity of the city. See Wallace S. Sayre, "Smaller Does Not Mean Better, Necessarily," *New York Times,* 8 April 1972, p. 29.

In this environment, the district manager cabinets could be portrayed as a "responsible," "concrete" step to improve services, in contrast to the "radical social engineering" of full-scale neighborhood government.

On the other hand, although the district manager cabinet plan had public political benefits, it also entailed immediate internal costs for the mayor. "This is," said one close advisor, "the biggest organizational change to come out of most of these Administrators since they've been on the job."[43] The mayor could only press his agency heads on a limited number of matters. Administrative decentralization would absorb energy and displace other items on his agenda. Was this where he wanted to spend his leadership capital? After an initial briefing on the strategy, Lindsay himself was uncertain. He was concerned that forcing agencies into a common administrative mold in community districts might prove inefficient for their separate service delivery systems. Most of all, he wanted to know what he would have to ask his administrators to do. And it was clear that he would not push them very far down the path to decentralization against their judgment.

The balance between the chief executive's authority and agency responsibility in developing decentralized areal administration was extremely delicate. Without the impetus of central leadership, nothing was likely to get off the ground. But from the beginning, ONG recognized the other part of the equation. As its first director stated: "If we were to be at all successful, the agencies would have to pick up the ball entirely and run with it. If you could describe this program solely as a mayor's office operation, then the program would probably be a failure."[44] There was no conceivable way that multiagency administrative decentralization could be directed on a day-to-day basis by the mayor or ONG. Both the politically appointed administrators and the ranking civil servants had to adopt the program as their agenda for administering the departments. It had to become a part of the bureaucratic culture itself.

---

43. Andrew Kerr, quoted in Lewis Feldstein, Memo to Files, "Meeting with Kerr," 24 August 1971.

44. Lewis Feldstein, quoted in "Command Decentralization (B)" (Boston: Harvard Business School, Intercollegiate Case Clearing House, 1972), p. 3.

THE AGENCIES AND UNIONS

In approaching the administrators, ONG stressed that the coordination possible through the district manager cabinet system was in the self-interest of their own field officers; it did not represent the assertion of mayoral control over agency service operations. The implications of areal administration for internal reorganization were not pressed very far. At a minimum, each agency had only to designate field officers to serve on the cabinets and formally define their decentralized authority to participate in the program. Even allowing for this relatively undemanding strategy, the responses of the agencies to the district manager cabinet concept were surprisingly positive, and there was little outright opposition. However, the motivations to support, acquiesce in, or resist the new approach varied considerably and fell into no predicatable pattern based on type of service or balance between area and function in agency organization. They depended more on the goals and management strategies of each agency administrator.

Despite the generally accepted pressures for centralization in government bureaucracies—the public responsibility of political executives for any and all problems under their purview, the fear of incompetence or corruption in lower-level officials—a number of agency heads were already planning to decentralize their internal operations. This group included an unusual mixture of the Police Department, the Human Resources Administration, and the Department of Recreation. For ONG, nothing could match in importance the fact that the police commissioner had taken the lead in initiating decentralization as a strategy to improve accountability and performance within his department. A word previously identified with black community control advocates was now proclaimed by the city's chief law enforcement administrator. As the most visible government workers dealing with the most worrisome concerns of citizens in all communities, the police were essential participants in the local cabinets. But the mayor would never have ordered the commissioner to decentralize the agency in the face of the commissioner's own objections. From the department's perspective, ONG presented few additional demands for internal reorganization and offered the possibility of tangible benefits in obtaining support and cooperation from other city departments and civic leaders in the communities.

In the Human Resources Administration, the new administrator was convinced of the need for a community-based delivery system that would integrate, rather than compartmentalize, social services for clients and families.[45] Decentralized areal administration could also be part of a strategy to gain control over his own fragmented agency. The institution of a "human resources district director" was one step in this direction, and ONG was a source of support to win backing for the agency's own goals within the Mayor's Office. Similarly, the Department of Recreation viewed ONG as an advocate that could help win approval for the agency's desire to add a new level of district officers to its internal structure. The motivation for this reform was not coordination; it was to put a relatively forgotten bureaucracy back on the map. As the commissioner later stated, the cabinets "greatly enhanced community recognition of the role, resources, capabilities, and in some cases, the existence of the Department of Recreation."[46]

For a number of administrators, ONG's demands were perceived as peripheral to the major management objectives of the agencies. Usually this was the case where the executives saw their opportunities for reform in developing new, specialized projects that would be mounted and controlled centrally. In some cases (Health and Highways), they participated only minimally in the cabinets until later in the experiment, when decentralization came to be high on their own agendas. In Housing, a reluctant administrator gave his backing only when it became apparent that the appointment of "area housing directors" and involvement in the district manager cabinets would win HUD approval for a federal neighborhood preservation grant that had previously been turned down. Of all city agencies, only the Sanitation Department seriously opposed the decentralization proposal. Many administrators were wary about the ability of their existing district officers to handle additional responsibilities. The sanitation commissioner favored increasing

45. See Jule Sugarman, speech delivered at a Conference of the New York City Inter-agency Council on Child Welfare, Andover, Massachusetts, February 1971.

46. Joseph Davidson, quoted in Robin Maas, *Decentralizing New York City Service Agencies, 1971–1973* (New York: Office of Neighborhood Government, May 1974), p. 95.

the authority of his borough commanders but felt that district decentralization was premature. He warned that ONG's requirement for reorganization could seriously disrupt services. "The department is very suspicious. The approach suggested here may raise the level of fear and suspicion so high that it will endanger collections."[47] In its experience, ONG had found many district superintendents to be competent and cooperative. But the prediction of problems from the agency that had come to symbolize the mayor's weakness as an administrator (because of its failures in a snow removal crisis during his first term) was a serious threat to the decentralization plan. Sanitation was second only to Police in public visibility. District cabinets without the capacity to deal with garbage collection or street sweeping would lose much of their relevance in the communities. The issue of administrative decentralization in Sanitation presented a choice between cautious management and the imperatives of the district manager cabinet approach. This was a decision only the mayor could make, but precisely the kind he had hoped to avoid.

After six months of planning and negotiations during 1971, ONG had reached the limits of what it could achieve without further backing. The groundwork for the simultaneous decentralization of city agencies had been laid, but it lacked closure. Two of the mayor's closest advisors—Edward Hamilton, then budget director but soon to be deputy mayor, and Jay Kriegel, the special counsel—stepped into the breach. All agency heads affected by the program were invited to a joint meeting at City Hall in early October. When Hamilton distributed and asked for comments on a "project milestone" chart that ONG had prepared for him, showing the steps each agency would have to take so that the first cabinets could meet in January, there were gasps around the table. The administrators now realized that the program would be a reality. Kriegel added his own gambit, which skillfully neutralized the mayor's qualms. He told the group: "The mayor is committed to this but he is nervous. He does not want to impose more priorities on his administrators

---

47. Herbert Elish, quoted in John Mudd, Memo to Files, "Meeting with Administrators," 8 October 1971.

when he is continually approaching them with internal agency issues. We need to get back to him and for the first time have his Cabinet take a proposal *to* him."[48] Revealing the weakness of ONG's backing in this way neatly boxed in any agency head who might have thought he could complain about the program privately to the mayor. To do so would have challenged two of the most powerful men in city government, who were in unique positions to do favors for, or undercut, each of them. After this appeal, the sanitation commissioner stated, and then swallowed, his worries about the implications of reorganization for his department: "I finally agreed that I would go along with the decentralization approach, [because] neighborhood government would not mean anything without the participation of the agency with the most frontline visibility."[49]

The one issue that could have blocked implementation of the program after the agency administrators' meeting was widespread opposition by the unions. But this did not materialize. Decentralization that involved citizen participation had become a red flag, but administrative decentralization was another matter. Some leaders, like those in the Patrolmen's Benevolent Association, privately blustered that the approach would inevitably lead to lateral entry (the introduction of civilian managers into a closed civil service hierarchy) and community control. Others (the American Federation of State, County, and Municipal Employees) saw strengthening the existing middle managers as critically important, since city employees were often blamed for problems caused by weak public management. Some of the most powerful unions (sanitationmen) represented only the lowest-level street workers, so that administrative changes for the supervisors only affected them indirectly. After a quick round of discussions, it appeared that publicly the unions would be neither hindrance nor help, at least in the early stages of the program, until they began to see whether the approach would affect their interests more deeply than they had imagined.

48. Jay Kriegel, ibid.
49. Herbert Elish, ibid.

ELECTED OFFICIALS AND CIVIC LEADERS

The strategy at the Office of Neighborhood Government called for no new form of citizen participation from the community boards or any other groups in the local districts. Its staff had carried out a laborious series of consultations with civic leaders on earlier decentralization proposals, and no additional steps were taken in planning the cabinet system. Community involvement would be developed informally as the program was implemented in each area.

The appropriate role for elected officials had the potential to raise much more serious problems. They might feel directly threatened by the district managers and cabinets and could well perceive them as the vanguard of a mayoral attack on their political bases. One agency administrator, a former state assemblyman, argued that although the mayor could act unilaterally at the start, in the long run city council members and borough presidents would play a major role in determining policy and budgets for the program. However, the mayor had strong personal views on this point. Administrative decentralization was a management program totally within the prerogative of his office as chief executive, and he adamantly opposed involving the political leadership in any substantive fashion. In his final review session to authorize the go-ahead for the district manager cabinets, he asserted that his administration should treat the approach as a "straight, technical, management program." If the politicians were involved, "they will ask for a piece of the action, especially if the program is not firmly in place already."[50] The mayor could afford to treat the elected officials this way, because ONG had received a federal "services integration" grant to help support the experiment.[51] These noncity funds would pay for critical extra expenses, like the district managers' salaries, which would

50. John Lindsay, quoted in John Mudd, "Notes to Files," 9 November 1971.

51. At the direction of the secretary, HEW funded over thirty separate "services integration" projects in various states and localities during Fiscal Years 1971 and 1972. In this period, a total of about $5 million was invested in research and demonstration efforts nationally. New York City received one of the largest initial grants: $320,000. See "Interim Report of the FY 1973 Services Integration R&D Task Force," (Washington, D.C.: Department of Health, Education, and Welfare), Table 1, pp. 4–5.

have been most difficult to get through the local legislative budget process.

Politically, the Office of Neighborhood Government program was uniquely a creature of the mayor and the Mayor's Office. The strategy was not developed as a result of direct public pressure. It represented an independent initiative by the city administration. As a federally financed executive reform, the introduction of the district manager cabinets involved none of the customary negotiations with elected officials. At its inception, therefore, the program was unusually free of the compromises inherent in the normal political process, but, conversely, it was dependent for survival and support on the mayor and a relatively small group of his closest staff.

SELECTION OF THE DEMONSTRATION DISTRICTS

The district manager cabinets were initially to be tested in a few demonstration districts. But ONG was determined to work in a sufficient number of communities so that the agencies would have to take the program seriously. Many New York bureaucracies were experienced in isolating small-scale experiments and using them as an excuse for not making broader structural changes in their operations. Testing too few areas would also create the danger of falling into a "hothouse" syndrome, where the special efforts forcing success in the target areas would make the model unreproducible. To be an adequate test of citywide applicability, the experimental districts would have to represent the variety of socioeconomic conditions found in New York as a whole. What might be effective in a middle-class area could well be meaningless in a slum. And given the politics of New York, it was important to demonstrate the potential of the program in all the largest boroughs. With their two votes apiece on the Board of Estimate, the borough presidents would have a strong voice in determining the future existence or extension of the cabinet system. In ONG's judgment between five and eight community districts appeared to be necessary to meet these objectives. Covering about 10 percent of the city and almost one million residents, this number would present a realistic test for the district manager cabinet approach, yet not overextend the management capability of ONG or the agencies. Most administrators disagreed. They argued for limiting the cabinets to two or three pilot districts. But each agency preferred a different community. By parlaying one's choice against another's, ONG was able to pyramid approval for five cabinets at the start, and gradually phased others into operation.

Eight community districts representing the political, ethnic, and economic variety of the city had been included in the district manager cabinet program by the end of 1972.[52] There were three transitional communities (Crown Heights, Washington Heights, and the Rockaways), two poverty areas (Bushwick, the South Bronx), and three predominantly middle-income districts (Wakefield-Edenwald, Maspeth-Ridgewood, and Bay Ridge).

After almost a year of detailed planning and politicking, the program was finally ready to get under way. The first cabinets met in January 1972. Their experience would begin to demonstrate whether or not decentralized administration could produce the projected improvements in the coordination and responsiveness of service delivery.

52. Data substantiating the rough representativeness of the districts to the city as a whole are reported in Stanley J. Heginbotham and Kenneth H. Andrews, *Between Community and City Bureaucracy,* pt. 5: *Problems and Prospects in Expanding to a City-Wide Program* (New York: Bureau of Applied Social Research, Columbia University, July 1973), pp. 58–69.

4
THE DISTRICT MANAGER CABINETS

*Looking at city neighborhoods as organs of self-government, I can
see evidence that only three kinds of neighborhoods are useful: (1)
the city as a whole; (2) street neighborhoods; and (3) districts of
large, subcity size. . . . This, I think is where we are typically most
weak and fail most disastrously. We have plenty of city districts in
name. We have few that function.*

—Jane Jacobs[1]

The Cabinets Meet

The Office of Neighborhood Government viewed the agency officers in the cabinets as the first constituency of the district managers.
This meant facing directly the civil servants' fears of outside meddling, especially by the Mayor's Office. Predictably, they were concerned that the introduction of the district managers would make
them responsible to two bosses—and open to criticism or second-
guessing by some long-haired arrogant newcomer who would place
additional (unfair and uninformed) demands on performance. ONG
had orchestrated a series of central briefings for the participating
field officers in each agency where they heard from their own
superiors the goals, mandate, and limits of cooperation in the
experiment. But the success of the program depended on the professional and personal relationships each manager would be able to

1. Jane Jacobs, *The Death and Life of Great American Cities* (New York: Vintage
Books, 1971), pp. 117, 121.

establish with his own cabinet members. To set the tone, the new district managers' first task was to visit all the field officers individually in *their* places of business. This gave the managers a chance to overcome the fear that ONG was appointing a group of capricious interlopers and to create some personal rapport, learn about the reality of service delivery in the district, and identify some immediate problems that could become the initial focus of the cabinet's work.

The district cabinets met monthly and immediately encouraged the kind of local communication among agencies that the city administration had lacked in the past. After the first session in Wakefield-Edenwald, the recreation supervisor leaned across the table to the district director of youth services and said something like: "It's good to finally have a chance to meet you. I knew you were working in the area but never knew who you were or where to find you. We have a lot to talk about." This kind of encounter occurred frequently: two district officers whose services either overlapped or were dependent on each other often had not previously met face to face. To the uninitiated, who do not realize the isolation and almost paranoid self-protectiveness that large bureaucracies often breed, this may seem surprising. Yet cutting through these barriers and attaching faces, names, and telephone numbers to the services represented around the cabinet table was an important accomplishment. Both the field officers and the district managers commented on this improvement in interagency communication. A police precinct commander felt that the cabinet provided "a meeting ground where we were not just titles. We became personalities to each other, and you were responding to an individual."[2] In the same vein, the observations in the South Bronx were typical of the first reports from many district managers: "One of the most important achievements of the experiment here has been getting the service chiefs to talk to one another across the same table. All of them acknowledged the value of such direct access to one another and the opportunities it opens to communicate the concerns, priorities, and needs from the other services."[3]

2. Adam Butcher, interview, 15 January 1975.
3. Victor Marrero, "South Bronx Monthly Report," 31 July 1972.

Communication was not the goal, but it set the stage for agency cooperation in improving service delivery. Cabinet members were drawn into helping each other solve specific problems. The district manager in the Rockaways described how this process developed among her cabinet officers:

> In the beginning, they were all reluctant and suspicious. How was this going to affect them? Are we going to be taking over their roles? Will they have two bosses? . . . The most significant change is that they became part of a group and that had a tremendous impact on them, in terms of their support for one another. We all have the same kinds of problems and we all have to deal with them. This provided a kind of moral support. They all sat around the table in the first two sessions and were bitching about how we can't do this or that because we need more staff. When that became a fairly common observation—and the fact that they weren't going to get any new resources—they together had to do the same kind of juggling that each one of them had to do separately. It was moral support in the sense that someone else has the same problem I do. I'm not alone. And, they began to see real ways in which they could be supportive to one another.[4]

Examples of coordination began to appear in all districts. Highways repaired the entrance to the parks beach, parks refilled oxygen tanks for health, sanitation sent its street sweepers through neighborhood playgrounds, police assisted sanitation by removing abandoned cars, and housing and health inspectors helped police close down illegal bottle clubs. These were not earth-shaking events in their impact either on the agencies or on the communities, but they represented the kind of nitty-gritty problems that daily plagued the field officers of municipal bureaucracies as they tried to operate in big city neighborhoods.

This mutual assistance between different agencies gradually began to occur without the district manager's involvement. One commented: "They didn't need me as a middleman anymore. . . . That was the real beauty of it. Not just that they began to find ways to

4. Janet Langsam, interview, 16 January 1975.

help one another, but that it happened almost routinely after a while. They didn't have to call me to intercede for them with each other. They did it themselves."[5] As the process unfolded, one district manager reported "a genuine espirit-de-corps in our Cabinet," and another, her cabinet's "growth from a loose-knit group of strangers to a fraternity, whose members are interested, willing, if not eager, to listen, recognize and support one another."[6]

In Wakefield-Edenwald, the manager of a local public housing project appeared at the cabinet for the first time.[7] She was desperate. Vandalism and trash fires had been increasing in a number of buildings, and, with her resources alone, she was unable to clear out the refuse fast enough to prevent dangerous accumulations. The semiautonomous Housing Authority provided its own sanitation and police services in the projects, and the regular city departments had no legal responsibility to cover these areas. The manager felt helpless as she watched a once proud project gradually deteriorate before her eyes. Interrupting the depressing litany, the sanitation superintendent quietly offered to send in his trucks and haul out the refuse, even though it wasn't his responsibility. The housing manager was apparently so amazed at this volunteered help that the superintendent literally had to repeat his offer several times before she understood and gratefully accepted. Across the table, the lieutenant from the local precinct asked if she knew the head of the Housing Authority police. When she said no, he offered to set up a meeting to review conditions in the project and, more to the point, promised to send his own men on patrols through the area, even though this also was not his responsibility. He then asked if there were any active tenant associations. A few were just being organized (with the involvement of the district manager's staff behind the scenes). The lieutenant said his crime prevention officer would help them develop a system of tenant patrols, along with other safety

5. Ibid.
6. The quotes are from two separate district managers. See John Sanderson, "District Manager Report Wakefield-Edenwald," 28 June 1972, and Janet Langsam, "Rockaways Monthly Report," August 1972.
7. Because the Housing Authority in New York was an independent agency not under the direct operating control of the mayor, representatives were invited but not officially assigned to the cabinets.

precautions they could carry out on their own. The Fire Department representative added his own commitment to investigate conditions in the project and identify potential hazards.

All of this occurred while the district manager was watching the voluntary interchange among the cabinet officers without saying a word. Such open communication, not to mention offers of assistance beyond the bounds of bureaucratic responsibility, was unheard of before the cabinets were established. And, as a staff member later reported, "It really worked. They cleaned that project up."[8] Trash and abondoned cars were removed, police scooter patrols were sent into the area, a threatening gang problem was resolved. The gang's leader was eventually assisted in entering John Jay College, and the tenants' association began weekly walks through the buildings with the project manager to plan joint action on new problems as they arose.

The district managers played a critical role in nurturing the growth of the cabinets. As career civil servants, the agency officers had been trained in the triplicate-form, buck-passing methods of traditional bureaucracies. The district managers had to encourage, cajole, and sometimes pressure them to break out of these old patterns, use their new authority, and assume new responsibilities. Most tried to motivate the local officers in a supportive, nonthreatening way. As one said: "I openly referred to the cabinet members as the commissioners for their services in the district. I never really challenged their expertise publicly but assumed they were professionals in their fields. . . . They didn't feel threatened by the whole process and that helped knit and gel the cabinet as a group."[9] Another district manager emphasized: "We had to boost those guys into making decisions. . . . If I tell them what to do, that's no gain. They've been told what to do all their lives. What we're trying to create is a situation where they *do* think it is their responsibility and their freedom to act on their ideas, even if it is a mistake."[10] On the other hand, if the field officers resisted being drawn out of their bureaucratic cocoons, the district managers did not always shy away

8. Alvoyd Doby, interview, 22 August 1978.
9. Sidney Jones, interview, 14 January 1975.
10. Edward Hiltbrand, interview, 14 January 1975.

from confrontation. At one meeting, an agency representative protested that he couldn't endorse a street lighting plan developed by the cabinet because "I'm only a foreman . . . [and] haven't got the authority to say yes, or no. . . . [I] don't want to step on anybody's toes." The district manager snapped back, "That's what this is all about. . . . We'll find out whose toes there are. If they have to be stepped on, they'll be stepped on."[11]

Typically, the cabinets developed through a number of stages. For the first three months, the members normally dealt with discrete, one-time problems or projects—street sweeping regulations for a particular trouble spot, or cleaning a specific vacant lot. In the next six months the cabinets evolved from working on single tasks to addressing larger problem areas requiring more complex long-term programs—developing vacant lots throughout the community, or strengthening the services available to the elderly. After twelve to eighteen months, some cabinets reached a stage of self-sustaining teamwork in which interagency cooperation took place as a matter of course, allowing the district manager to focus on the larger developmental issues affecting the community.

As the cabinets evolved in programmatic complexity, they developed a more structured internal organization. Task forces or subcommittees of relevant agency officers were established to handle larger issues. The district managers and their staffs generally had to give direction to such efforts. Agency representatives were reluctant to assume a position of leadership over their peers on the cabinets, and none had the staff or the inclination to arrange meetings, prepare plans, and monitor the implementation of decisions they had reached. By absorbing these responsibilities, the district managers held the interagency groups together and maintained their momentum. Most of the operational work of the cabinets took place in the task forces. The monthly cabinet meetings became forums for progress reports from the working groups and the identification of new issues. And they provided the opportunity for informal contacts among the officers during coffee breaks when many minor problems were resolved on the spot.

11. Victor Marrero, quoted in Ralph Blumenthal, "Neighborhood Units Help Local City Services Department Heads Solve Problems Without Red Tape," *New York Times*, 27 June 1972, p. 21.

The eight district manager cabinets became involved in hundreds of identified "projects" during their first two years. Their mandate was diffuse, and so were their activities. One district manager commented that "the program is more than the projects; it is a process" establishing new relationships among agencies and citizens in their communities.[12] The products of this process varied according to the styles of the managers, the competence and resources of the field officers, and the composition of the different districts. Idiosyncratic efforts—solving a particularly complicated traffic safety problem, handling a gang crisis, supporting the revitalization of neighborhood merchants, developing a youth center for delinquents, promoting child health testing, getting curb-cuts installed on street corners near nursing homes—tended to dominate. It would be impossible to describe all that was done, yet it is difficult to categorize its diversity. Although the traditional, centralized administrative system could have generated a few of the programs, the breadth of the actions stimulated by the decentralized district manager cabinets is significant in itself and important to convey.

Common Coordination Projects

The work of the cabinets involved most of the usual types of coordination problems: operational dependence, divided responsibility, gaps in accountability, duplication, and lost opportunities for complementary action. Systematic conflict was less evident in field operations, although agencies might bitterly disagree over the solution to specific local problems, or over central policies. The district managers generally found they could not get away from administering systems to respond to individual citizen complaints. But they discovered unanticipated opportunities to coordinate the identification of problems so that agencies could "pro-act," rather than only react, to community concerns. The common projects were concentrated in the sanitation, transportation, parks, and police services. Social, health, and housing issues tended to be specific to certain types of neighborhoods.

---

12. Robert House, quoted in participant observer notes by Peter Roggemann, "Report of DM Meeting—ONG Central," 2 October 1973.

STREET SWEEPING AND ALTERNATE SIDE PARKING
The interagency coordination required to clean the city's streets presented the classic problem that decentralized areal administration was designed to overcome. One agency was responsible, but it depended on two others to do its job effectively. The Sanitation Department operated a fleet of mechanical brooms, but to allow them to reach the refuse near the curbs there were regulations that prohibited automobile parking from 8 A.M. to 11 A.M., or 11 A.M. to 2 P.M., for specified days on alternate sides of almost every street in the city. Theoretically, sanitation designed the sweeper routes, traffic installed the no-parking signs, and police ticketed the violators.

In the past, policies had been set centrally and operations carried out without consultation or communication among the responsible local officers from each agency. If cars consistently blocked the curbs on some streets, there was no coordination with the police to target enforcement in the trouble spots. The sweepers just drove uselessly down the middle of the road. Equally maddening to local residents, people often moved their cars back into the cleaned areas after the brooms had gone through and then received tickets. In one community, merchants complained that a midday sweeping schedule made early morning deliveries from their suppliers more difficult (because cars were parked) and prevented customers from shopping during lunch hour (because cars couldn't park). In another district, three-fourths of the streets were marked for cleaning in the morning and one-fourth for the afternoon, even though the same men and equipment worked in both periods. Schedules appeared to be bureaucratic artifacts handed down unthinkingly from civil servant to civil servant through the years. Routes were rarely adapted to shifts in population density, new construction, or changed resources. Citizens throughout the city ranked dirty streets as one of their greatest problems.[13]

To ONG, street sweeping was a clear case where policy and operations should, and could, be coordinated by the three agency

13. Theresa F. Rogers and Nathalie S. Friedman, "The Quality of Big-City Life in 1972," in Allen H. Barton et al., *Decentralizing City Government* (Lexington, Mass.: Lexington Books, 1977), p. 189.

representatives in each district with their newly decentralized powers. In practice, all the experimental cabinets were involved with the issue. The changes varied in their impact, from a few blocks on a single street to revisions for entire areas. But the apparent simplicity of the district manager cabinet's capacity for the decentralized coordination of service delivery gave way to a much more complicated reality.

At the first cabinet session in Wakefield-Edenwald, a Neighborhood Police Team commander reported numerous citizen complaints about the lack of street cleaning along a stretch of White Plains Road near the Westchester County border. The sanitation superintendent verified the problem. His equipment couldn't get through because commuters parked their cars there early every morning to be near the subway station. He recommended extending no-parking 8 A.M. to 9 A.M. signs, which were in effect on his sweepers' route lower down the same street, into the troublesome area. The traffic representative resisted. The department had a citywide policy to use such regulations only where there were parking meters, and the upper part of White Plains Road had none. The district manager argued that a major purpose of the cabinet experiment was to adapt citywide regulations to local needs. He insisted that traffic approve the sanitation and police recommendation. In the process, the district manager demonstrated that he would not be a weak coordinator who unquestioningly accepted the constraints of existing department rules but would be prepared to fight for change and for the interest of one agency against another when it appeared to be justified. Eventually, although not without balking and delays, the Traffic Department capitulated, and the necessary signs were installed.

Continued departmental centralization of a different variety faced the Washington Heights cabinet. The sanitation commissioner had introduced a group of central management specialists in a new Bureau of Industrial Engineering to revise the outdated street sweeping patterns throughout the city. In theory, these technical experts would work with the operating officers in the districts to devise new routes. In practice, such consultation sometimes broke down. It led in Washington Heights to the announcement of regulations that would have required a community of Orthodox Jews to move their cars on the Sabbath. The district manager and ONG, prodded by an outpouring of opposition by civic and political leaders, convinced the commissioner to delay implementation until acceptable schedules could be designed locally. Another kind of issue appeared in the Rockaways. There, the sanitation district superintendent proposed an elaborate plan revising the boundaries of his collection routes to adjust to the large shifts in residential population during the past decade. Despite the formal authorization in the decentralization guidelines to take this kind of action, his recommendations were bottled up in the bureaucracy. Apparently, the borough and central staff officers not only were threatened by this initiative but were offended that an internal departmental proposal had been submitted "with the approval of the District Manager."[14] The commissioner had to step in personally and order that the hierarchy approve the superintendent's plan.

The many street cleaning and parking enforcement projects implemented by the cabinets showed that it was possible to adapt the service delivery system to meet community needs within the existing level of resources, although evidence about the extent of the projects' impact is largely subjective. But they also demonstrated how difficult it could be to cut through the formal and informal pressures against decentralized action, even on the most mundane service problems.

PARKS REFUSE

The district managers could resolve the coordination problems of parks refuse disposal simply by encouraging local interagency communication, without getting embroiled in challenging central policies or procedures. Through administrative agreement, the Parks Department collected debris in the parks and placed it on adjacent streets for pickup by the Sanitation Department, which was then responsible for moving the waste to the city incinerators or landfills. In district cabinet meetings, it became clear that the parks general foremen and the sanitation superintendents did not talk to each

14. From an ONG staff study quoted in Robin Maas, *Decentralizing New York City Service Agencies, 1971–1973* (New York: Office of Neighborhood Government, May 1974), p. 59.

other in coordinating the timing of the pickups. As a result, the refuse gathered in the parks was often left rotting, to be blown by the wind or used as ammunition by local children. In most cabinets, this issue was quickly resolved. The mechanism developed in the South Bronx was typical. After meetings between the parks and sanitation district officers,

> Parks agreed to place refuse in plastic garbage bags instead of the baskets or drums previously used and to have it ready for pick-up by a specific time every day. The Sanitation Department committed itself to pick up the bags at the specified time each day, and the Superintendent gave his telephone number to the Parks foreman so that if the bags were not collected on any given day, he could be contacted to arrange for pick-up by the night crew the same day.[15]

PARK SAFETY

The issue of safety in the parks increasingly concerned many communities. Vandalism was rampant, and whole sections of parkland were unused by local residents who feared everything from harrassment to mugging or worse. But in general, police and parks officials had not had face-to-face discussions about where to direct patrol activity. Although most districts were affected, the problem was unsually acute in Washington Heights, which had extensive park areas and a large population of elderly people who felt particularly vulnerable. The district manager established a Parks Vandalism Task Force. Ironically, he wrote that their work was delayed because "the office of the District Parks Supervisor was vandalized and his records destroyed."[16] Nevertheless, the project eventually went forward.

After Police prepared a spot map locating the extent and nature of crimes commited in the parks last summer, new scooter patrols

---

15. *Project Report: South Bronx Office of Neighborhood Government* (New York: Office of Neighborhood Government, December 1973), p. 18.

16. This and the subsequent quote are from Donald J. Middleton, "District Manager's Status Report," March 1972.

were planned. Since there was a high concentration of crimes around the Cloisters, the 34 Precinct Commander agreed to scooter coverage in the area seven days a week from 8 A.M. to midnight. A plan is currently being prepared to re-deploy other scooter patrols.

Paralleling these steps by the police, the cabinet worked with the Bureau of Gas and Electricity to replace broken park lamps with unbreakable heads, planned to install burglar alarms in recreation facilities which had been regularly vandalized, and arranged with the Highways and Traffic Departments to break through a curb so that patrol cars could have access to a park. In addition to these essentially negative efforts to reduce crime and vandalism, some cabinets attempted to initiate new recreation programs to encourage people to use the parks again. This positive attack on the problem of park safety was less successful because the Recreation Department had limited resources. The police were able to redirect their patrol forces to some extent within their existing allocations of men and equipment; recreation did not have that much flexibility.

VACANT LOTS

There were (and are) thousands of vacant lots throughout New York. The problem was particularly severe in the poorer communities where demolished buildings and fires generated many more empty spaces every year. In the early 1970s, Bushwick alone had over three hundred abandoned parcels of land, most still privately owned. When neglected, these areas quickly attracted garbage, weeds, and other refuse. Vacant lots often became an aggravating safety or health hazard in a community, a visible and provocative symbol of neighborhood decline, and a lost opportunity for recreation, off-street parking, and other constructive uses. A police commander raised the problem in a cabinet meeting because there had been complaints of muggings near one overgrown lot. A recreation superintendent might call for the development of a basketball or bocce court, or even a garden. Block associations frequently reported pests and other health problems caused by illegal dumping. Given the trash, rats, and fires, the sad irony of the vacant lot problem was that it actually cost the city money (one estimate put the total at $3,850 in carting, fencing, and fire-fighting expenditures for a single year) to maintain these community eyesores.[17] Sometimes the solution to a particular problem involved nothing more complicated than getting the Highways Department to bring a mower and cut down the tall grass where muggers hid. On the other hand, it often entailed much more elaborate planning to determine who owned a lot, cart off massive amounts of refuse, blacktop the surface, and install recreation equipment.

The city procedures for dealing with vacant lots were centralized and cumbersome; they made action almost impossible. Most land was still in private hands, but the Sanitation Department was only authorized to go into private property on an order signed by the commissioner of health. ONG negotiated with the Health Department to station a health inspector in some communities and allow the district health officer to authorize entry into privately owned lots. Simultaneously, the Sanitation Department assigned the borough lot cleaning crews regularly to certain areas so that the district superintendent could integrate their activities with the local men and equipment he could spare for this work. In Bushwick, these new procedures made a difference. During a five-month period, one health sanitarian, working under the district health officer and cooperating with citizen groups and other agencies, was able to identify hazards in 159 lots and certify them for cleaning.[18] The Sanitation Department managed over time to clear most of these areas at least once.[19] But removing refuse was just the first step in dealing with vacant lots, because without some active use by the community, they rapidly became dumping grounds again. Lot development, on the other hand, usually required additional resources which the district officers on the cabinets did not control.

In the South Bronx, double- and triple-parked cars seriously

17. Curt Meade, quoted in "Model Projects" (ONG files, n.d.).

18. Patricia Nolan and Anthony C. Mustalish, "Environmental Health Tactics for the Inner City" (paper prepared for the 102d Annual Meeting of the American Public Health Association, New Orleans, October 1974), p. 6.

19. The description of the old and new procedures is vastly simplified. For a more detailed analysis of the process and the results, see Ronald Brumback, "Service Integration at the District Level: Seven Examples," in Barton et al., *Decentralizing City Government*, pp. 52–56.

hindered clients' access to the local welfare center and made the entry of emergency police, fire, or ambulance service almost impossible. Cabinet representatives identified the worst blocks, and the district manager's staff located city-owned vacant lots in the vicinity. The Highways Department agreed to level the lots and spread crushed stone so that they would be suitable for free off-street parking. Three lots were actually converted.[20] On the whole, however, the attempt to develop constructive uses for this vacant land had disappointing results.

SUMMER YOUTH PROGRAMS

Spurred by the fear of riots and other racial disturbances in the mid-1960s, the city government made a major effort to mount a large number of youth programs every summer, but resources were always inadequate to address the need for jobs and recreation as over a million students left the schools every June. The problem was exacerbated because the funds and responsibility for summer activities were splintered among many different agencies. The Recreation Department developed programs in the parks and scheduled over twenty mobile vans which brought puppet shows, roller skating, and other entertainment to the neighborhoods; the Youth Services Agency administered the Neighborhood Youth Corps employment programs as well as its own set of mobile vans; the Board of Education sponsored summer activities in some schools; Community Action Agencies made special allocations for youth projects in poor communities; the Mayor's Urban Action Task Force, the Housing Authority, and Model Cities all financed hundreds of one-day bus trips to beaches and parks outside the city. In addition, many private organizations were active in developing programs. There was no systematic way to assign these diverse, but scarce, resources in a cooperative or coherent fashion at the community level. No one knew, for example, whether some active block associations had bargained separately with the various departments to obtain an inordinate number of bus trips or mobile recreation vans, while others had received nothing.

In all the experimental areas, the district managers recognized

20. *Project Report: South Bronx*, p. 17.

the need and opportunity for interagency coordination to make the most of the limited resources available. The cabinets became the focus for concerted local planning which could prevent either the duplication of effort or the neglect of specific subgroups or geographic areas. In Bushwick, for example, the district manager reported:

> Every agency in the district, from the Board of Education to the Salvation Army, was asked to define program resources and, through their membership on the Cabinet's Summer Program Task Force, join in a review to: (1) avoid duplication of efforts; (2) focus on those parts of the district where programming was thin or non-existent; (3) share and exchange program supplies; (4) provide sufficient notification to the local police and sanitation services for support for street activities; and, (5) attempt, on an on-going basis, to identify program gaps and omissions and take prompt corrective action.[21]

Coordination was often hindered by the lack of decision-making authority in the district. But the decentralized allocation of program resources involved sensitive community politics. In Wakefield-Edenwald, there was intense competition for summer jobs between the older Italian organizations and newer black groups. Rather than continue to have the assignments made centrally, the district manager and his deputy convinced the Youth Services Agency to delegate this authority to its district director in the community. Together they negotiated a formula with all youth organizations in the area, which prevented an anticipated blowup. The traditionally dominant Italian program received the largest single allocation of jobs, but various black groups were assigned a number of slots that gave the minority poor a greater total share of the resources.[22] Such a delicate balance of program purposes and community interests would have been unlikely, if not impossible, without decentralized decision-making through the district manager cabinet structure.

21. Sidney E. Jones, "Monthly Report to the Mayor," July 1972.
22. John Sanderson, "Monthly Report to Mayor Lindsay," 7 August 1972.

CITIZEN COMPLAINT SYSTEMS

The processing of individual complaints became an important consideration for each of the local offices, despite ONG's initial inclination to stay away from the ombudsman role. It was soon evident that no district manager could operate with credibility in a community if he refused to deal with the individual issues worrying the residents. Usually one person on the ONG office staff was designated to deal with citizens' complaints. Depending on the community, the amount of this work varied from twenty-five items a month to hundreds per week. ONG generally did not publicize this kind of activity in the early stages of the program so that the cabinets would not be overwhelmed with individual casework. Nevertheless, some districts gave serious attention to these concerns. Wakefield-Edenwald developed a Quick Response Citizen Complaint Service through which problems were channeled to the appropriate agency for action and the resident received a postcard notifying him or her when the issue would be resolved.[23] In contrast to earlier complaint systems in New York and other cities, the problems were taken directly to the responsible agency officers in the district—not shuttled through the elaborate, centralized systems that had proved time-consuming and ineffective in the past.

ENVIRONMENTAL INFORMATION SYSTEM

Most departments depended on citizen complaints to pinpoint a wide range of common environmental problems. These included potholes, clogged catch basins, abandoned cars, leaking fire hydrants, broken street lights, defective traffic signals, unsafe buildings, and so forth. Few agencies had the capacity or desire to establish a system that could report these matters before citizens became sufficiently aggravated to pick up pen or phone and complain. ONG worked with the cabinets to develop a way to anticipate the breakdowns, rather than waiting to respond to complaints. If the Traffic, Highways, and Water Resources Departments did not have adequate personnel to gather information about service needs

23. *Wakefield-Edenwald, Office of Neighborhood Government Project Report 1973* (New York: Office of Neighborhood Government, 1973), p. 7.

themselves, the city government as a whole put thousands of police and sanitationmen on the streets every day. They could spot the problems and report them to the ONG office, whose staff would consolidate and channel issues to the appropriate agencies for action. With weekly or monthly information, the managers in each of the operating departments could plan the allocation of scarce resources rationally, rather than haphazardly according to incomplete data from random citizen complaints.

The central ONG staff developed a small reporting form, which could easily be carried in the pocket of a patrolman or any other agency's field personnel, listing over twenty of the most common street condition problems. All eight experimental districts utilized this system, with varying degrees of effectiveness. In some areas, hundreds of specific issues were reported and resolved every month, but in others only a few score. The South Bronx used the data to develop a new service monitoring and management planning technique. With the cooperation of the local City Planning Department, the incidence of specific problems was plotted on large transparencies that could be placed over a base map showing all streets, addresses, and tax lot numbers. This enabled ONG and the cabinet agencies to identify recurrent trouble spots and examine the interelationships between services. For example, by comparing locations with frequent potholes, car accidents, planned sewer repairs, and housing construction, the district manager and cabinet specified priorities for street repaving in the area. This aggressive approach in identifying service delivery problems also began to affect the internal operations of some agencies. Sewers expanded its preventive maintenance activities in the cabinet communities. And for the first time, the Traffic Department conducted district-wide surveys of all street intersections. Over four hundred traffic control devices were replaced or installed in the cabinet areas as a result.[24]

THE NEIGHBORHOOD SOCIAL SERVICE INFORMATION SYSTEM
There was an obvious logic in trying to extend interagency reporting systems to include social as well as physical problems. People as

24. Joel D. Koblentz and Ronald Brumback, "An Analysis of the Service Integration Projects of the District Offices," in Barton et al, *Decentralizing City Government*, p.81.

well as streets had multiple needs, but citizens were often lost in the maze of separate service agencies. Despite the enormous public and private investment of resources in health and social welfare programs, there was no system to insure that a mother who gave birth to an addicted child at the local hospital would be guided to appropriate treatment programs, or that family disputes might be channeled to counselors rather than cops. Although individual departments were developing elaborate computerized information systems, the only institutionalized form of interagency communication was the telephone. Referrals between agencies were intermittent, and no one monitored the process to determine if clients directed to a second office ever reached their destination.

This was a generic problem in every area, but the district manger in Crown Heights proposed testing a "neighborhood social service information system" in his community. Cabinet representatives were guardedly enthusiastic about the idea. It would help them shift responsibility for problems they couldn't handle and would prevent individual clients from getting lost in the cracks between departments. The district manager hoped to develop common intake procedures for all participating agencies and a direct interchange of computerized information about client backgrounds, referrals, and service needs. Institutional resistance to this suggestion was overwhelming. Agencies refused to change existing forms, which were often tied to federal or state reporting requirements. The new computer systems being introduced by separate departments were incompatible with each other, and the expense of reprogramming to enable communication between them was deemed prohibitive.

In the face of this opposition, ONG central staff specialists helped the district cabinet members design a manual referral monitoring system using multicopy forms. Eight agencies agreed to participate, and the local human resources staff assumed responsibility for managing the project. A test was initiated in January 1974, but during the next five months only three dozen referrals were made through the system, mostly between the local housing office and ONG.[25] For a troubled community that had thirty-five thousand

25. "Final Report for NSSIS Referral Service" (New York: Office of Neighborhood Government, 4 December 1974), pp. 3–4.

welfare recipients, the effort was a failure. The system was apparently not of sufficient help to the city workers to overcome their resistance. Local employees were inhibited by the confidential nature of many problems and objected to the added clerical burden of filling out new forms. Upper echelon agency managers were never sufficiently committed to press for more active involvement from their field personnel.

In general, the district cabinets continued to focus much of their energy on the traditional city service problems where they had been able to develop projects with some success. As a leading city politician once remarked to a district manger: "You give me somebody who can keep the streets clean, fix the potholes, and increase safety, and he can be elected to anything."[26] But gradually, as the district managers settled with more confidence into their new roles in the cabinets and communities, they began to work on more varied and ambitious plans.

Community Projects: Flexibility and Responsiveness

The district manager cabinet system was intended to increase the flexibility of the city administration in addressing the special needs and concerns of local communities. Responsiveness implied that the district managers could mold this capacity so that agencies' service plans and activities would conform more closely to citizen preferences. In contrast to the consistent emphasis on strengthening the coordination among field officers assigned to the cabinets, ONG allowed the managers a great deal of discretion in developing relationships with civic leaders and elected officials in each area. The assumption was that community organizations would gradually be drawn into working with the cabinets as a way to improve local services. There was no formal procedure either within the cabinets or between the cabinets and the communities to set priorities for action. ONG expected that the socioeconomic conditions in each district would set the parameters both for the kinds of projects and ultimately for the success of the program. It underestimated the importance of differences in district managers' styles and experi-

26. Quoted by Edward Hiltbrand, interview, 14 January 1975.

ence, local civic cultures, field officers' competencies, and unanticipated service needs in shaping program development. The variation among similar socioeoconomic communities was often as great as the diversity between types of areas.

DISTRICT MANAGER AS BROKER: THE MIDDLE-CLASS AREAS

Three of the eight experimental districts were predominantly middle-income.[27] Wakefield-Edenwald was an older Italian and Irish community on the northern tip of the Bronx. Over the previous two decades, a number of middle-class, home-owning black families had purchased property in the district. There were two public housing projects. Maspeth-Ridgewood was a blue-collar area in western Queens originally settled by Germans and East Europeans with Irish and Italians following later. It was a community with small, well-kept patches of green in front of frame buildings on which owners had added new facades that displayed their traditional pride in house and home. This deliberate care seemed almost an act of defiance when contrasted to the deterioration of similar housing stock in the poor, minority communities just to the south in Brooklyn. The district had effectively raised a rigid barrier against any influx of blacks or Puerto Ricans. Bay Ridge, located on the southwestern edge of Brooklyn, was a solidly middle-class community with apartment houses and large comfortable homes that appeared more typical of the suburbs than the inner city. Ethnically, the area was again primarily stable Italian and Irish, with a small Scandinavian minority.

The civic culture in such areas was dominated by long-established neighborhood homeowner and taxpayer associations. In Wakefield, middle-class blacks had developed a number of block associations, but the poor had almost no groups to press their interests. There was little interrelationship between the civic and the political organizations in the community. Each group kept to its own separate sphere. The civic associations held meetings and worried about maintaining their neighborhoods; the clubhouses were ingrown and

27. Sketches of the history, population composition, and land use patterns, but not the politics, of all community planning districts are found in the *Plan for New York City*, vols. 2—6 (New York: Department of City Planning, 1969).

quiescent, except to preserve a cadre of loyalists for work in the primary and general elections. Their tone was defensive and their politics conservative. Wakefield elected one of the few Republican state legislators from the city, and Bay Ridge regularly returned the Republican minority leader of the City Council to office. Service needs expressed by the citizens and local leaders in these areas reflected the relative well-being of the residents: street cleaning, potholes, recreation, and safety—the major concern of every community, despite the great differences in crime rates.[28]

John Sanderson was the first district manager in Wakefield-Edenwald when the cabinet got underway in January 1972. He was as little like a Lindsay longhair as one could imagine. Middle-aged, balding, and cigar-chomping, Sanderson was an Irish Catholic and served as head of his neighborhood parish council in Queens. After directing a Navy test lab for many years, he had worked on the mayor's Project Management Staff, where, in his supportive, non-authoritarian style, he involved the civil servant parks managers in a major reorganization of their maintenance operations. From his approach and appearance, one sensed that but for an accident he could have been a police captain or fire battalion commander. He neither scared nor offended the district officers on the cabinet but had demonstrated an ability to move career civil servants in new directions. From the start, Sanderson and his deputy, Robert House, also set out on a "road show" to involve the community. Three or four nights a week, they attended meetings of neighborhood associations, block associations, police precinct councils, or any other organizations that would invite them to explain the program and hear citizen concerns about services in the area.

Ed Hiltbrand (Bay Ridge) and Emil Rucigay (Maspeth-Ridgewood) were appointed district managers during October 1972, in

28. The Bureau of Applied Social Research at Columbia University sponsored public opinion and community leadership surveys in four of the eight experimental districts (Wakefield-Edenwald, Crown Heights, Bushwick, Washington Heights) and three control areas. The data were compiled in separate reports (for example, "A Community Profile of Bronx Community Planning District 13," December 1972) and summarized in Nathalie Friedman and Naomi Golding, *Urban Residents and Neighborhood Government* (New York: Bureau of Applied Social Research, Columbia University, June 1973).

the last of the eight areas approved for the experiment. Both were residents of their respective communities and neither had previous management experience in city government. They were professionals (school teacher and lawyer, respectively), had been active in civic organizations, and had successfully developed a number of cooperative projects with city agencies through the urban action task force. Neither was exclusively identified with a partisan political faction or leader. Hiltbrand and Rucigay were nominated by broad-based community councils in their areas. Thus, although Bay Ridge and Maspeth were intensely anti-Lindsay, the district managers had a builtin civic constituency of influential local leaders, including the publishers of the neighborhood newpapers.

Many of the cabinet projects in these middle-income communities predictably emphasized the environment and recreation. What citizens often wanted was an honest broker, an intermediary who could match their relatively moderate demands to the appropriate suppliers of services in government. Before the program started, an ONG staff organizer wrote:

> Maspeth-Ridgewood simply doesn't have productive outlets and vehicles for expressing anger and seeking redress of grievances. Yet, because their problems are rarely emergencies or massive grievances, their expectations are relatively low. . . . Maspeth-Ridgewood doesn't need to see a sharp upward jump in their service delivery graph—just some upward movement as contrasted with the perceived steady downward movement.[29]

And citizens were willing to participate actively in this process.

Environmental monitoring in Maspeth-Ridgewood. The Real Estate and Housing Committee of the Community Council devised an elaborate form for residents to monitor services and report refuse collection, street lighting, traffic sign, storm sewer, pothole, housing, and other problems in designated subdistricts in the area. Two years later, forty-two volunteers were still working with this environmental monitoring system, which in 1974 alone dealt with twelve

29. Robert Mitchell, "Progress Report," 9 February 1972.

hundred sanitary code violations by local homeowners and merchants.[30] One of these issues illustrated how the district manager cabinets adapted citywide policy to neighborhood mores. In New York, commercial businesses were legally required to dispose of their own refuse. To improve storage and loading efficiency, the private cartmen developed a closed one-cubic-yard metal container that could be wheeled by the store owners onto the sidewalks. The sanitation commissioner had strongly urged the expansion of this practice throughout the city, since it was more sanitary than leaving a number of cans or loose refuse on the street. But in Ridgewood, the residents objected to the containers on their sidewalks, and a number of civic organizations protested their continued use. The district manager first brought the problem to the sanitation district superintendent, but knowing the commissioner's attitude, the superintendent felt helpless to do anything. The manager continued to press the issue through higher-ups in the department until, finally, the commissioner himself came to the area and personally reviewed the situation. Recognizing that a policy valuable for the South Bronx or for sections of Manhattan was inappropriate in a traditional family community like Ridgewood, he authorized the district superintendent to negotiate with the storeowners and private cartmen to get rid of the metal containers. Dozens of the offensive receptacles were removed from the sidewalks and did not reappear.[31]

Shoelace Park in Wakefield-Edenwald. On a walking tour with the district manager and the president of a local taxpayers' association, the general parks foreman commented that an abandoned seventeen-block strip of an adjacent parkway road could be developed into a needed recreation area for the neighborhood. Sanderson encouraged him to present his ideas to the cabinet. This was very unusual for a district officer whose normal responsibility was managing maintenance laborers. Planning for new facilities was

---

30. "Community Government Report," *The Ridgewood Times*, 6 February 1975, p. 2. A committee study showed a 79-percent success rate in getting the violations removed.

31. Robert Mitchell, interview, 13 November 1978.

the purview of a central bureau in the Parks Department, which usually took years to push a project through the required sixty-four implementation steps. The other members of the Wakefield cabinet responded positively to the foreman's suggestions, and a task force of seven related agencies was established under his leadership to work out detailed plans for the "Shoelace Park." With technical assistance from the City Planning Department, he prepared design sketches for the area and agreed to install basketball stanchions, volleyball and bocce courts, horseshoe pits, and touch football fields with his own maintenance forces. The sanitation district superintendent cleared the area and modified the proposed plans to insure access for his equipment on a regular cleaning schedule, the water resources foreman agreed to clean and repair catch basins to provide adequate drainage, the highways foreman arranged to resurface the roadway, the recreation supervisor designed game areas and made a commitment to assign staff, and the police captain established regular patrols. Additional lighting was essential, and, with the other parts of the project in place, the district manager successfully negotiated with the Bureau of Gas and Electricity to install it.

In addition to coordinating the planning by various city agencies, the parks foreman also actively participated in neighborhood meetings to discuss the project—a role usually reserved to the agency's central community relations staff. Although civic leaders had been supportive, a number of residents near the park began to fear for their safety, if many children from outside the community would come to use the new facility. At a long and sometimes tense session in the local Catholic church, the foreman and the police lieutenant, with the backing of a local priest, were able to assuage these fears. In contrast to the Manhattan-oriented community relations staff, the district officers came from the same kind of ethnic community that surrounded the park. They were able to overcome the residents' suspicion of city government and give them a sense that commitments would be honored.

The next day, the parks foreman proudly made a presentation at the district cabinet. As an added dividend, the citywide commissioners from the Parks, Transportation, and Sanitation Departments all attended. These officials rarely came in contact with their middle managers, and if they did it was not to hear a crisp, organized "chart-show" describing how a new project had been conceived and planned. District officers began to see the potential for personal recognition within their own agencies as a result of work on the cabinets.

The Shoelace Park opened amid public fanfare on July 7, 1973, only eight months after the first meeting between the parks foreman and the taxpayer association president. Normally, such a project might drag on for two to five years before completion. Many of the resources for developing the facility were obtained by reallocating existing personnel and equipment; but central authorization for lighting, additional asphalt, and new recreation staff was necessary. Nonetheless, the district manager could report with legitimate pride that this was "the first park in the city to be totally designed and planned by local agency officers."[32]

On very different, unpredicted matters—direct assistance to residents in dealing with social entitlement programs and other regulatory aspects of government—the district manager cabinets revealed more serious gaps in the city's approach to middle-income communities.

Direct services in middle-income communities. As a second-generation Croatian, the district manager in Maspeth knew that the well-kept facades of the homes lining the peaceful streets hid a great deal of human need and poverty, particularly among the elderly. They qualified for a range of social services that they did not receive because of ignorance (many still had difficulty with English), pride, or fear, which kept them from seeking help in the welfare center located at the end of a long bus ride in an impoverished black area of Queens. He and his staff proposed a series of "one-stop service days" in which applications and, where possible, certification for food stamps, income maintenance (welfare), Medicare, and rent increase exemptions for the elderly would be available at a location in their community. The Human Resources Administration agreed to send a mobile van into the district for a test. With advance publicity in the local newspaper and flyers distributed through civic

32. *Wakefield-Edenwald Project Report 1973*, p. 5.

organizations and churches, the outpouring was surprising. Over one hundred people came for assistance on the first day, which was a larger turnout than the HRA staff had seen in any other area of the city, including the most poverty-stricken. Given this demonstrable need, the manager arranged for the appropriate social service and housing agencies to assign staff two times per month at a local YMCA, church, or community center easily accessible to the residents.

Bay Ridge experienced even greater success in providing assistance to residents with a broad range of government permits and applications. In the first year, the local office issued 9,000 senior citizen reduced fare cards for buses and subways, 4,000 applications for rent increase exemptions, 500 applications for property tax exemptions, 6,000 rent control forms, and 1,000 golf and tennis permits for parks. They issued 100 food stamp certifications in the first month.[33] The district manager felt that providing these direct services in the area was "the biggest thing that made [the ONG program] acceptable to Bay Ridge." As he explained:

People with a sense of alienation found a place in the community where they could get all of the smaller things [which were] important to them. A senior citizen who gets a rent exemption form is in many cases just absolutely bewildered by how to fill it out—not only whether it is correct or not but what do I put down, what are they really asking me? A trip downtown to them is torture, mostly because of the time, the money, and the feeling that downtown is dangerous. They feel safe dealing with what they consider their own kind.[34]

Wakefield-Edenwald had a different, but analogous, experience. While attending neighborhood meetings, the district manager and his staff became aware that many residents were deeply troubled about finding employment and job training opportunities for their children leaving high school. The city government did not provide a place in the community for work counseling and placement services,

---

33. Edward Hiltbrand, "Letter to Community Leaders," 12 November 1973.
34. Edward Hiltbrand, interview, 14 January 1975.

which were appropriately concentrated in poorer districts. Yet, particularly among the blacks in the area, many families were only marginally middle-class and struggled to maintain their status with both adults working at one or two jobs. Inflation and recession increased their worries for themselves and their children. To address this need, the district manager assigned a member of his staff to develop an employment program. By making direct contact with a number of private companies throughout the city, he discovered many jobs and training positions available for the young adults in Wakefield-Edenwald. By the end of 1973, almost one thousand young people had used this service, and over four hundred were placed in paid employment.[35]

The city administration was not structured to deal with these multiple, direct service needs in middle-income communities. Many agency procedures were overly centralized, and those housing or social service field offices that did exist were predominantly targeted in poverty areas. A district manager could help to fill these gaps in the service delivery system partially through his own staff and partially by periodically scheduling outstationed personnel from the central agencies.

THE DISTRICT MANAGER IN POVERTY AREAS: TECHNICIAN
OR COMMUNITY ORGANIZER?

District manager cabinets were tested in two poverty areas—the South Bronx and Bushwick—but the differences in community politics, district manager styles, and cabinet functions were more revealing than the socioeconomic similarity of the communities. The South Bronx and Bushwick were both desolate and desperate urban slums. Deteriorating tenements, abandoned and stripped buildings, refuse-strewn vacant lots, and streets overflowing with trash were depressingly familiar sights along with the drunks and drug addicts. Ethnically, the vast majority of the South Bronx were poor Puerto Ricans; Bushwick was split almost equally among Spanish-speaking people, blacks, and remnants of the once-dominant Italians. To some, the South Bronx was symbolized by the name the police gave to the local precinct—"Fort Apache."

35. *Wakefield-Edenwald Project Report 1973*, pp. 15–16.

Bushwick was infamous for the fires which ravaged the wood-frame houses that lined its streets. Flames from one house would shoot down an entire block through the "cock lofts" (interconnected attics), consuming ten to twelve houses at a time. The South Bronx was the target for many supplementary federal, state, and city programs. Designation as one of only three Model Cities neighborhoods brought an additional $20 million a year in funding for public services. In contrast, Bushwick at that period remained largely ignored and forgotten, despite its desparate need. Political development in the two areas reflected this difference, both as cause and consequence. The transformation of politics in the South Bronx was rapid and volatile. New Leadership parlayed power in the multiple poverty programs into elected representation in the City Council and the regular party organization. Bushwick, on the other hand, was still represented by an Italian councilman. The first Spanish-speaking representative from the area was not elected until 1973.

Initially, ONG did not plan to operate in any of the Model Cities neighborhoods. But the district manager cabinet seemed to offer a technique for integrating the traditional service bureaucracies more effectively with the supplemental programs in the community. Victor Marrero, the Model Cities neighborhood director, was also appointed to serve as district manager. He had earlier worked on the mayor's staff and had successfully maneuvered his way through the politics of the South Bronx to push the stalled Model Cities program into action. Given the intense political conflict in the area, Marrero decided to project the cabinet as a purely managerial experiment with no community involvement. In the environment of the South Bronx, the district manager cabinet never gained the focal position it came to occupy in a number of other areas. It was essentially a technical appendage of Model Cities, but it did succeed in extending the impact of some programs in new directions.

School safety in the South Bronx. At one of the first Cabinet meetings in July 1972, the police precinct commander covering the South Bronx complained about loss of manpower because he was forced to assign uniformed patrolmen to guard duty in the local schools. This seemed inefficient, since the men cost the city over twenty thousand dollars a year but had no special ability or training to deal with school children. Marrero knew that Model Cities was allocating funds for the police department to employ sixty "community service officers" (CSOs), young adults from the area who would provide escort and other nonenforcement safety services in the district. He asked the obvious question: Why couldn't CSOs be placed in the schools to free the regular police for street patrol duty? The captain agreed wholeheartedly with the suggestion but complained that the CSOs were administered from a special project office at police headquarters in Manhattan. They were not under his operational control, and he felt powerless to deal with the bureaucratic politics necessary to reassign them. Marrero immediately asked his deputy to prepare a specific plan with the police, the school administrators, and members of the various parents' associations. In consultations over the next six weeks, the representatives from the elementary schools felt the substitution of CSOs for uniformed patrolmen could be helpful. Since CSOs were younger and came from the community, they would be able to relate to the students more effectively. But the change was judged inappropriate for the older population in the high schools. On the recommendation of the precinct commander and the district manager, CSOs were authorized to work in six elementary schools in the fall of 1972, and the uniformed patrolmen returned to the streets. Although the numbers affected in the South Bronx were relatively small, this mode for utilizing CSOs instead of police patrol forces became citywide policy during the next year as a way to deal with the increasing problem of safety in the schools.[36]

Lead paint poisoning in Bushwick. The district manager cabinet developed very differently in Bushwick. Without question, it was the most difficult area for the administrative decentralization program. Many in city government were skeptical whether any institutional system that did not bring major new resources into the community could survive. Sid Jones accepted the appointment as district manager. He knew bureaucratic politics from the inside and had been tested in sensitive community situations. For over a decade, Jones had worked as a welfare social worker; then he served

36. *Project Report: South Bronx*, p. 23.

as a special assistant to the commissioner of social services, developing an experimental program in the South Bronx. His latest position involved troubleshooting for the Model Cities administrator in Harlem. As a career civil servant, he was careful, experienced, resilient, and committed. As a black, he gained the respect of the predominantly white district officers on the cabinet and earned a reputation for fairness among the Italian and Spanish-speaking leaders in the area. His problems with community politics were almost precisely the opposite of those in the South Bronx. The many recent migrants into Bushwick were underorganized and underrepresented in civic and political activity, and the older residents had given up on the area. From the early days of the program, Jones used his own small staff to help organize and stengthen block associations, which could begin to provide a basis of broader participation in the public life of the community. He held monthly leadership briefings to involve as many elected officials and neighborhood organizations as possible in the cabinet's work. The local community board had been viewed as an irrelevant institution. Jones made a calculated effort to revitalize it with new members and successfully lobbied to join it himself.

For the district manager, local politics was not the problem in Bushwick; services were. Jones searched for feasible projects that could demonstrate some constructive action by the cabinet, but this did not begin to deal with the underlying concerns of the community in employment, schools, and housing. The tension between these needs and the capabilities of the cabinet officers with their limited resources was discouraging. As he wrote in an early report shortly after taking office: "It is difficult to take pride in the enormously successful inter-agency coordinated street cleaning project, for example, if the basic need of 10,000 new housing units in the neighborhood is ignored."[37] In later stages, Jones fought successfully to speed construction of planned public housing and to include the district in the city's neighborhood preservation program, but his efforts to mount a coordinated attack on lead paint poisoning best revealed the strengths and weaknesses of the cabinet in Bushwick.

The Bushwick health district had fewer than two hundred thou-

37. Sidney Jones, "Bushwick Monthly Report," 1 March 1972.

sand residents but accounted for more than 15 percent of all children discovered to have lead poisoning in the entire city during
1972.[38] The standard operating procedure for handling these cases
was extremely cumbersome. Blood was drawn when children were
brought into the district health center for examination. If the sample tested positive, the child was treated in a city hospital. Simultaneously, the Health Department's central Bureau of Lead Poisoning Control was notified. The Bureau sent one of its sanitarians
to take paint chips from peeling surfaces in the child's residence.
These in turn were tested for lead content by the central labora-
tory services. If the paint was shown to contain a toxic level of lead,
the health commissioner issued an order to the landlord to make
necessary repairs within a specified time. The sanitarian returned to
check whether there was compliance. If not, the Health Department notified the Housing and Development Administration to
cover the surfaces on which lead paint had been discovered through
its Emergency Repair Program. When HDA reported completing
the job, the health sanitarian would check back once more to verify
elimination of the hazard. HDA was left to try to recoup the cost of
the repair from the landlord. In some cases, a child might be kept in
the hospital throughout this entire process, which could go on for
months.

In tackling this bureaucratic complexity, the district manager had
a number of different concerns. The centralized control over health
inspections and housing repairs seemed to invite delay and uncoordinated action. More important, the whole approach was oriented
toward treatment; no attention was given to changing the housing
conditions that caused poisoning before it occurred. Few efforts
were made either to search for undiscovered cases or to follow up
and make sure that children were not recontaminated. The district
manager's staff prepared a comprehensive proposal with members
of the cabinet to overcome these weaknesses.[39] It called for assigning sanitations to the district health officer so that he could speed
investigations and granting him the authority to order landlords to
remove lead paint *before* children were poisoned. To cut down the

38. "Model Projects" (ONG files, n.d.).
39. "Bushwick Lead Control Proposal" (ONG files, August 1973).

delay between authorizing an emergency repair and having it carried out, the area housing director would be given the power to contract for this work locally. In addition, decentralized housing inspectors would begin to investigate other apartments in buildings where a case of lead poisoning had been discovered, gather paint samples on their normal rounds, and eventually make comprehensive surveys of housing in designated areas. Finally, the powers of the housing administration to set rent levels and provide rehabilitation loans would be used as carrot and stick to encourage landlords to take preventative action.

The results fell far short of this goal. The Health Department did outstation a lead paint sanitarian from the central bureau to work full-time in Bushwick under the direction of the district health officer. Additional paraprofessional aides were reallocated within the local health center to help in outreach and follow-up. Existing field staff in the community corporation (the local CAP agency) and the HRA participated in a public health campaign to spread the word about the dangers of lead poisoning in selected target areas of the community. In comparison with other areas of the city during 1973, Bushwick's testing program had by far the highest percentage of contaminated cases discovered in proportion to the number of blood samples tested, and in 1974, the district had the most children discovered with lead poisoning in the city.[40] However, the more ambitious aspects of the plan to improve housing conditions were stymied. The Housing Administration balked at decentralizing either control over inspectors or authority to order emergency repairs. The cost of de-leading an apartment was prohibitive, given the available technology. There was no way to detoxify paint once it had been applied. The only solution was to cover the surface with new wallboards, a process that could cost thousands of dollars per room. Under these conditions, pressuring landlords to make repairs might only encourage them to abandon their properties, and paying for the repairs with public funds was well beyond the capacity of the city's finances. Although there was some increased attention to

40. The comparative data were derived from statistics provided by the Bureau of Lead Poisoning Control in a personal communication to the author, 19 September 1978.

testing children in the district, Jones later commented about his efforts: "We probably took on too many issues and too many agencies at one time"[41]

TRANSITIONAL COMMUNITIES: THE DISTRICT MANAGER AS ENTREPRENEUR[42]

The district manager cabinets were introduced in three older residential communities that had undergone profound socioeconomic transitions over the previous two decades: Crown Heights, Washington Heights, and the Rockaways. Although large minority populations migrated into each of these areas, none of them exhibited the pervasive poverty of Bushwick or the South Bronx. Needs varied from the traditional service concerns typical of middle-class communities to the larger developmental problems presented by the new immigrants. The underlying question for the city was whether these areas could be preserved, or whether they would gradually deteriorate into slums. The district managers and cabinets faced unusual challenges, made more complex because the process of change had invariably increased the stakes and heightened tensions in community politics.

Crown Heights, an area of over two hundred thousand residents located in the heart of Brooklyn, was one of the city government's greatest concerns. Standing midway between the heavy minority populations in Bedford-Stuyvesant and Brownsville to the north and the mostly white homeowners living in the southern part of the borough, its future would have a major impact on the social, economic, and political forces affecting millions of people. In one decade, from 1960 to 1970, the district had shifted from a 70 percent white, predominantly Jewish community to 70 percent black, many of West Indian origin. Racial tensions compounded by sensitive religious issues threatened to engulf almost every issue. The stability of the remaining whites depended to a great extent on the

41. Sidney Jones, interview, 30 January 1976.
42. For both the "broker" and "entrepreneur" analogies used in a somewhat different context, see Stanley J. Heginbotham and Howard G. Katz, *Between Community and City Bureaucracy*, pt. 3: *Patterns of Community Involvement in the Experiment* (New York: Bureau of Applied Social Research, Columbia University, February 1973), pp. 4–9.

decision of the Lubavitcher Rebe, leader of a twenty-thousand-member Hasidic sect, to stay in the community. Having opted for Crown Heights, the group consciously moved beyond its religious focus and became increasingly aggressive politically. It had a remarkable capacity to mobilize votes. Tensions in the area were further exacerbated by a growing rift between the middle-class black homeowners and the black poor. There were a number of black elected officials from the area, but the competition between rival factions pervaded the civic and political life of the community, with the Hasidim often left to determine the balance of power. In contrast, Washington Heights, on the northern tip of Manhattan, had experienced a large increase in the number of blacks and Spanish-speaking people in portions of the district, but their impact on the older Jewish and Irish communities had been less profound. The major civic organizations were dominated by an active but self-contained white middle-class clique. Unlike Wakefield, this leadership maintained close, almost byzantine connections with elected officials and the regular and reformed political clubhouses. Few blacks and practically no Spanish-speaking leaders had gained acceptance into this closed circle.

The Rockaways, a ten-mile long peninsula parallel to the border of southern Queens, exhibited all the problems of rapid, unsettling growth. Between World War II and the 1970s, the population had almost tripled to ninety-nine thousand. Because of its underdeveloped land, scores of coop apartments had been built that attracted many elderly retired Jews. This development was accompanied by major public housing programs, including some "model" urban renewal disasters. Most troublesome, the Rockaways had become a relocation dumping ground for people forced from their homes by public construction projects throughout the city. Thousands of the poor were shunted into dilapidated former beach houses without adequate heat and plumbing for year-round living. These problems were compounded by an increase in private nursing homes and other proprietary health institutions far out of proportion to the needs or capabilities of the area to sustain. Neither the physical infrastructure nor the social service system had kept pace with these developments. Sewers overflowed, and both welfare recipients and the elderly went unattended. Yet the middle class was defensive and ambivalent, if not overtly hostile, to the introduction of services that would make life more bearable for the minority poor.

In these transitional communities, the district managers faced an entrepreneurial challenge—the need for new combinations of political and administrative resources—with all the risks such a role inevitably entailed.

The neighborhood preservation program in Crown Heights. The Office of Neighborhood Government had already targeted special capital budget funding into Crown Heights through the city's Neighborhood Action Program, and its local director, Dick Duhan, became the district manager for the area. Duhan had previously worked for a nonprofit community association involved with housing, economic development, and education in the ethnically polyglot Lower East Side of Manhattan. As a manager, he had an open, participatory style, which he encouraged in the cabinet and the community. Early on, he sensed the opportunity to develop a comprehensive housing rehabilitation program in the district. It seemed a logical and propitious choice. Housing, with its broader implications for the stability of the community, was the one concern which could draw together all the disparate ethnic and political factions in a cooperative venture. Both city and federal officials were shifting their attention from the renewal of the poorest areas to the preservation of existing neighborhoods. New York was losing more housing units each year through fire, demolition, and abandonment than it was gaining through new construction.[43] For some time, the City Planning Commission had been fighting the HDA's focus on new production and was urging the mayor to devote more resources to rehabilitation and neighborhood preservation.

With the turbulent demographic change in Crown Heights, the problem of a basically sound but rapidly deteriorating housing stock

---

43. The dimensions of the problem were staggering. In 1972 there were 15,000 units of publicly-aided new construction—a relatively large number. But it was estimated that *annually* the city lost 10,000 to 15,000 units through abandonment and 5,000 to 15,000 due to fire and other emergencies; and an additional 10,000 to 15,000 were demolished to make way for public improvements. See *Neighborhood Preservation in New York City* (New York: Department of City Planning, October 1973), pp. 51–53.

was particularly severe. The signs of neighborhood decline began to appear: vacant storefronts, commercial areas closing early, a sharp decline in sales, landlords milking buildings for income and neglecting maintenance, the unavailability of bank mortgages or home improvement loans due to "redlining."[44] Both the city and federal governments had a number of techniques to address these pressures, but they had rarely been applied in a coordinated way. On the one hand, code enforcement could make landlords repair existing violations, but experience indicated that this frequently encouraged abandonment. On the other hand, there were positive inducements to help landlords or allow them to leave the scene gracefully: loans for renovation, tax abatement, mortgage insurance, and ownership transfer through co-oping. But focusing solely on the rehabilitation of the housing stock appeared to be self-defeating in the long run. Bricks and mortar did not stand in insular isolation from the surrounding social system. If a renovated apartment house were immediately overloaded with welfare tenants, who were viewed as dangerous and received inadequate sanitation services, the building would rapidly return to its deteriorated state.

For the first time, the district manager cabinets gave city government a system to mobilize and coordinate existing municipal service agencies to complement a concentrated housing rehabilitation program. The HDA had been negotiating with HUD in Washington to obtain funds for an area maintenance program, and with the addition of the district cabinets and the active involvement of the City Planning Commission in the proposal, New York received a $310,000 contract in August 1972 to plan the new approach in Crown Heights. City Planning Department staff took the lead in analyzing the process of neighborhood decline. The evidence pointed to "small pockets of deterioration" where there was "a significant correlation of families on public assistance to buildings with high levels of reported building code violations." The study continued:

The process begins when the first families on welfare move in. These families require services which are largely absent. The

44. See *Crown Heights Area Maintenance Program*, vol. 1: *CHAMP Strategy* (New York: Department of City Planning, December 1972), p. 58.

problem is intensified when more follow. This in turn, triggers the departure of long-term residents. Landlords fill the vacancies with welfare families. Residents and owners of adjoining buildings become frightened and the destructive dynamic accelerates. A pocket of deterioration results. It spreads, meets similar pockets, and wrecks a neighborhood.[45]

To block this cycle, the proposed neighborhood preservation strategy required concentrating housing programs and social services on these pressure points of incipient decline. The mayor agreed to focus city housing rehabilitation loan funds in these areas. Through the cabinet, the decentralized area housing director and the human resources district director would coordinate their activities in specific buildings and subsections of the community. Social services would be directed not simply in response to individual need but on the basis of community welfare. The district manager, in consultation with a citizens' advisory board, also proposed a number of supplemental programs to strengthen civic organizations. In Crown Heights as in other transitional communities in New York, block associations were a powerful force in resisting the blockbusting activities of real estate interests. The neighborhood preservation plan, therefore, included the appointment of "block superintendents" in target areas to organize these local groups and work with them to monitor service delivery problems. In addition, paraprofessional "community security officers" under the police department would be assigned to these same subdistricts to improve residents' safety in their neighborhoods. To help small landlords with the high cost of maintenance services in their buildings, a nonprofit community-based housing management corporation was designed. While the city mobilized its own resources, there was a parallel effort to work with private bankers. The major clearinghouse banks established a planning group, which agreed to create a subsidiary corporation to channel mortgage funds into neighborhood preservation districts.

The Crown Heights neighborhood preservation program was

45. Ibid., p. 52.

ambitious and enervating. For six months the district manager and his staff gave it most of their attention as they worked with community representatives and cabinet agencies to develop extensive plans. When HUD backed away from funding the project and President Nixon placed a moratorium on the relevant federal housing programs, it was a bitter disappointment. The city later announced its own program in five districts to be financed by targeting $45 million from existing Municipal Loan funds, but even this effort proved impossible to sustain as New York faced its looming financial crisis. Eventually a cut-back program was mounted in a number of areas with federal community development funds. But the inability to implement the project in Crown Heights at that time was a serious political as well as programmatic failure. The district manager was not able to overcome the aloof defensiveness of the Hasidic community. Jewish and black leaders who had begun to cooperate in this effort did not have the same stake in burying their rivalries and suspicions on other issues, and the area was subsequently split into two separate community districts.

Public employment jobs in Washington Heights. Don Middleton was appointed to be district manger in Washington Heights. He had grown up in an Irish Catholic family in the area but was later executive director of the OEO−funded Community Action Program in Nassau County. He had joined city government as a planner in charge of innovations for the rapidly expanding Addiction Services Agency. Middleton was bright, able, and aggressive. He wanted to accomplish something and, despite ruffled feathers, usually did. Naming an outsider as district manager was a threat to the closed circle of local influentials in Washington Heights, but the protest which greeted Middleton's appointment was unexpectedly intense. His ambitious and authoritarian style, which might have been an advantage in other areas, compounded the problem of establishing a working relationship with civic leaders in the district. The degree of antagonism aimed at him is revealed in the comment of a former community board chairman, which appeared in a neighborhood newspaper eighteen months later: "We take pride in the success with which we have destroyed Don Middleton in this community."[46]

Facing harrassment from community leaders, the district manager turned his attention to projects developed internally with the cabinet. One of the more unusual efforts involved decentralized planning for the use of personnel hired under the increasing number of public service employment programs. As the economic recession deepened, the federal government authorized Emergency Employment Act funds to localities. The city had developed a Work Relief Employment Program (WREP) providing part-time jobs for employable welfare recipients and had cooperated with the VERA Institute to initiate a "supported work" project for former addicts through the Wildcat Corporation. With his background in poverty and drug agencies, Middleton recognized the problems in making these public employment programs operate effectively, and the opportunities that were lost when they did not work. Although departments constantly complained about their lack of manpower, they usually viewed WREP and similar workers as a burden and placed them on unconstructive make-work or dead-end jobs. Traditionally, planning and design for these programs was highly centralized. Field commanders in the agencies had no involvement in the process either to specify the type of work needed or how many people they could use effectively. A district officer would simply be informed that on a specific date he would receive X number of personnel who would do Y.

In Washington Heights, Middleton turned this planning process upside down. Instead of local officers following central mandates, he involved the district cabinet in planning how public employment workers would be used. Approximately 175 WREP personnel were eventually employed by city agencies and various non-profit organizations in the area.[47] The district officers themselves initiated discussions with community representatives for the more venturesome use of these workers in the local health center, the schools, and recreation facilities, where they had normally been relegated to

46. Susan G. Sawyer, "Was Decentralization Here Just an Exercise of Will," *Washington Heights—Inwood Advocate*, 23 May 1974, p. 1.

47. Brumback, "Service Integration at the District Level," in *Decentralizing City Government*, p. 68.

menial, cleanup tasks. Washington Heights had six hundred acres of parkland, almost one-quarter of the total in Manhattan, and much of it was understaffed and deteriorating. Scores of public employment jobholders were involved in maintenance and renovation work. The parks officer on the cabinet was willing to use the former addicts from the Wildcat Corporation to help in an erosion control project for the park around the Cloisters Museum. As the district manager reported:

> He made the decisions. He worked up the development of the proposals. He met with community groups interpreting what was going to happen there, including the community board, to convince them we weren't going to unleash a horde of sex-crazed dope fiends in the parks—that they had a real job to do and were capable of doing it.[48]

Integrating capital and expense budgets in the Rockaways. The fragmented disruption of the Rockaways at the hands of private and public developers cried out for some concerted, long-term planning. Janet Langsam, the district manager, had been born and raised in the area. Although she did not have prior work experience in city government, as the chairman of a community board in another area of Queens she had been intimately involved with the politics and bureaucratic intricacies of capital construction projects. The time was ripe for a review of government policies and services in the peninsula. Langsam persuaded the chairman of the City Planning Commission to assign staff to work with her and the district cabinet on the project. The resulting study, *The Rockaways: A Report to the Community,* was the first of its type.[49] Like other cities, New York is legally required to have separate "capital" and "expense" budgets. This split not only exists on paper but permeates the administrative structure of individual departments where planners and operational managers are segregated into different divisions. Although there may be some coordination between these

48. Donald Middleton, interview, 14 January 1975.

49. *The Rockaways: A Report to the Community* (New York: Department of City Planning and Office of Neighborhood Government, November 1973).

divisions in the central offices, local operating officials are rarely, if ever, consulted about development plans for their districts. This allows parks to be developed with no provision for upkeep, or housing construction planned without considering the implications for sanitation services. As the Rockaways report itself stated: "Implicit in a park system. . . . but often overlooked, is the cost of operations and maintenance. Ten-acre parks, for instance, entail operation and maintenance cost of about $100,000 per year."[50]

The process of preparing the report forced many agencies to reconsider and modify their existing plans. The substance covered the full array of concerns in the community. Some examples:

■ The total number of units projected for the Arverne urban renewal site was reduced and the Housing and Development Administration made a commitment to use new low-rise housing designs.

■ Sewer cleaning and construction would be speeded and no new housing construction would be approved without adequate sanitary facilities.

■ City zoning policy was modified to provide more stringent criteria for approving new nursing homes and other domiciliary care facilities.

■ Realistic priorities for developing parkland and recreation were outlined and accompanied by necessary changes in maintenance facilities.

■ Sanitation projected management changes and increases in equipment to handle new development in the districts.

■ New procedures were devised for cooperation between local social service and housing inspection personnel to reduce the number of welfare clients in substandard housing and increase landlord compliance with existing codes.

■ Expanded clinics and a mobile-unit outreach program were designed to improve health and social services for the elderly.

50. Ibid., p. 57

The process of developing the report changed communications between field officers and central planners within the city departments. Janet Langsam commented later on this effect of the report:

Line officers got involved in matters that were going on around them within their own agencies about which they had no knowledge. Now [District Supervisor of Parks Operations] John Budzek calls and tells me the [construction] bids have gone out on the west-end section of the boardwalk. . . . He's gotten to know this person in planning and that one in engineering. . . . and the information is beginning to flow.[51]

Although many of the recommendations which appeared realistic in 1973 subsequently succumbed to other budget realities after the city's de facto financial default in 1975, the concept of neighborhood planning gained increased acceptance. The City Planning Commission rejected the idea of a single, static "Master Plan" for the city as a whole in favor of continuing "mini-plans" oriented to local communities.

ONG: The Central Role in Decentralization

At one of the weekly meetings, a district manager commented: "The irony of decentralization is that you need a strong central office."[52] ONG was inevitably drawn into the pushing and hauling required to get almost anything done in the bureaucracy. Despite formal administrative decentralization, most projects required some intervention in the hierarchy by the district manager or the central staff to change procedures or shift resources. The experience showed how difficult it was to cut operational responsibility into neat horizontal layers and how pervasive the sharing of functions was within the bureaucracies. City administration was as much a marble cake of multilevel actors as was intergovernmental relations.

---

51. Janet Langsam, interview, 16 January 1975.
52. Dick Duhan, quoted in Roggemann, "DM Meeting—ONG Central."

District managers were sometimes proud of their accomplishments, and often frustrated. One wrote of their "uphill, practically bare-handed battle to gain recognition for the experiment and for themselves from city agencies, local officials, and communities."[53] ONG had sloughed many of the toughest issues of administrative and budget decentralization, coterminality, and district manager powers in order to get the program into operation. But to move forward aggressively on any of these difficult questions, ONG was dependent on its narrow central constituency—Mayor Lindsay and his principal staff.

Mayor Lindsay himself gave broad policy backing and important symbolic support to ONG, but he did not actively manage or direct the program. He announced the experiment in an elaborate press conference surrounded by all the agency administrators and commissioners, insisted that a district manager make a presentation at every session of his citywide cabinet, and personally attended many local district cabinet meetings. His presence lent prestige to the program and boosted the morale of the district officers. In Bushwick, he listened with increasing impatience as the sanitation superintendent outlined his problems in getting legal permission to enter privately owned vacant lots. Finally the mayor interrupted and said (approximately): "To hell with the legality. Go in there and get the lots cleaned. By the time the absentee landlords try to catch up with us through the courts, none of us will be here any longer, and at least we will have accomplished something for the community." The district manager reported the impact of such a visit on the cabinet members:

There was enormous talent around that [cabinet] table. . . . Joe Thelen, the sanitation district super, was a fantastic guy. He put twenty-five to thirty years in the department, and he knew his job. But he was just doing his job. Mayor Lindsay came out to the cabinet meeting, and it dawned on Joe that this thing was for real. The guy moved mountains. He had his men doing things that were not in the sanitation book. They were volunteering to go on private property to clean lots. He added his own lot-cleaning

53. Marrero, "South Bronx Monthly Report,"

crew, and they went into basements, into backyards—whatever needed to be done—as long as it had the sanction of the cabinet.[54]

This kind of mayoral involvement brought recognition to ONG and was a stimulus to the local officers, but it did not produce the bureaucratic reorganization and commitment from the agencies that were essential to the long-term success of the program. After hearing about a problem at a district cabinet meeting, the mayor was more likely to exercise his "executive ax" and demand that the commissioner of water resources have six catch basins cleaned than he was to order an organizational change to prevent such difficulties from occurring again in the future. To a great extent, this style of using power for limited, discrete ends, rather than for institutional reform, permeated the highest levels of the Mayor's Office in its relation to ONG. With the multiple crises of city government falling into their laps every day key mayoral advisors were likely to slide into the pattern of the old urban action task force system where city commissioners used their political and bureaucratic clout to resolve neighborhood complaints. But this desire for quick results produced by central direction and an impatience with long-term institution building could conflict with a strategy to create a system of decentralized administration.

In this context, ONG acted as the internal advocate for the decentralization and geographic coordination of public services. It could count on general support for its goals and concrete backing on discrete issues, but not on consistent use of mayoral authority to reorganize the structure of city agencies. Since the district manager cabinets required a wide-scale effort to modify the bureaucratic culture of all operating departments, ONG had special problems in sustaining dynamic forward movement. In an environment where the daily pressures of administration forced the chief executive to deal with his top staff and agency heads on relatively narrow issues, the demand for organizational change, with its high immediate costs and vague promise of future benefits, was particularly difficult to manage. As a consequence, ONG was able to make only marginal changes to strengthen administrative decentralization, expand the

54. Sidney Jones, interview, 14 January 1975.

powers of the district managers, or create coterminous service boundaries during the two years of the demonstration project. Of all the major program development objectives, only budget decentralization showed some significant progress.

DECENTRALIZED BUDGETING

Two techniques for budget decentralization were tested by ONG: revenue-sharing grants to communities and formula budgeting for specific services. Although the dollar amounts affected by these efforts constituted only a small fraction of the total city expenditures in any given area, the attempts represented the first concrete experience in developing comprehensive district budgets.

The Highways Department funded general street repair and resurfacing through a lump-sum capital budget appropriation for each borough. Decisions on which streets would receive attention during any year were usually made by the borough engineers and the commissioner's office. Working closely with ONG, the department agreed to prorate these central funds for each of the district manager cabinet areas so that resurfacing priorities could be set at the community level. Since there was no accurate inventory of street condition or maintenance needs, the project staff was forced to budget funds using a crude formula based on each district's overall street mileage as a proportion of the borough total. For the eight experimental areas, amounts ranged from $152,000 in Bushwick to $382,000 in Wakefield-Edenwald. In addition, the staff developed information on unit costs, planned construction, and technical guidelines. The highways district foremen were given the responsibility to work with the district manager cabinets and the community boards in each area to select which streets would be repaved within these constraints. Never before had there been a formal process which allowed other city agencies or civic representatives not only to be consulted but to make these decisions.

Generally, implementation of the Highways experiment with decentralizated budgeting was successful, although there were marked variations among districts. With its elaborate "environmental information system," the South Bronx was able to pinpoint streets with pothole problems and relate these to planned sewer construction, traffic flow patterns, and new housing in developing final recommendations with the community board. In some areas the lack of data and the unwillingness of the highways foremen to assert their professional judgment in the face of community pressure led to local decisions that had to be overruled. For the eight districts as a whole, however, the department was impressed that over 70 percent of the recommendations could be implemented, an achievement which demonstrated that the district manager cabinets and community boards could "select technically feasible projects within budget constraints—and they did so in only one month."[55] The response of the districts was less restrained. Most of the community boards agreed with the statement of the chairman in Wakefield: "We've waited for a long time to receive this type of recognition from the city. . . . None of the community boards have ever been called upon to participate in a program of this magnitude in the past."[56]

The highways experiment was limited to capital budget funds and did not involve personnel. The Health Department tackled the complexity of developing a district "expense" budget that granted the district health officers unprecedented authority over the hiring and assignment of local staff.[57] The commissioner set citywide goals for departmental activities (increasing the proportion of children receiving dental treatment or school admission physical exams, for example). Standard unit costs for each service were prepared and, on the basis of estimated needs, a consolidated personnel budget was set for every district. Within this allocation, the district health officers were free to plan clinics and programs to meet their local goals. If improved efficiency enabled the officers to realize savings in fulfilling service targets, they were authorized to reassign funds and personnel to other special projects. One former district health officer reported that he was able to shift resources unilaterally to deal with the growing number of young children in an area two miles from the existing health center: "From an early analysis of the

55. Paul Belliveau, Memorandum to Manuel Carballo, "Neighborhood Budgeting Experiment—Preliminary Evaluation," 16 November 1973.

56. Bernard Butler, quoted in Robert Lane, "Louder Voice Planned for John and Jane Q.," *Sunday News,* 3 June 1973, p. 38.

57. See *Decentralized Budgeting in New York City* (New York: Office of Neighborhood Government, January 1974), pp. 28–34.

need, a Child Health Station was expanded to almost full-time capacity within a three month period. After another four months, the Child Health Station was converted to a Pediatric Treatment Center. All of which, I believe was only possible because of decentralization."[58] In theory, similar formula budgeting procedures could have been developed for other agencies. In practice, it required a heavy investment in complex planning, and the gains in flexibility were seriously constrained by civil service regulations and line-item budget controls. No other agency made the attempt.

Since 1970, ONG itself had administered a special capital budget allocation to finance small-scale projects in designated transitional neighborhoods. It recommended that this revenue sharing strategy be extended to the district manager cabinet communities in their second year of operation. A $2 million "line" was approved in the citywide capital budget, which gave each demonstration area about $250,000 for projects and equipment. Every expenditure required the approval of both the district manager cabinet for the city administration and the community board representing local residents and business interests. Projects developed by the city agencies and community representatives with these decentralized, lump-sum budgets covered a broad range of activities. Washington Heights approved the purchase of a large van to serve as a mobile "precinct-on-wheels" for the local police; Maspeth-Ridgewood put the bulk of its funds into improvements for a neighborhood park and equipment for a geriatric health facility; Bushwick arranged to seal abandoned buildings and acquired special sanitation equipment to clean vacant lots; Bay Ridge focused on a building to house a mental health clinic for local children and a mobile health van to serve the elderly in the area; Rockaways gave special attention to developing a youth center and installing a television security system in a junior high school; and Wakefield used its funds to renovate an old police precinct house for use as a local "Town Hall" where the district manager and officers from a number of other city agencies could be located.[59]

The amount of money in this lump-sum budget was intentionally

---

58. Anthony Mustalish, interview, 17 January 1975.
59. *Decentralized Budgeting in New York City,* pp. 15–22.

kept relatively small to prevent a diversion of cabinet attention away from its primary task—improving the coordination of ongoing agency operations. But the flexible funding did solve a number of problems for the field officers. It enabled them to obtain specialized equipment necessary in one area but not applicable citywide. It cut the time required to meet immediate operational needs in circumstances where a district officer's budget recommendations would normally be submitted in the spring of one year for a capital budget that came into effect fifteen months later. And finally, it allowed the agency officials to respond directly to the requests of community leaders without always having to buck these matters to headquarters.

Later in the experiment, an effort was made to strengthen the district managers' role in setting broader budget and development policy for their communities. ONG argued that on internal district affairs "the recommendation of the district manager should be paramount within the Administration."[60] There was some initial progress in this direction. The Bureau of the Budget issued a memorandum to the heads of all mayoral agencies directing them to consult with the district managers on key matters affecting their neighborhoods: the location of capital projects (a new police precinct house); the design for new construction (a park renovation); the rental of office space (a drug program); and "purchase of service" contracts (funding neighborhood day care centers).[61] In addition, the chairman of the City Planning Commission directed his staff to refer all proposed development plans and projects significantly affecting ONG areas to the district managers for their "review and comment."[62]

The immediate impact of these new procedures was minimal. They led to some budget review sessions with the heads of important agencies (transportation, sewers), in which the district managers could argue their priorities. But in general, there was not enough

60. John Mudd, Memorandum to Mayor John V. Lindsay, "Neighborhood Government Progress Report," 20 November 1972.

61. David A. Grossman, Memorandum to All Mayoral Agency Heads, "Coordination of Agency Operations at the Neighborhood Level," 30 April 1973.

62. John E. Zuccotti, Memorandum to Commissioners, Borough Chiefs, Section Heads, "Neighborhood Government—CPC," 17 May 1973.

time to see whether it would be possible to use these new consultation procedures to increase the influence of the managers, and through them the district cabinets and communities, in the governmental system of the city. Limited in its ability to improve the qualitative strength of the district manager cabinet program, ONG turned to increase its quantitative base in the communities and its support among political leaders.

Institutionalizing District Manager Cabinets

In the spring of 1973, when Mayor Lindsay announced he would not seek reelection, ONG was forced to ponder its prospects for survival. The district manager cabinet system had made some inroads into the established bureaucracies, but the program, which operated in only eight of sixty-two planning districts, did not have sufficient weight either within the city administration or with the public to maintain itself under a new mayor. In addition, in mid-1972 the state legislature had established a commission to review and revise the New York City Charter. Its mandate suggested some move toward decentralization, and its leadership was sympathetic to ONG. But as it began intensive work during 1973, what direction it would take and whether the voters would approve its recommendations were very open questions. ONG, therefore, worked both to extend the public constituency for the district manager cabinets and to encourage their inclusion in any charter reform.

Despite the mayor's lame-duck status, ONG recommended a major expansion of the district cabinet program in late April 1973. Some months earlier, the mayor's closest staff political advisor, Jay Kriegel, had revived the moribund Urban Action Task Force in many communities throughout the city. A few of the more aggressive city commissioners appointed as task force chairmen had formed district cabinets of local service chiefs. Without funds to hire full-time district managers, ONG estimated that it would be possible to form similar "Commissioner Cabinets" in eighteen new communities. Kriegel endorsed the idea, and with his active leadership in obtaining agency cooperation, ONG expanded from the original eight demonstration districts to a total of twenty-six cabinets covering almost half the city by the end of August 1973.

The expansion strategy also included the first formal connection between the cabinets and the traditional political institutions in the communities. In most areas, the district managers had developed a semistructured but informal relationship with the civic leaders and elected officials. But in September 1973, Mayor Lindsay issued an Executive Order that made the chairman of each local community board, the city councilmen from the district, and the borough president ex officio members of the cabinet in each area.[63] With an election imminent, no one expected any visible shift in the attitudes of the elected officials, who would already be laying the groundwork for bargaining with a new administration. Their participation might simply mute some suspicions and demonstrate the concrete value of the system for decentralized administration.

The Office of Neighborhood Government had much higher hopes for mobilizing a political constituency through the community boards. They were *the* single official institution established by the city charter in each planning district to represent the community in advising municipal government on matters of local concern. As such, they were the logical political counterpart to the administrative district cabinets. From experience, it was clear that the boards should be strong supporters of the program. Their membership was based in the civic organizations that had the most interest in the kinds of service improvements which the district managers and cabinets could produce. But the boards' narrow neighborhood orientation, reactive styles, and dependence on the borough presidents had inhibited their vision and aggressiveness on citywide issues in the past. And ONG's attempt to mobilize a public constituency for the program through them in the present was a flop. Although seven of the eight chairmen from the original demonstration districts agreed to consult with their full fifty-member boards to map out a citywide strategy, there was no follow-through. It was clear that although some civic action to defend the district manager cabinet program would occur, it would occur independently in each community and not as part of a broader approach, either in the upcoming mayoral election or the charter reform process.

63. Office of the Mayor, Executive Order No. 85, "In Relation to the Establishment of District Service Cabinets," 13 September 1975.

MAYOR BEAME AND THE CHARTER COMMISSION

Abraham Beame was elected to succeed Mayor Lindsay in November 1973. He did not make ONG a campaign issue, although a denunciation of "neighborhood city halls," "political patronage," or "another layer of bureaucracy" easily would have produced headlines. The local civic leaders had apparently given the district manager cabinets a sufficient community constituency so that candidates treated the program gingerly. The question for ONG no longer appeared to be one of survival, but survival on what terms. These terms were evident soon after the new mayor took office. As an old party loyalist from the Madison Democratic Club in Brooklyn and a longtime municipal administrator with years of service in the Budget Bureau and as the elected City Comptroller, Beame's orientation to government was fundamentally at odds with ONG's notion of decentralization. He represented the traditional view that government services should be managed hierarchically through the established agency bureaucracies and adapted to community needs through the local party organizations. His deputy mayor was quoted as saying that "if the city departments did their job right, there wouldn't be any need for an O.N.G."[64] Efficient, centralized administration would replace the need for an integrator like the district manager who could cut across bureaucratic lines to coordinate agency activities. Local political clubhouses, district leaders, and elected officials would replace ONG's nonpartisan effort to work with the broader civic community. Beame eventually authorized an expansion of commissioner cabinets to fifty-one districts citywide, but with a much reduced level of staff support under a renamed Office of Neighborhood Services. Political clubhouse presidents, party district leaders, and their relatives began to appear on the payroll. The shell of the administrative decentralization system survived, but more for patronage purposes than as a strategy to reorganize the delivery of city services.[65]

64. Quoted in Robert McG. Thomas, Jr., "Local City Offices Soon to be Closed," *New York Times*, 19 October 1974, p. 33.

65. See Steven R. Weisman, "Beame to Reorganize Neighborhood Cabinet," *New York Times*, 14 December 1974, p. 17; John Darnton, "U.S.–Financed Work for Jobless in City Being Used as Patronage," *New York Times*, 10 April 1975, p. 1.

But while the operation of the district manager cabinets gradually atrophied under Beame's administration, they became part of a larger debate over the future structure of city government in the charter reform process. The 1972 legislation creating the State Charter Revision Commission for New York City tilted toward decentralization. It included three guidelines for the commission's work: (1) Encourage genuine citizen participation in local city government; (2) Ensure that local city government is responsive to the needs of its citizens; and (3) Achieve effective local self-government.[66]

The chairman (State Senator Roy Goodman) and executive director (Dennis Allee) viewed the district manager cabinet system positively.[67] It offered a model for the administrative side of any decentralization plan. Their problems on this issue were twofold. What political decentralization would parallel this administrative structure? And would any of their recommendations have a chance at the polls? At the beginning of 1974, their prospects were not bright. It seemed likely that the winning combination at the last election, Mayor Beame and the regular Democratic party, would oppose decentralization. This opposition did not change, but the financial collapse of the city drastically shifted the patterns of influence in the eventual referendum on the proposed charter reforms.

The Charter Commission itself was permanently split on the decentralization question. Of the twelve members, four pressed for a return of power to the borough presidents, one insisted on a radical shift of budget and operating authority to neighborhood governments, and a bare majority of seven favored some moderate form of decentralization. By mid-1975, after two and a half years of study and debate, the chairman was able to engineer an artful compromise among these factions in the final recommendations. The commission unanimously approved six propositions covering a wide range of managerial and structural reforms. On decentralization, these included an expanded formal advisory role for the com-

66. *Final Report of the State Charter Revision Commission for New York City* (New York: State Charter Revision Commission, 1975), p. 1.

67. See *Office of Neighborhood Government* (New York: State Charter Revision Commission, 1974).

munity boards in budget and land use matters, a mandate for service agency coterminality in forty to fifty community districts, and a provision for local cabinets of district officers. But in a significant shift, the boards were also given the exclusive power to appoint the district managers and their staff. In return for the unanimous backing of these sections, the commission allowed separate propositions calling for borough government and neighborhood government to appear on the ballot but without any official recommendation. The voters could choose among these conflicting alternatives.

Although debate over the question of decentralization underlay the formation of the Charter Commission, its authorization included the responsibility to review the entire structure of government in the city. As New York was rapidly engulfed in the financial and political traumas of default during 1975, the commission's proposals for managerial reform became increasingly important in giving credibility to its overall package of charter amendments. Many of the recommendations were highly technical provisions concerning accounting systems, management performance reports, and personnel procedures. On the larger governmental level, the commission called for increasing the power of the elected city legislators vis-à-vis the mayor in formulating and approving the budget. More important than the details, the aura that permeated the commission's official recommendations was technical management expertise and moderation. Administrative decentralization, with its new jargon about "coterminality," complemented this tone. The one visible political loser, the mayor, was publicly tainted by his inept handling of the deepening budget crisis, and by the assumption of financial control over city affairs by the state.[68] The more controversial charter alternatives were presented separately at the end of the ballot, both diverting and dividing the opposition to the majority proposals.

As expected, the mayor opposed the Charter Commission provisions on decentralization, "ambushing" the proposed reforms in Chairman Roy Goodman's view through a series of "orchestrated"

68. A penetrating description of New York's road to default is found in Charles R. Morris, *The Cost of Good Intentions: New York City and the Liberal Experiment* (New York: Norton, 1980).

attacks by high administrative officials.[69] Less expected, the so-called "goos-goos," the good government civic groups that often rally to mobilize public opinion on complex reform issues in New York, were deeply divided on the question of charter revision. Some supported it and others recommended that decisions be deferred until after the fiscal crisis. Amidst the confusion, the *New York Times* made a major effort to inform, and then mold, public opinion. Beginning in September 1975, it published a series of lengthy articles explaining the proposals and sorting out the arguments pro and con. These were followed in the days preceding the vote by four editorials strongly supporting the Charter Commission's unanimous recommendations for fiscal management reforms and moderate decentralization. The series culminated with the clear instruction, like the classic political palm-card, to vote "Yes on Questions 1 to 6" and "No on questions 7 to 10."[70] Despite this unusual publicity, city councilmen reported little interest in the communities and predicted that all the propositions would be defeated.

The results of the referendum on November 4, 1975, came as a surprise to many observers. With a turnout of about 25 percent for a ballot filled with complex questions, the six Charter Commission recommendations passed and the alternatives were turned down. While an average of over 60 percent favored the central management reforms, 55 percent supported decentralization with district service cabinets and strengthened community boards. The more radical political decentralization proposition, which would have placed operating control over city services in the communities, was rejected by 65 percent of the voters.[71]

The decentralization provisions of the new charter were to be phased into operation over a period of years. New community districts had to be designated by January 1, 1977, and coterminous service areas with decentralized management authority were re-

69. Frank Lynn, "City Hall Reported Ready to Fight Charter Revision," *New York Times*, 28 September 1975, p. 1.

70. "The Charter Proposals," *New York Times*, 31 October 1975, p. 32.

71. Raw voting figures on each proposition are reported in "Tally on City Charter," *New York Times*, 6 November 1975, p. 33.

quired three years later by January 1, 1980. New land use and budgeting procedures would be developed in the process. Thus, the full implementation of the charter reforms would come during the administration of yet another mayor, Edward Koch, who succeeded Beame at the beginning of 1978. The original district manager cabinets had functioned with strong mayoral backing for only two years in the early 1970s. They gained sufficient credibility and constituency to be incorporated into the structure of city government but with a significant shift in their relation to the local community boards. Clarifying the lessons of this earlier experience is important both to evaluate the potential of decentralized management techniques in general and to understand the strengths and weaknesses of the district manager and cabinet system as it was eventually implemented in New York under the new charter.

5
THE IMPACT OF DISTRICT CABINETS

The cabinet "represents interagency cooperation at the grass roots level. . . . Each program becomes a small, workable community project rather than a bureaucracy-laden, city-wide undertaking.
—General Parks Foreman[1]

Some analysts have warned that coordinating councils tend to get lost in "special projects to demonstrate the ability to coordinate."[2] During the first two full years of their work, the district manager cabinets carried out hundreds of projects, ranging from improved methods for detecting and repairing clogged street drains to comprehensive plans integrating capital construction and agency service operations in local communities. What did these varied activities add up to? Were they make-work or did the city officials, community leaders, and citizens find them worthwhile? Who gained or lost by the creation of the cabinets, and to what extent and at what cost? From the available evidence, some broad consequences of the program are clear.

1. Quote from a general parks foreman in Susan S. Fainstein and Fran LaSpina, *District Service Cabinets and the Office of Neighborhood Government* (New York: Bureau of Applied Social Research, Columbia University, 1973), p. 14.
2. The quote is by White House Counselor Daniel P. Moynihan, commenting on the plans for Federal Regional Councils during the Nixon administration. It is taken from the minutes of the Under Secretaries Group, 13 June 1969, and cited in a chapter written by Gary Bombardier, in Martha Derthick, *Between State and Nation* (Washington, D.C.: Brookings Institution, 1974), p. 169.

Lessons of the Experiment

Political viability. The district manager cabinet program made decentralization politically acceptable in New York. In a city where the approach had become identified with the turmoil and polarization surrounding the struggle over community control of the schools in Ocean Hill–Brownsville, this was no small achievement. Less than a decade after the extensive school strikes opposing political decentralization in the education system, a majority of the voters approved the system of strengthened community boards and district service cabinets for inclusion in the city charter as a formal part of the structure of government in New York.

Agency officers' support. A remarkably high proportion, over 80 percent, of the civil servants who participated in the demonstration program found the cabinets "useful" or "very useful."[3] Most reported that the new institutions were "somewhat" or "very important" in promoting communication and cooperation among agencies in the area. Fewer, but still a majority, found them helpful in resolving conflicts with other departments. A similar proportion reported that the district managers were "effective" or "very effective" in facilitating cabinet work in the community. Almost unanimously, the agency representatives from the established bureaucracies favored continuation and expansion of the district manager cabinet system of decentralized administration. Why? Some quotes from individual field officers give the flavor of their attitudes toward the new approach.

---

3. The data in this paragraph are drawn from two separate surveys carried out by independent researchers at the Bureau of Applied Social Research, Columbia University. One included all cabinet officers in five of the original eight demonstration districts. It is analyzed by Susan Fainstein and Fran LaSpina Clark, "A Survey of District Service Cabinet Members' Attitudes toward ONG," in Allen H. Barton et al., *Decentralizing City Government,* (Lexington, Mass.: D.C. Heath and Company, 1977), pp. 177–80. The other is based on a survey of 107 officers in both cabinet and control districts. The results are discussed in John M. Boyle, "Local Operating Officials' Responses to the Experiment: Service Integration, Agency-Community Relations, and Overall Attitudes," in Barton et al., *Decentralizing City Government,* pp. 173–77.

Max Votreflich, assistant supervisor of recreation, Maspeth-Ridge-wood, Queens: The cabinet cuts red tape; it allows service chiefs to sit down face to face and discuss common problems. . . . I am now in better touch with the community.[4]

Anthony Mustalish, district health officer, Washington Heights, Manhattan: The uniqueness of the district cabinet was that it provided the only time that representatives of the city agencies get together. . . . Nowhere in the other districts without cabinets was there an opportunity to meet on a regular basis.[5]

Joseph Mezzardi, district superintendent of sanitation, Bay Ridge, Brooklyn: Before I joined the cabinet, the other agency chiefs were just names, not faces. Now I know them and can work with them.

Chuck McDowell, area director, Housing and Development Administration, Washington Heights, Manhattan: The cabinet takes the blinders off agency people.

Lieutenant David Walsh, 47th Police Precinct, Wakefield-Eden-wald, Bronx: I now think much more favorably about other agencies. . . . We all work together since we are all part of the same community. . . . ONG has helped us quite a bit with our own work. Previously we would report a condition which needed rectification and that was it. We reported it and received no feedback as to whether or not the condition would be taken care of. We now have face-to-face contact with the people in the agencies responsible for correcting those conditions. Now when we need traffic signs or potholes repaired, the agency tells us the disposition of our request.

A Traffic Department engineer: The cabinet's function is to filter complaints . . . it can sort out the reasonable ones; it can defuse an angry community.[6]

4. Except where noted, this and the following quotes were gathered under the direction of Susan Heilbron for an internal Office of Neighborhood Government evaluation.
5. Interview with the author, 17 January 1975.
6. Quoted in Robin Maas, *Decentralizing New York City Service Agencies* (New York: Office of Neighborhood Government, May 1974), p. 62.

Glen Barrett, human resources district director, Bay Ridge, Brooklyn: Because we were all committed to this cabinet . . . you don't feel that you're imposing on the other man, to call him up on his time, so to speak. He's here for this purpose. I don't mind talking to him about how my problem relates to him. I don't have to feel afraid that he's going to turn off.[7]

Not all the agency participants were unequivocally favorable, however. A district health officer who had to cover multiple cabinets in Queens said: "It's a waste of time . . . since the complaints that come up on the agenda could be brought back to me by a clerk."[8] Police commanders often expressed frustration at having to deal with representatives of other agencies who did not have comparable authority or resources. Some civil servants mentioned the district manager cabinet's inability to bring pressure on member agencies to change their ways. These problems were not seen as definitive defects in the system; rather, the officers said they wanted the approach stengthened through the formation of common service boundaries and greater clarity and consistency in the powers of the district manager and agency representatives.[9]

Community leadership approval. Over three-fifths of the civic and political leaders interviewed in four communities rated the overall impact of the district manager cabinet program as "good" or "very good."[10] An even higher proportion wanted to see it continued and stengthened. Only four percent of those questioned thought the program should be stopped. Except for one area where the appointment of the district manager caused serious political conflict with local leaders, there was little variation in this high rate of approval between middle-class and poor communities, blacks and whites, or civic and government officials. There was some tendency for blacks

7. Interview with the author, 15 January 1975.

8. Maas, *Decentralizing New York City Service Agencies*, p. 105.

9. A summary of the most frequently mentioned recommendations is found in Fainstein and LaSpina, *District Service Cabinets*, pp. 27–30.

10. Evidence on the response of local leaders to the program is reported in Susan S. Fainstein et al., "Community Leadership and the Office of Neighborhood Government," in Barton et al., *Decentralizing City Government*, pp. 119–22.

and lower-class representatives to express stronger support, but the poll found unusually high agreement across socioeconomic lines in supporting decentralized administration. Again, some individual comments help to explain why.

From Wakefield-Edenwald: ONG is one place where community problems are heard and acted upon. . . . It's a place where I don't get a run-around. . . . I think we have started turning Edenwald around. . . . We have had extraordinary cooperation.[11]

From Bushwick: They have helped to get better street lighting and the sewer lines are getting unclogged. Of course, they haven't solved the big problems, like housing, but they are working on it. . . . ONG has in a sense brought the [racial] groups together because it takes a stance in the center. . . . It does not favor any one group but tries to find the common issue in every problem.[12]

From Crown Heights: ONG responds to requests as best they can; they're an intermediary between you and the city. They cut the red-tape and provide services that centralized agencies downtown can't or won't deliver. They have improved the responsiveness of the city government to the community.[13]

From Bay Ridge: Practically every reporter's study on this city's ills comes up with a parallel solution to halt municipal decline and stem the flight to the suburbs: put the citizens in touch with government, particularly place the services he needs—such as sanitation, police, parks—within his reach so that he won't think his fate is in the hands of the distant uncaring bureaucracy. . . . To cure this infectious feeling of insignificance and to restore the dignity of being an individual . . . we in Bay Ridge now have an answer. . . . Far from competing with existing facilities . . .

11. Various civic leaders are quoted in "ONG Unit Hopes for Continuation," *Bronx Press-Review,* 6 December 1973, p. 1.

12. Susan S. Fainstein et al., *Community Leadership and the Office of Neighborhood Government in Bushwick, Crown Heights, and Wakefield-Edenwald* (New York: Bureau of Applied Social Research, Columbia University, 1973), pp. 28, 30.

13. Ibid., pp. 57–58.

ONG provides that vital link—the heretofore missing link—between the citizen's problem and its solution.[14]

Even a city councilman, who might be expected to feel threatened by the program since the district manager cabinets handled citizen complaints, a traditional source of constituency-building, supportively stated: "It frees me to do my other work to be able to refer service complaints to them. I do work with them closely, however, in developing long-range plans for the district."[15]

On the other hand, a healthy proportion of the local leadership gave the district manager cabinet system only a "fair" or "poor" rating. Their criticisms reflected a variety of perspectives. One elected official bluntly commented, "I consider it a patronage set-up."[16] Some institutional interests were challenged. For example, a local poverty program official said, "ONG is duplicating the Community Cooperation; it's a waste of energy."[17] Some social groups felt threatened. An Hasidic rabbi voiced the fears of many Jews during this period in New York when he stated: "With decentralization and community boards, only the most vocal are heard. . . . I don't see better services when the activists get in. They only get for themselves."[18]

Other leaders were concerned that the cabinets were not known in the community and were not able to address the deeper problems of housing, employment, and education in poor neighborhoods. Although favorable about their current relationships with ONG, many feared the lack of a formal role for residents in determining the future direction of the program. As one said, "If those people should change it could become a buffer, it could become just another game. . . . A more permanent form of citizen participation is needed."[19] Most of the criticism by local leaders was not based on the feeling that the new system of decentralized administration was

14. Charles F. Otey, "Focus," *Home Reporter and Sunset News*, 12 April 1974, p. 10.

15. Fainstein et al., "Community Leadership" (1977), pp. 120–21.

16. Ibid., p. 121.

17. Fainstein et al., *Community Leadership* (1973), p. 56.

18. Ibid., p. 62.

19. Ibid., p. 31.

bad, but that it was not strong enough. They wanted to see greater power vested in the district offices, more publicity to encourage wider access, and a structured role for community and citizen influence.

Limitations. Despite the very positive attitudes among the district officers and the local leaders, the district manager cabinets did not penetrate deeply into the service delivery system or the consciousness of the public. One attempt to measure quantitative shifts in the frequency of contact, cooperation, and conflict resolution picked up little reported change in behavior among the agencies officially represented on the cabinets or other city departments in the area that were not regularly included in the program.[20]

Publicity about the district manager cabinets was intentionally downplayed at the start in order not to raise expectations too high, and predictably, the public in four of the demonstration communities had little awareness of the program. More important, however, neither the public nor the local leadership reported any significant improvement in city service delivery compared to control districts.[21] In fact, citizens reported in almost every area that both their problems and city services, including safety, housing, sanitation, and so forth, had gotten worse during the two years of the experiment. During this period, from 1972 to 1974, the national inflation and recession were becoming the dominant concerns of many citizens,

---

20. See Boyle, "Local Operating Officials' Responses to the Experiment," pp. 162–63. These data are particularly tricky to interpret. The questionnaire asked for information about the relationships between *offices,* not *officers,* and therefore probably elicited opinions about low-level, routine activities rather than those issues of special interest to the district officers themselves. In addition, the sample did not include most of the regular cabinet participants; the correlations are so low (the highest is .2) that it is not evident the survey instrument picked up much at all; and the statistical groupings of areas reduce the distinction between district manager cabinets, commissioner cabinets, and control districts. This may be a case of social science precision without much significance. On the other hand, the conclusions conform with experiential judgment. The changes introduced by district manager cabinets were not primarily quantitative modifications in behavior.

21. This comparison is blurred because, through no fault of the researchers, the city introduced commissioner cabinets (without district managers) into two of the three control areas during the second year of the program.

but this was prior to the de facto default that brought the major layoffs and cutbacks in city departments. The one measurable improvement reported by the public in district manager cabinet areas was an increase in the proportion of citizens who were satisfied when they contacted city agencies about their most important problems.[22] Although the experiment demonstrated only marginal impact on the overall service delivery system, both the public and community leaders continued to favor the decentralization of city government. And administrative decentralization received much more widespread support than the more extreme forms of political decentralization entailed in community control or full-scale neighborhood government.[23]

Balkanization. The fears that decentralization would lead to "balkanization" (increased conflict within or between communities, marked disparities in service among districts, or inconsistent policies within functional program units), corruption, loss of productivity, or parochial pressure to divert major resources to the demonstration districts were not borne out in practice. There were no unusual incidents of conflict, no allegations of favoritism or corruption connected with the program, and no evidence that professional service standards were distorted or that productivity was reduced. By and large, the attempt by the ONG managers to prevent a diversion of extra resources into the communities was successful. One estimate found some additional parks and street maintenance allocations, but much of this resulted, not from political pressure, but from technical mistakes in estimating the amount of asphalt required for street resurfacing.[24] The fact that corruption or distorted resource allocation did not appear in a two-year demonstration program is not evidence that these problems would not

---

22. For a comparative analysis of the public's attitudes on problems, services, and satisfaction rates, see Nathalie S. Friedman and Theresa F. Rogers, "Decentralization and the Public," in Barton et al., *Decentralizing City Government*, pp. 219–25.

23. Ibid., pp. 236–37. The views of leaders are presented in Fainstein et al., "Community Leadership," (1977), p. 123.

24. Joel D. Koblentz and Ronald Brumback, "Costs of the Program and Resource Allocation Effects," in Barton et al., *Decentralizing City Government*, pp. 102–23.

arise over a more extended period. It does suggest, however, that political leaders can implement a strategy of decentralized administration without exaggerated concern about potential negative consequences.

Costs and benefits. The additional cost for the district manager cabinet program was minimal—less than one dollar per capita for the districts, including not only the direct expenses of the central Office of Neighborhood Government, the district managers, and their staff and offices, but the time of the participating agency officials as well. Crude estimates of the dollar benefits found that the decentralized administration system almost paid for itself through service improvements even during its initial period and had the potential to produce greater savings in the long run.[25] However, some projections for changing agency administrative boundaries to provide common service districts showed that the cost of achieving perfect coterminality could be very high, both in initial start-up and ongoing expenses. And the benefits that could reasonably be expected from coterminality would be minimal, unless accompanied by significant administrative decentralization in the operating bureaucracies to increase the management flexibility of field officers.[26]

Who won and who lost. The district manager cabinets did not produce a noticeable change in the quantity of services, but they did improve the quality of the service delivery system for those most closely involved—the front-line field officers from city agencies and the civic leaders in the communities. The cabinets increased interagency coordination in ways that the mayor and the district officers valued; and the community leaders reported that access to a new institution of decentralized administration like the district cabinets increased city government's responsiveness to their concerns. The program was implemented without any great political conflict, and cost estimates indicated that it could pay for itself through increased

---

25. Ibid., pp. 113–14.
26. Robin Maas, *Service Integration and the Problem of Redistricting* (New York: Office of Neighborhood Government, 1973), p. 110.

efficiency in the use of existing resources. Far from being incompetent, many field officers from the specialized bureaucracies demonstrated unexpected managerial capability, initiative, and potential in working with the district managers. The strategy strengthened the central (mayor) and local (field officer, civic leader) levels within the larger political system of the city—and threatened the intermediary politicians and administrators. It offered a new mechanism for nonpartisan civic activists to influence service delivery in ways that the remnants of the political clubhouse could no longer provide.

Overall, there were fewer potential losers, or big winners, among the major interests in this decentralized administration strategy. The gains were incremental in selectively improving services to citizens in their communities; they were not dramatic. As a system to coordinate multiple, specialized agencies with significant additional resources to confront complex problems like neighborhood preservation or community development, the district manager cabinets suggested potential but were untested. The combination of cutbacks in federal funding and increasing budget pressures in New York thwarted the plans for major new programs to be managed at the community level. The district manager cabinets strengthened the administrative capacity of city government and the institutional infrastructure of urban neighborhoods. The system indicated an untapped potential for development among the middle-level field managers of the civil service bureaucracies. It successfully demonstrated an organizational technique to integrate the activities of the increasingly fragmented functional specialists at the point where services are delivered to citizens in their communities.

In addition to these broad conclusions, the ONG experience in New York offers rich insights into three underlying issues: the nature of the coordination problem in big cities, the difficulties and potential of administrative decentralization, and the impact of organizational reforms in shifting patterns of citizen influence.

The Coordination Problem

The experience with district manager cabinets in New York helps increase the understanding of numerous issues raised in discussions of coordination among government agencies.

First, why is a coordinator, and a coordinating institution, necessary? Won't these problems, to the extent that they exist, simply work themselves out through voluntary negotiation and bargaining among the affected agencies?

Second, what powers should a coordinator have? Does he need line authority, a boss's capacity to give orders and expect action, or is some lesser mediating role adequate and perhaps even preferable?

Third, what are the limits of coordination? To what extent can it reasonably be expected to affect the performance of specialized agencies? Would the energy and resources devoted to the issues and institutions of coordination be better spent in resolving basic policy questions and then perfecting the simplest possible hierarchial organization to carry them out?

WHY IS A COORDINATOR NECESSARY?

Implementation of the district manager cabinet system repeatedly demonstrated multiple reasons why a coordinator, and a coordinating institution, can be valuable in improving big city service delivery, and why the problems of coordination do not just resolve themselves, guided by some invisible hand in the administrative marketplace. Among the most important are the following:

Functional parochialism. Bureaucratic cultures foster administrative introversion, a narrowing of vision and relationships in which the inhabitants tend to look for sustenance, help, and rewards almost exclusively within the confines of a specialized hierarchy. It results in the kind of attitude expressed by a police commander about his relations with other agencies: "We aren't looking out to help them, and they aren't looking out to help us"—even if such assistance is needed or desired.[27]

Reciprocal fears. Interagency relations are viewed as a kind of Pandora's box. If not handled with great care, they can loose many evils on the bureaucrat's head. Requests by one field officer for cooperation from a peer in another agency may lead to a reciprocal request for assistance at some point in the future, with unknown consequences. Criticism of another's operations may subject the

27. Adam Butcher, interview, 15 January 1975.

critic to attack in return. Agency officials' willingness to engage in open discussions about their own or others' problems, to seek or give assistance, and to listen to suggestions from community leaders increased noticeably during the development of the cabinets. The participating officers learned to trust each other and to trust the district manager to enforce some restraint and provide support in the deliberations. Interviewers in Bushwick found cabinet members who were aware of this problem commenting that the new organizational system "removes inter-agency fears and rivalries."[28]

No effective interagency procedures. In theory it should be possible to remove some of these fears by establishing depersonalized bureaucratic routines, or standard operating procedures, to handle interagency relations. In practice, this tends to work only on the most conventional kinds of problems, like reporting a broken traffic light, and even in these cases it can break down in triplicate-form busywork or neglect. In analyzing sixty-five of the more far-reaching projects undertaken by the district manager cabinets, researchers found that in over 80 percent of the cases there was either "no procedure" to handle the issue or established practice was "unreliable and cumbersome."[29]

Overcentralization. Administrative centralization often constrains field-level supervisors from working cooperatively with their peers in other agencies to realize common goals. A district health officer did not have the authority to certify that a vacant lot surveyed by health department sanitarians was a health hazard. A housing inspector investigating another complaint in an apartment was not authorized to take a chip of paint from a wall to test for its lead content. Even after an intensive effort to decentralize general administrative authority, the district managers had to work with local cabinet members to obtain approvals from agency decision-makers above the local level in 85 percent of the larger projects studied.[30]

28. Fainstein and LaSpina, *District Service Cabinets,* p. 18.
29. Joel D. Koblentz and Ronald Brumback, "An Analysis of Service Integration Projects of the District Offices," in Barton et al., *Decentralizing City Government,* p. 82.
30. Ibid., p. 84.

The district officers themselves commented that the district manager cabinets provided "internal leverage for each agency to decentralize and puts pressure on them [the agency commissioners] to
give their representatives authority to act."[31]

Disparities in power, prestige, and resources. There is a pecking
order not only within but between agencies. These differences may
be a reflection of public opinion, professional status, organizational
power, resources in personnel or budget, and current political
attention. The result is that a bureaucratically weak or undisci-
plined agency may be ignored by a strong, tightly managed department. A recreation supervisor expressed this plaint, and described
the changes brought about by the new system, when he said, "Before the cabinet, I occasionally tried to deal with the cops, but
they didn't take me seriously; they gave me the runaround. Now,
through the cabinet, I am heard, responded to."[32] From this perspective, the weakest departments had the most to gain from a
system of interagency coordination. But this presented the district
managers with the converse problem—what would the strong agencies, whose officers were often heard to complain that others could
not produce anything, get from the cabinets? One study found that
social and health service representatives were more likely to estimate that the lack of cooperation hurts them and that cooperation
would improve their performance, than were police, sanitation, and
fire officials.[33] This imbalance in needs and resources presented
a challenge to the district managers.

Unidirectional dependence. The need for assistance is often "unidirectional rather than mutual."[34] One agency may systematically

---

31. Fainstein and LaSpina, *District Service Cabinets*, p. 18.
32. Maas, *Decentralizing New York City Service Agencies*, p. 96.
33. John M. Boyle and Stanley J. Heginbotham, *Dependence, Cooperation, and
Conflict* (New York: Bureau of Applied Social Research, Columbia University,
January 1975), p. 7.
34. This important analysis is developed in ibid., p. 3. Also see John M. Boyle,
"Decentralized Administration of Municipal Services: An Assessment" (paper prepared for the 1977 Annual Meeting of The American Political Science Association,
Washington, D.C., September 1977), p. 18.

require help from a second, but the second agency may just as consistently not need support from the first. What may be a pressing problem for one may only be a peripheral concern for the other. For example, housing inspectors sometimes required police assistance in gaining access to a building, the Department of Relocation needed written notification from the Fire Department in order to house tenants thrown on the streets in a burnout; social service agencies may need police protection in operating their offices. But in each of these cases, the "petitioner" agency has little or nothing to offer the "respondent" in return for his trouble.

This systematic imbalance in the needs, priorities, and resources of the specialized bureaucracies is perhaps the most significant single reason why voluntary bargaining and negotiation among agencies will not solve the coordination problem. Aside from all the other habits, fears, and disparities that work against cooperation, one of the necessary parties to a negotiation may consistently be uninterested and see little benefit in getting involved. Without intervention, cooperation may appear to be a zero-sum (or even negative-sum) game for individual players. The role of a coordinator in creating a system of multiple payoffs for the agency participants is, therefore, crucial.

THE COORDINATOR'S ROLE AND POWERS
The role. Faced with the imbalances between single pairs of agencies, district managers had to expand the network of parties involved in the bargaining process so that all of them could see the potential for winning something in the new game. If Social Services needed Police for protection, perhaps Police needed Highways to clear vacant lots, and Highways needed Parks for grass trimming, and Parks needed Social Services to work with youth gangs. Finding and completing these circles of reciprocal interest was not the only role for the coordinator, but it started a process moving. This brokering among agencies set the stage for overcoming the inertia and fears that prevented direct, voluntary dealings between the agency representatives themselves. In effect, it established a forum in which institutionalized logrolling was acceptable, and this exchange of favors began to occur without the need for mediation by the district managers. As one police captain put it: "The cabinet

eliminates a big stumbling block—the reluctance of people to under-take projects because of the difficulty of getting in touch with each other. It sets up *the turnpike effect.* Once someone works with another agency on a cabinet project, he feels he can do it again on other matters.[35]

Evidence that a coordinator is necessary to this process comes from a comparison of cabinets that had a full-time district manager and expansion cabinets that were chaired by a city commissioner, who performed the coordinating role usually for only a few hours a month in addition to his normal departmental duties. In every case, agency officers reported that the cabinets with a district manager had more impact on improving interagency communication, co-operation, conflict resolution, and community relations. And the difference was markedly greater on the more difficult coordination tasks.[36]

If the cabinet needed a district manager to set the coordination process in motion, the district manager also needed a cabinet to be effective. The coordinator was not simply a free-floating entrepre-neur, even though, as district manager, he was an official agent of the mayor. A coordinator needs to be tied into the system he is coordinating, not simply by his designation as its titular head but through the legitimizing sanction of its specialized parts. One local agency official commented:

If Ed Hiltbrand [the district manager] was down here simply as the mayor's representative . . . if he just called my office, really I would have had pity on him. I'd say, "Oh could we do a job on you because you don't know what the hell is going on." And I could snow you seven days from Sunday. The beauty of this [cabinet] is that everybody has been brought together.[37]

With both the approval of the agencies and the institution of the cabinet, the district manager could move beyond the role of broker to energize the system—to fill in gaps between agencies' major

35. John Watters, ONG Evaluation Files (emphasis added).
36. Boyle,"Local Operating Officials' Responses to the Experiment," pp. 174–76.
37. Glen Barrett, interview, 15 January 1975.

responsibilities (joint inspections of illegal bottle clubs), change individual agency procedures (preventive safety surveys in Traffic), develop new programs (local assignment and job development for public employment workers), and mobilize community participation in decision-making (street paving priorities).[38] In some cases, the explanation of why particular projects had not been implemented prior to the district manager cabinets was nothing more than the mundane need for staff to provide the glue to support joint activities. In other cases the district manager had to change the rules of the game. Agency district officers often did not have the clout to get their ideas heard or accepted within their separate hierarchies. The district manager could provide backing and access to higher levels of the various specialized departments on matters that were in the self-interest of the local officials. On occasion, however, the district manager had to challenge these interests. Both the agencies and the officers needed to be pushed to action by an outside party who had sufficient weight in the system to command respect and response. Coordination, in this sense, is not simply a passive process of accommodation among established, unchanging program units. At times, the district manager and cabinet moved against a member agency's position. A traffic engineer's decision on parking regulations was challenged and reversed, Sanitation Department policy on the use of bulk containers by private carters was modified for a particular community, and an ineffective social services field supervisor was replaced. The district managers generally intentionally adopted a nonthreatening posture to gain the confidence and cooperation of the functional agencies. But they were not patsies of the system. What power and authority was necessary to play out this energizing role?

The powers. As coordinators, the district managers were given some of the weakest formal powers in the bureaucrat's book— convening power, access power, information power. But they were also given a mantle of authority and respect by virtue of their

38. For the "energizer" analogy, see *Integrating City Services: The Role of the District Manager* (New York: Office of Neighborhood Government, March 1974), p. 61.

appointment and recognition by the mayor. Was this enough? Does the role of a coordinator require direct line authority or merely the capacity to mediate? Can mere mediation amount to much at all? It is a convention of good public administration that power must be commensurate with responsibility. It follows from this presumption that if someone is given the task of coordinating agency activities, that person must be given the power to order agency actions—and some district managers adopted this stance. Aside from its political improbability, other district managers argued that the line-authority approach was inappropriate. They reasoned that a district manager would never be able to match the technical skills and expertise of all the cabinet officers covering the full gamut of city services. To be the boss would be overwhelming. Rather, the job called for the capacity to motivate, to integrate with persuasion and managerial techniques, and only very selectively to use access in the highest levels of the administration to force action—but to use this power when necessary. To judge by the later comments of some district officers, this was a wise decision. Many of them feared that the district manager would try to become a boss and that this would lead to the same kind of turmoil as school decentralization did. One parks foreman said:

> We had a bad taste with school decentralization. There was conflict over hiring and firing. Others in the department felt ONG was going to take over discipline. . . . Their fear was that the district manager would take control, set schedules, shift someone from this playground to that. . . . At first our union took a stand and formed a committee. But with the good experience in the program, this didn't go anywhere. It was nowhere near like the Board of Education.[39]

A later district manager perceived the same problem but from the opposite vantage point. He felt that "the courtship of the cabinet is probably the only way you will get into the flow of agency life in a community quickly." And to do this, "the cabinet officers have to

39. Frank Roseti, interview, 17 January 1975.

see you as a partner, not as a threat [or] some kind of CIA agent."[40] It would appear, therefore, that part of the success the district managers were able to achieve was a consequence of their *lack* of formal power over local operations.

A more serious inadequacy to many managers was their lack of what might be called "policy authority" within the larger governmental system. Top level administrators in the agencies (or the mayor, or the city planning commission) could make major personnel or program decisions without even informing the managers, or obtaining their approval. The district manager in the Rockaways complained that she was not being consulted on matters for which she had to assume responsibility in the community: the transfer of a police captain, the closing of a fire company, the installation of new street lights, the award of service contracts, and plans for new construction projects.[41] The effort to increase administrative decentralization within the agencies would improve this situation to some degree, but on many larger policy, planning, and budget issues the district managers themselves had to be tied into the central decision-making process of city government. One manager suggested that the ONG districts should be "officially designated for special treatment along the lines of Urban Renewal or Model Cities areas." Such a step would "constitute notice to city officials that their activities within these areas would thereafter be planned and carried out with the input of the local Neighborhood Government Office."[42]

Implicit in this line of reasoning was a powerful expansion of the district manager's role. Instead of simply serving as the catalyst for local interagency service projects, the managers would be involved in setting city policy for their neighborhoods. Such a step required the decentralization of mayoral power. The district manager would not only represent the mayor in a community but share his authority in determining district-wide policies and priorities. There was some movement beginning in this direction toward the end of the demon-

40. Roger Martin, interview, 14 January 1975.

41. Janet Langsam, "Rockaways Monthly Report," 29 December 1972.

42. Victor Marrero, Memorandum to John Mudd, "Neighborhood Government—More Monothematic," 10 October 1972.

stration program, but it did not proceed very far. That it went anywhere at all depended on the fact that the district managers were appointed by the mayor. It was one thing to order consultation or even approval of major policy decisions by your own appointees; it would be very different if the manager were named by the community.

THE LIMITS OF COORDINATION

The original accommodation with the specialized bureaucracies, which was a source of strength for the district manager cabinets, also set limits to their potential achievements. As a system, decentralized urban administration essentially depends on the resources and organizational capabilities of the established agencies. In general, coordination operates at the margins of bureaucratic turf— what one analyst has labelled the "no-man's land," the "interior fringe," and the "periphery" of "bureau territoriality."[43] On the whole, it is in these areas that a coordinator should be expected to act most effectively. However, to view coordination as confined exclusively to marginal operations, and as ineffective in more significant policy-making issues, would also be a mistake. The addition of a coordinator into the organizational environment can affect larger questions of structure and policy in ways that on occasion reach into the "heartland" of the existing bureaucracies.

District managers quickly appreciated the natural limits of their position in relation to the cabinet officers. Putting an optimistic perspective on the situation, one reported after only a few months in the field that "agency service chiefs are showing a willingness to initiate and work together on issues, particularly where those issues do not strike deeply into their domains."[44] Another district manager gave a similar assessment of the system three years later: "It was my feeling that the cabinet process worked best on new programs or service integration projects that would never have happened before, or trying to patch up breakdowns in the standard service provisions such as lot cleaning and things like that."[45]

43. Anthony Downs, *Inside Bureaucracy* (Boston: Little, Brown, 1967), 212–14.
44. Dick Duhan, "Crown Heights Monthly Report for March," 20 April 1972.
45. Sidney Jones, interview, 14 January 1975.

Many issues go beyond this kind of peripheral action and require more extensive changes in the organization and direction of the service delivery system. A coordinating institution can be expected to throw up those problems and conflicts that require resolution by higher authorities. Some can be handled by elaborating existing systems. For example, with the support of ONG, the Traffic Department received authorization to open field offices in each borough so that it could work more effectively with other agencies and respond more rapidly to community complaints. Other problems may call for a reintegration of specialized bureaucratic responsibilities to broaden, or narrow, the scope of action in the major administrative units. Instead of coordinating *joint inspections,* there may be a need to create a new bureau staffed by *joint inspectors,* each of whom could enforce the health, housing, and sanitary codes.

Such structural issues quickly become central policy questions that must be decided by the elected chief executive and the legislature. Yet, to conclude that policy comes first, and implementation and coordination follow, is too simple. The existence of a coordinating institution can contribute to the policy-making process by affecting which issues are raised, how they are resolved, and whether the solution can be carried out effectively. The district manager cabinets significantly affected the city administration's decision to create a "neighborhood preservation" program. In this situation, the housing development bureaucracy favored new construction. The city planners argued the need for rehabilitation of existing structures. The mayor was caught in a serious conflict between his highest executive appointees. District managers in transitional communities wanted a concentrated housing rehabilitation program to be integrated with complementary services available through other local agencies. With the cabinets in place, HUD in Washington reversed its earlier negative decision and agreed to fund the detailed analysis and design of a neighborhood preservation project in New York. Given this support, the mayor and his administrators agreed to develop a program. In this case, the existence of a decentralized coordinating unit facilitated the formulation of a new central policy to deal with a complex problem like the deterioration of transitional neighborhoods. It also provided the organizational capacity necessary to implement the proposed solution.

Decentralized Management

There are two common misconceptions about government organization that divert attention from the importance of decentralized field administration in coordinating the delivery of public services in urban neighborhoods. The first might be called the fallacy of central control. New York's experience in regrouping existing departments into broad superadministrations demonstrated that whatever their strengths in improving central *policy* coordination, service delivery *operations* continued almost unchanged through uncoordinated, compartmentalized bureaucratic units in the communities. Sewers and Sanitation were both in the Environmental Protection Administration, but that did not get the catch basins cleaned any faster so that street sweepers could move through flooded intersections. Youth gang workers and job trainers were both in the Human Resources Administration, but that did not mean that a kid in trouble had a better chance of being prepared for employment. Shuffling the bureaus in the bureaucracy may have implications for central policymakers (and delusions for reorganizers), but it has only an indirect impact on those who manage or deliver services in the field.

The second confusion might be labeled the fallacy of physical proximity. There is often an assumption that if central agencies have personnel or offices in the field, especially if they are housed in the same multiservice center, this will promote coordination among the local units. Again, the experience in New York and other areas reveals that this supposition is unrealistic. Agencies within a multiservice center do not necessarily communicate with each other, and a special health program in the center may operate with little relation to the activities of the established Health Department in this same area. The *decentralized delivery of services* through field offices is not the same as the *decentralized management* of the service delivery system, which the district manager cabinets attempted to institutionalize.

In ONG's model, two elements were thought essential to enable district managers to turn their cabinets into effective instruments of service coordination. The first was decentralization of administrative authority to field officers within each agency. The second was the creation of coterminous service boundaries.

ADMINISTRATIVE DECENTRALIZATION

Independent surveys found that the degree of administrative decentralization ("decision-making autonomy") did have a measurable impact on increasing contact and communication between agency field officers at the district level. However, an awareness of overlapping responsibilities and the need for assistance from others was even more important in explaining the frequency of interagency relations.[46] Front-line supervisors often had more ability to work with others than the informal bureaucratic cultures encouraged them to use. Thus, even without great additional powers for its members, the district manager cabinets could nurture increased interagency coordination. But the new environment did expand the field officer's conception of his own role. As one sanitation superintendent put it, "I feel that the cabinet has elevated my position from that of a supervisor to an administrator. . . . It has elevated me to a higher managerial position."[47]

Although the decentralization of authority did not occur to the extent that the Office of Neighborhood Government leaders had hoped, the development of formal administrative decentralization procedures provided an important, authoritative sanction for local officials to operate in new ways. One commented:

It would have been different if there had been no guidelines for us. [They] set it off the ground; you had to cooperate. [District Manager] Sanderson might have been able to get cooperation because he had a fantastic knack to work through people, but others probably not. . . . The guidelines also freed me up. At first we didn't know what we were getting into, but then once we got started it made us freer to speak up and take new ideas to the department.[48]

46. Boyle, "Local Operating Officials' Responses to the Experiment," pp. 153–54. For confirmation of the increased interagency communication produced by administrative decentralization, see Robert K.Yin, Robert W. Hearn, and Paul Meinetz Shapiro, "Administrative Decentralization of Municipal Services: Assessing the New York City Experience," *Policy Sciences* 5 (1974): 67.
47. Quoted in Maas, *Decentralizing New York City Service Agencies*, p. 47.
48. Frank Roseti, interview, 17 January 1975.

Yet there were striking variations in the agencies' ability to decentralize operational authority effectively. In all cabinet areas, the big hierarchical departments dealing with relatively homogenous services—Sanitation and Police, and to a lesser extent Parks and Highways—were able to participate most effectively. The large conglomerate superagencies like the Human Resources Administration or the Housing and Development Administration had the greatest problems.

The differences in organizational characteristics that were noted in planning the program continued to explain the problems in implementation. Most important proved to be the degree of functional specialization in the agency, the preexistence and scale of field districts, the extent of top-level managerial control and commitment, the competence of the field officers, and the professional or interest group identification of the bureaucracy. Where a committed, strong commissioner was combined with capable local officials already operating at the district level, as in the Police Department, administrative decentralization and coordination was natural, and relatively straightforward to implement. Where the reverse was true—a high degree of specialization in centralized baronies without a consistent field delivery system in the districts, as in the Human Resources Administration—even a committed administrator could not easily implement decentralized administration. ONG had encouraged both HDA and HRA to create a new, local official who could represent the superagency as a whole. This strategy essentially failed. The district managers saved their harshest criticisms for these two agencies. A typical comment echoed in many reports spoke of "the continuing inability of HDA to clarify the role and responsibility of the Area [Housing] Director . . . and their inability to expedite the outstationing of their area staff."[49] About HRA and its social service agencies, another manager wrote in desperation, "I assume that they are still part of the city, but it is hard to tell."[50] The resistance of the constituent departments to ceding authority to someone outside their existing hierarchies continued unabated throughout the two-year experiment. The area

49. Donald J. Middleton, "October Status Report," 1 November 1972.
50. Dick Duhan, "Crown Heights Monthly Report for March," 20 April 1972.

housing directors became, in effect, project managers for the neighborhood preservation programs, and advocates without authority over the local operations of the departments managing code enforcement, rent control, relocation, and development. Similarly in HRA, the human resources district directors had a mandate to plan, coordinate, monitor, evaluate, and mobilize community involvement around social services, but they had neither the formal authority nor the informal clout within the agency to affect the actual delivery of those services, such as the assignment of homemakers, family planning counselors, foster care, adoption, or protective services for children; day-care centers; youth programs; consumer education; special programs for adults; and food stamp, welfare, medicaid, or medicare certifications. As one ONG analyst put it, their "effectiveness depended almost entirely upon personal style and contacts."[51] The departmental baronies survived with their independent professional allegiances, federal funding sources, and special interest or ethnic constituencies.

However important it may have been as a long-term objective, the ONG superagency strategy produced conflict, frustration, and few concrete results in the short run. Ironically, the specialized department field personnel were often more willing to work directly with the district manager, as a representative of the Mayor's Office, than to accept the imposition of a new superagency official like the human resources district director.[52] Without legitimacy in his own bureaucracy, one new appointee said simply: "I lack the muscle to get things done."[53] Theoretically, a strong citywide administrator could have compensated for the fragmentation of agencies under his purview and enforced the delegation of authority to his representatives at the district level. But a number of social service departments had become enclaves for special political interests, and neither the mayor nor his staff were prepared to back the administrator in establishing control over these departments.

51. Maas, *Decentralizing New York City Service Agencies*, p. 118.
52. Robert E. Blanc, *A Comparison of the Office of Neighborhood Government and the Department of Community Development (Human Resources District) Experiments in Decentralization and Local Integration of Services* (New York: Bureau of Applied Social Research, Columbia University, December 1974), p. 11.
53. Maas, *Decentralizing New York City Service Agencies*, p. 118.

Where decentralized management goes beyond the delegation of authority within an existing hierarchy and requires the transfer of power to a new official outside the normal departmental lines of authority, the resistance can be extreme.[54] To make such a new position function effectively would have required a much greater investment of substantive analysis and political clout than either ONG or the agency administrators were able to muster. The experience illustrates the thesis that administrative centralization is a precondition for administrative decentralization. In the case of the conglomerate superagencies, there was insufficient central control to enable the titular agency heads to decentralize operational authority to the field.

COTERMINALITY

The creation of common service boundaries was viewed by ONG as an important ingredient in improving service coordination. Others have considered coterminality so crucial that it could produce significant service improvements on its own and in effect substitute for administrative decentralization in the agencies or the need for a coordinator. In practice, ONG produced few concrete changes in administrative boundaries as it attempted to develop coterminous service districts, and the realignments which did occur were of minimal value. The experience did more to illuminate the resistance to and costs of coterminality than to demonstrate its presumed benefits. Despite the initial agreement of agency heads to develop plans for conforming these local boundaries as part of the overall decentralization program, it was necessary to report after almost two years that, "since there had never been a rigorous analysis of the problems of redistricting, most of the commitments . . . proved to be wildly optimistic and incapable of implementation."[55]

Coterminality was an appealing ideal and most agencies agreed with the goal, particularly if their own boundaries were accepted as the basis for the common field districts. But when faced with

54. See Stanley J. Heginbotham and Robin Maas, *Between Community and City Bureaucracy*, pt. 2: *Responses of City Agencies to the Experiment* (New York: Bureau of Applied Social Research, 1973), pp. 12–14.

55. Office of Neighborhood Government, " 'How to' Conclusions on Coterminality" (report submitted to HEW, 29 October 1973), p. 5.

the necessity to modify their existing system, commissioners and their staffs immediately elaborated the costs: the relocation of physical facilities, changing established work-load criteria for middle managers, increasing or decreasing the number of district officers, modifying emergency response patterns, altering the basis for gathering statistical data on social needs or agency performance, the diversion of management's energy from other projects, and the inevitable disruption of service delivery during any transition period. In examining specific recommendations, those objections often proved to be not simply a defensive bureaucratic smokescreen but an accurate assessment of real problems. Police would point out their heavy investment in existing and planned precinct houses, the expenses in reprogramming the computerized "911" response system, and the essential requirement for speedy response to emergencies—a criterion also critical to Fire but not, for example, to Sanitation.

On the other hand, from some district managers' perspectives the existing crazy-quilt pattern of agency boundaries undercut many possibilities for improving the coordination and responsiveness of city service delivery. Crown Heights presented the worst case among the demonstration areas. One study identified parts of forty-three field districts included within the boundaries of the "community," just counting those agencies directly represented on the cabinet.[56] The mere size of the cabinet meetings, with an average of over forty participants, inhibited the district manager's ability to develop effective interagency action. But this was an extreme.

Faced with the high costs of modifying agency boundaries, and the lack of widespread pressure for change, ONG was able to encourage only a few limited experiments with redistricting, not a full-scale test of coterminality. On the surface, agencies without an established field delivery system at the local level appeared to have more flexibility in developing a new structure. The Human Resources Administration designated community planning districts (or aggregates) as the basis for the field operations of all constituent social service departments. But this only affected the planners and social workers specifically assigned to these areas. Most of

56. Maas, *Service Integration and the Problem of Redistricting*, p. 31.

the specialized service bureaus continued their delivery systems without discernible change. Boundary changes in departments like Police, Parks, and Sanitation, which had large field forces and elaborate networks of precinct houses, garages, and other physical facilities, were more difficult to implement, and only marginal changes were achieved during the two years. Police made one minor adjustment of a forty-square-block area to conform to cabinet boundaries in Bushwick and consolidated two precincts in Crown Heights, a move that the department planned independently and which still left three commands covering the community. In the one case where ONG pressed for a test of more radical redistricting, the consolidation of five separate sanitation districts covering Crown Heights, the planning process raised so many issues and took so long that the consolidation was never implemented.[57]

However, the most important lesson of ONG's experience was that the district managers were generally less concerned about the failure of coterminality than they were about the district officers' (and their own) lack of decentralized authority within the service delivery system.[58] It was evident that problems caused by the patchwork pattern of administrative boundaries would increase, if the cabinets were extended from selected demonstration areas to a citywide system. Without common districts, front-line field officers would find themselves involved in more and more separate cabinets at the same time. But while full coterminality could represent a commonsense ideal, it would be costly, and without other organizational reforms to decentralize and coordinate field administration, it would very likely bring few returns in improved service delivery.

THE STABILITY OF ADMINISTRATIVE DECENTRALIZATION
The district manager cabinet system was unstable. But the cause of this instability was rooted less in the centralizing pressures of bureaucracy, as some had predicted, than in the instability of the mayoralty. There was some recentralization of authority within the

---

57. For a detailed case study of the experience in Crown Heights, see ibid., pt. 3: "Expense and Efficiency: An Agency's Perspective on the Problem of Redistricting," pp. 62–88.
    58. Ibid., pp. 6–8.

ranks. A police commander found his superiors beginning to say, "Notify me before you send them anything, before you accept anything from them, or before you do anything for them."[59] However, the gradual recapturing of authority by the bureaucracy was relatively minor compared to the consequences of the transfer of power from John Lindsay to Abraham Beame. Lindsay styled himself as a manager, and he won the election of 1969 as a fusion candidate. Despite its unconventionality, the district manager cabinet system served both programmatic and political interests. It was a managerial innovation that maintained Lindsay's position as a leader in decentralization, and it provided a nonpartisan appeal to independents and opponents as well as allies in the neighborhoods. Beame, in contrast, brought into office a faith in traditional, hierarchical, civil service administration and an allegiance to the regular party clubhouse. The cabinets came to be viewed neither as an instrument of administrative reform nor as an opportunity to respond to those not normally included in the partisan political process, but merely as a service adjunct to the party apparat. Without backing, the effectiveness of the district manager cabinet system deteriorated.

Coordination between major service agencies is essentially a problem for the chief executive. Decentralized administration therefore depends on strong central leadership that is institutionalized in something like an Office of Neighborhood Government at the top and in something like the district manager cabinets at the bottom. But the electoral system makes a mayoral commitment inherently unstable. This is the Achilles' heel of the New York strategy for decentralized urban administration. If the leadership and participants are not committed to make the structure work, it probably will not work.

Neighborhood Responsiveness

The district manager cabinet system increased the influence of organized local interests, especially the nonpartisan civic activists in

59. Adam Butcher, interview, 15 January 1975.

the demonstration districts. The neighborhood, taxpayer, home-owner, and civic associations were active precisely on those con-crete service delivery issues which the cabinets were best designed to handle. Many civic leaders initially feared that their intermediary function between the citizen and the government would be replaced, not strengthened, by the new program. They later became the strongest advocates for continuing the approach. ONG's commit-ment to function as a nonpartisan service agency and the ability of the district managers to mediate between ethnic groups, rather than taking sides both contributed significantly to the program's success in winning a civic constituency in most communities.[60] In some areas, however, there was active and continuing opposition, or barely restrained hostility, among certain groups. Variations in the nature of citizen organization in each community (its extent, com-petence, power, level of consensus or conflict, and relation between civic and political groups) had more effect on the reception and operation of the program than did the socioeconomic differences among the various areas. District manager cabinets could assist local leaders in their dealings with the city administration, but they were an independent power center in the community that could upset the existing distribution of influence. The stronger the local organizations, the higher the consensus among them, the more they conceived of themselves as *the* representatives of the district or the exclusive defenders of besieged interests, and the more extensive their prior access to government officials, the greater their opposi-tion to the new system.

The responsiveness of the district manager cabinets to organized local interests led to two identifiable ways in which the service delivery system could be systemically skewed. First, there were differences between the priorities of community leaders and the concerns of the public. Leaders were unaware of the importance placed on environmental problems (dirty streets and sidewalks, polluted air, noise) by the general public, and rated the issues of

60. For the ethnic mediation role, see Fainstein et al., "Community Leadership" (1977), p. 128; and for the impact of nonpartisanship, see the "Editorial Comment" from the most politically conservative and anti-Lindsay district in the (Bay Ridge) *Home Reporter and Sunset News,* 28 December 1973, p. 12.

schools and recreation comparatively higher.[61] Second, ethnic groups differed in their level and style of organizational membership. In New York communities, blacks tended to participate in block or tenant associations; Hispanics had a relatively low level of organizational membership, but gravitated toward the PTAs; the Irish were generally not joiners, although they were involved in the Church; and Jews were active in union, professional, and ethnic associations.[62] Such intermediary organizations perform a critical role in making government responsive, but they introduce a bias in determining which concerns are articulated with what weight. Recognizing this reality invites a more difficult question: Who organizes the unorganized so that they can have their interests represented?

District managers tried to compensate for the organizational bias of the cabinet system to some extent. Staff encouraged the creation of block and tenant associations in poor and transitional communities. Offices in two of the middle-class districts devoted major attention to the provision of direct services (food stamps, Medicaid certification) for the hidden, elderly poor. Such efforts constituted only minor steps in facing the problems of the specially vulnerable groups, and in themselves introduced another issue: Who would give guidance and hold the district manager accountable in making these decisions about community affairs?

PARTICIPATION AND ACCOUNTABILITY

Civic leaders in urban neighborhoods want concrete service improvements, not abstract power.[63] Both leaders and the public in New York communities said they wanted to participate in policy decisions (give advice, be consulted), but *not* to control operations

---

61. Allen H. Barton et al., *Interim Report on Results of New York Neighborhood Study* (New York: Bureau of Applied Social Research, Columbia University, April 1974), p. 7.

62. See, for example, Nathalie Friedman and Naomi Golding, *Neighborhood Variation: The Implications for Administrative Decentralization. An Analysis of Subcommunities in Manhattan Community Planning District 12* (New York: Bureau of Applied Social Research, Columbia University, February 1974), p. 35.

63. For a similar conclusion, see Douglas Yates, *Neighborhood Democracy* (Lexington, Mass.: D.C. Heath, 1973), p. 99.

(determine budgets, hire and fire personnel).[64] On the other hand, they distrusted a decentralized system that denied them any formal role or influence. Most seemed to favor some middle ground between the extremes of traditional, centralized city government and full-scale community control. Among New Yorkers, there was widespread support for decentralized administration and some parallel institutions for citizen involvement. There was little or no evidence that the public wanted to spend much time in discussion, debate, and deliberation about city service operations. Rather, it appeared that they wanted the services performed by those in charge, some place to complain to and get response from when there were breakdowns, an opportunity to have their opinions considered on local service or land use questions, and some capacity to hold those responsible for government activities accountable for their performance.

These conclusions fit the available evidence and the New York experience, but data on public attitudes concerning government organization or citizen participation are particularly suspect. Questions on interview schedules are often unclear, the implications are rarely specified, and responses are often conflicting. For example, although ONG conceived of the district manager cabinets as a technique to coordinate government action, almost no civic leader mentioned improved coordination as a benefit. Rather, they viewed the approach as a more effective complaint response system.[65] This is significant because it implies that even the most active community leaders may not understand the importance of *organizational* changes within the administrative system to increase access and accountability in the service delivery system. And consequently, these leaders will provide support for this kind of reorganization strategy only *after* they perceive the practical impact of decentralized management. The district manager cabinets also helped the

64. For data on the public, see Friedman and Rogers, "Decentralization and the Public," p. 237; and for the leaders, see Norman I. Fainstein and Susan S. Fainstein, "The Future of Community Control," *American Political Science Review* 70 (September 1976): 910.

65. Fainstein et al., "Community Leadership" (1977), pp. 127, 142.

agency district officers overcome their fears and increase their support for citizen participation. After working with the program, 70 percent of the career civil servants said that they favored creating a formal mechanism for community representatives to advise on, but not control, city service operations.[66] This contradicted those predictions that administrative decentralization would block further political decentralization.

Overall, the experience of the district manager cabinets pointed to the need for a balance of power between the mayor and the neighborhoods that involved a complementary centralization and decentralization of the organization of big city government. An analysis of alternative appointment procedures for the district manager illustrates this thesis. Conventional wisdom holds that responsiveness will flow along the channels of political accountability. Whoever appoints the district manager will control his behavior and influence. On this theory, many decentralists have called for the community to appoint or elect such an official exclusively. Experience with the demonstration cabinets suggests, however, that since urban neighborhoods depend on institutions and resources at the citywide (or higher) level, sharing power over the district manager with citywide officials would be likely to increase the responsiveness of the service delivery system.

There are many alternative methods for the selection and appointment process. Each may seriously affect the role the district manager is able to play. Mayoral appointment implies the ability to control citywide service agencies, but the capacity to be unresponsive to neighborhood concerns. Community appointment implies the advocacy of local needs and demands, but not the authority to require response from the operating bureaucracies. Political appointment by local elected officials implies support on legislative issues like budget approval, but raises the dangers of narrow partisanship and unresponsive agencies. To the extent that improving service delivery is the major issue at stake, the New York experience indicates that the official who controls the bulk of the relevant

---

66. Derived from data reported in Fainstein and Fainstein, "The Future of Community Control," p. 920.

service agencies should have the dominant role in the appointment of the areal manager. If the mayor controls, the mayor should predominate, with some form of advice, consultation, or veto power vested in the community. Many formulas giving different weight to different interests are theoretically possible. But such procedures, if they combine too many interests, may produce the least common denominator, not a strong district manger. Implementation of the 1975 Charter reforms provides a clear test of these conclusions.

6
EPILOGUE

The 1975 Charter made a major difference. . . . It gives the Community Boards an opportunity. The agencies court the boards for their support, and the communities can then negotiate with the agencies on their priorities.

—Lorraine Holtz[1]

The New York City Charter amendments of 1975 tried to combine the two very different earlier strategies for improving the actions of city government in local communities: (1) the citizen participation structure consisting of advisory community boards appointed by the borough presidents, and (2) the decentralized management system of mayorally appointed district managers and district service cabinets. But the charter reforms not only strengthened the traditional advisory role of the community boards in land use and budget decisions, it also gave them the authority to appoint the district managers. This dramatically shifted the political dynamic of the decentralized system. The district manager cabinets were no longer essentially a mayoral management mechanism to improve the coordination and responsiveness of city service delivery operations. Rather, a nonmayoral community advocate tied to appointees of the popularly elected borough president was placed in the position of presiding over mayoral service agency field officers. This organizational change significantly affected both the politics and the content of the decentralized system, probably more than the Charter

1. Lorraine Holtz, interview, 9 July 1982.

Commission envisioned. Its members did not seem appropriately sensitive to the profound implications of making the district manager exclusively a community appointee.[2] With respect to improving local service delivery, the Commission produced a seemingly impotent compromise somewhere between a mayoral system and full neighborhood government. It did not give the community boards sufficient power over services to enable them to make significant changes on their own, but it also undercut both the ability and the motivation of the mayor to focus on improving neighborhood services through better coordination. Without any role in appointing the district managers, the mayor had little immediate incentive and no direct responsibility to make the decentralized system work. Thus the Commission's compromise in effect fundamentally crippled the new system's ability to meet its goal of coordinating the planning and operation of neighborhood services.

The charter reforms clearly placed the community boards at the center of government in the community, and the characteristics and concerns of the boards became the predominant characteristics and concerns of the system. Community boards are political, and they politicized the decentralization process in a very distinct way. As appointees of the borough presidents, the boards are clearly perceived as the instruments of the borough presidents (or in some cases of the local city councilpersons) in their competition with the mayor. On the whole, community boards are reactive. They tend to respond ad hoc to individual projects, rather than initiate proposals or plan in a comprehensive, long-term fashion. Traditionally, the community boards have been most involved in land use and capital budget issues, and it is not surprising that they continue to concentrate most of their energy on and have most of their impact in these areas. The intended potential of the charter reforms for improving local service planning and service coordination has been much less developed. This gap in the system could be viewed as an opportunity for action in the future. Improvement in managing local service operations would require much more aggressive leadership by the mayor and the Mayor's Office. But the organizational

2. See "Recommendations: City Government in the Community" (New York: State Charter Revision Commission, 5 February 1975), p. 18.

framework designed by the Charter Commission does not provide much motivation for the mayor to invest energy and resources to strengthen the current community government system.

After the desultory inaction of the Beame years, the Koch administration initially proceeded with an intensive effort to implement the charter mandates. Soon after taking office in January 1978, the mayor established the Community Board Assistance Unit (CBAU) as part of his immediate office and appointed one of his strongest young assistants to head it. This new director orchestrated an aggressive planning process to implement the key charter reforms in land use review, geographic budgeting, coterminality, and management decentralization. But gradually in succeeding years, partly through accident and partly through design, leadership has been divided among the Mayor's Office and other city agencies. No one agency provides overall direction or holds the ultimate responsibility for the decentralized system.

Currently, three agencies provide support functions and technical assistance to the community boards. The City Planning Department has assumed the primary role in implementing the procedures for land use review and, more recently, in providing some technical help to encourage the preparation of district needs statements by the boards. The large role performed by the Office of Community Board Relations within the Office of Management and Budget in designing and implementing a carefully elaborated budget consultation process has been both unusual and important. Its instruction manual detailing timetables and procedures for community board input in the city budgets is a model. The third agency, the mayor's Community Board Assistance Unit, changed leadership and became embroiled in bitter conflicts surrounding proposals for the coterminality of police precinct boundaries soon after its formation. These struggles left little energy for pursuing management decentralization and service coordination among the operating agencies. In addition, the fiscal crisis, which forced severe manpower and service cuts, seriously inhibited efforts to deal with the decentralization and coordination of services. CBAU's successor agency, the Community Assistance Unit (CAU) has recognized these continuing defects. A management decentralization process is under way in a number of departments, and CAU is also working to train the boards, district managers, and agency officers to move beyond individual service complaints to examine broader service coordination goals. But progress on both fronts is slow. The deputy mayor for operations now holds quarterly meetings with the district managers from all communities in the city. However, no one is attempting to tie the bits of the decentralized system together in a comprehensive whole so that the logical connections are made between needs statements, land use decisions, service plans, and budget recommendations. The mayor gives benign support sprinkled periodically with caustic criticism but shows no indication that he is deeply committed or actively involved in developing community government. He evidently does not see decentralization either as a management tool to increase control and improve agency service operations or as a political strategy to create a constituency.

Although it is now many years since the voters approved the charter reforms, there is remarkably little objective evidence about its impact. There have been a number of guides and manuals prepared to help communities implement the changes but almost no rigorous evaluation of what has actually changed.[3] Despite this, there seems to be an unusual degree of agreement among those close to the operations of the community government system about its impact in land use, budgeting, and service coordination.

Land Use

The community boards' expanded advisory role in land use decisions was spelled out in detail by the City Planning Commission in the Uniform Land Use Review Procedures (ULURP). This process has been an important source of authority and influence for the boards in many communities. As one former district manager put it: "Land use is critical. And is real power."[4] Previously the boards

3. The Nova Institute, a nonprofit organization in New York, has taken the lead in developing a number of guides. See, for example, *Helping Community Boards Monitor the Delivery of Municipal Services* (December 1977); *Tracking Community Services in New York City* (June 1978); *Guide to Community Board Participation in the Budget Process for the Fiscal Year 1980* (September 1978); *Guide to the District Resource Statement* (November 1980). References to other Nova materials are included in subsequent notes.

4. Tom Cusic, interview, 23 June 1982.

only had a diffuse mandate to consider the districts' "needs" and "welfare," and city agencies had few concrete requirements to work with them. The 1975 amendments to the City Charter (Section 197−c) authorized the boards' involvement in ten specific land use areas, including the key issues of site selection for city projects; the sale, lease, or disposition of city property; the designation of zoning districts and permits for zoning variances; and the approval of housing and urban renewal plans. The charter required that the City Planning Commission refer all applications on these matters to the boards and set a timetable for the boards to review, hold public hearings, and send recommendations back to the commission on each proposal. The Planning Commission had to provide a written explanation for any changes it made in the boards' recommendations. These powers went into effect relatively early in the reform process on July 1, 1976.

The total number of ULURP applications referred to all community boards has increased significantly from 423 in Fiscal Year 1977 to 699 in Fiscal Year 1983. Even these numbers understate the magnitude of the tasks faced by the boards, since one proposal could include recommendations for the disposition of as many as a hundred city-owned, in rem (taken over due to tax default) buildings. Including non-ULURP issues, the total number of items sent to the boards came to almost 1,200 in fiscal 1983.[5]

The number and type of ULURP applications vary markedly from community to community, and consequently the opportunity, or burden, of using the procedure is very different for different boards. In Midtown Manhattan, the board might deal with a number of multimillion-dollar office and residential development projects every month. In downtown Manhattan and on the East or West Side, questions about the explosion of requests for sidewalk cafes dominate the referrals. In the poverty areas of all boroughs, city decisions to dispose of tax-delinquent, in rem property are key. And in areas of Staten Island, there are scores of proposals for street mapping and certifications to allow new development. But many communities have almost no land use applications. Including

5. Department of City Planning, Land Use Review, Mimeograph, and Peggy Kingsbury, interview, 17 September 1984.

both ULURP and non-ULURP matters, over one-third of the boards have less than one referral per month.[6] Even in these predominantly residential, middle-class areas, however, the location of a sanitation garage, the rehabilitation of a park, or the introduction of a group home for the mentally retarded could arouse significant community concern which would be expressed through the review process.

Overall, City Planning Department staff estimate that the Commission approves more than 90 percent of the community boards' recommendations, although there are no rigorous data to substantiate this estimate.[7] In a report to the mayor, it was noted that the Board of Standards and Appeals, which rules on requests for zoning variances, agreed with the community boards' recommendations in 82 percent of its cases in 1980.[8] And even where there is disagreement among the various parties, it is often not total. The boards and their district managers have moved beyond simple yes-or-no responses to proposals. They frequently specify conditions for approval, for example, by saying they will support a new office building if the developer makes particular changes. The Planning Commission might then approve the application conditionally by requiring some of the amendments recommended by the community board but not all of them.

The formal ULURP procedures have also led to equally important informal processes. City agencies and private developers now often consult with community boards about their proposals *before* submitting official applications to the City Planning Commission. In this way, ULURP puts the boards in a position to negotiate changes that are important to the community. In one transitional area, the ULURP procedures gave the district manager and board the leverage to redirect developers into geographic areas where the community was making a concerted revitalization effort. It has enabled boards in poverty communities to give specific advice on the disposal of city owned in rem property. They might recommend au-

6. "Community Board Workload by Application Type" (Computer printout, Department of City Planning, 12 August 1982).

7. Laurence Parnes, interview, 28 July 1982.

8. David Lebenstein, "A Report Card," in *Community Boards: How Are We Doing, New York Affairs* 6 no. 1 (1980): 11.

thorization to auction certain buildings but note that a particular facility was being used by a church and should not be sold or should be sold only to the church, or that a particular property had been leased by a soccer club for ten years and should only be sold for athletic use, and so forth. As a whole, it appears that the boards are becoming increasingly sophisticated in using their advisory authority under ULURP. The procedures set up a situation in which community representatives can negotiate to make development plans sensitive to the scale, texture, and social life of the city's neighborhoods. Those affected by decisions must be consulted as part of the decision-making process and therefore are less likely to feel violated by the results. On the other hand, the boards' role is still advisory, and final decisions on land use are made by the central city political institutions. In this sense, ULURP has not led to what some feared would be a stalemate in citywide land use and economic development policy. There may be ways to speed up the process. Perhaps the boards should have the right to waive local public hearing requirements under certain conditions. But these are marginal changes. Perhaps the strongest indication of the perceived value of ULURP to the communities is the boards' overwhelming opposition to any proposals that would weaken the procedures. For example, when the city administration recommended legislation to exempt in rem property from the full review process, the boards forcefully and successfully resisted. When asked for their views in one survey, they strongly rejected any reduction in the scope of their responsibilities under ULURP.[9]

At a broader level, however, a number of participants and observers note that most boards continue to function in a reactive fashion on land use questions, just as they have in the past. Generally, they respond to applications on a case-by-case basis and do not put these individual project decisions in the larger context of comprehensive, long-term planning for the community. There is usually little long-range perspective and little initiative from the boards as they deal with the opportunities presented by the ULURP process. Given their history, orientation, and current low-level staff sup-

9. *ULURP: A Community Board Perspective* (New York: Nova Institute, February 1981), pp. 13–15.

port, it is not likey that there will be any change in this style. The boards would need a great deal more encouragement and assistance to tie their land use decision-making to broader budget or operational service plans.

Geographic Budgeting

The requirements for geographic budgeting added by the 1975 charter amendments were potentially powerful levers for the community boards to influence government policy in their districts. Specific provisions for an overall budget planning and reporting system were spread throughout various sections of the revised charter.[10] Agencies were required to consult with community boards in preparing their own expense and capital/community development budget requests to the mayor. The boards themselves were mandated to hold public hearings on these departmental estimates and to submit their budget priorities to the mayor, the Board of Estimate, the City Council, and the City Planning Commission. The mayor's executive budget was required to show direct local expenditures for each community district, and the boards were specifically given the right to appear and be heard at legislative hearings on the proposed budgets. Finally, after the budgets were adopted and implemented, agencies and the comptroller were required to report actual expenditures in each community district. Although their authority was still only advisory, these charter mandates guaranteed the boards an unusual amount of information and access to influence the city's capital and expense budgets, if all of the provisions were used effectively.

The city's Office of Management and Budget played the leading role in developing the decentralized budgeting system. Traditionally, budget offices have focused on the "macro" issues of citywide functional agency accounts and not on the "micro" levels of budgets and expenditures for subcity geographic units. Yet by accident of history and personality, OMB in New York moved ahead to implement the charter's geographic budgeting provisions with increas-

10. For a summary of the major provisions, see *Guide to Community Board Participation in the Budget Process*, p. 58.

ingly elaborate designs. Just a few months before the end of the Beame administration, when the mayor was especially vulnerable to criticism for his inaction in putting the charter reforms in place, the deputy budget director set up an Office of Community Board Relations (OCBR) within OMB. Subsequently delegated primary responsibility for implementing the system of community board consultation in the budget process, this office started with one staff member in 1977, and by 1983 it had seventeen full-time people.

Where there was a need for a structure to enable the community boards to have input, OCBR provided it, with detailed information, guides, manuals, and timetables instructing both boards and agencies how to work through the complex and lengthy budget-making process. For community boards that were essentially reactive, OCBR gave them more than they could have imagined to react to. And this was developed thoughtfully and carefully. The 160-page manual for Fiscal Year 1984 provides specific guidelines and organizing hints for a process that lasts almost a full year.[11] The boards are encouraged to start their budget activity with an analysis of community concerns and the preparation of a district needs statement. To provide background information that can be the basis for the boards' recommendations, OCBR gives them a detailed District Resource Statement that spells out for sixteen agencies the personnel and equipment available in the district, as well as selected performance indicators for service delivery. With these data in hand, board members and district mangers hold individual district-level consultations with local agency field officers. This is followed by borough consultations in which board members and their staff meet to discuss their priorities with relatively high-level representatives from the sixteen agencies. At this stage many of the service departments are represented by commissioners, deputy commissioners, and division chiefs. On the basis of these consultations and further meetings in the community, the boards are asked to submit three sets of recommendations: their capital budget priorities, expense budget priorities, and priority ranking among sixty-five sepa-

11. *MANUAL for Participation in the Budget Process* (New York: The City of New York, Office of Management and Budget, Department of City Planning, Community Assistance Unit, May 1982).

rate city services. After seeing how their recommendations fare in the mayor's executive budgets, the boards are encouraged to testify at the Board of Estimate and City Council hearings before the final capital and expense budgets are adopted.

The effect of this community board involvement in the budget process is difficult to determine precisely. In consultations for the Fiscal Year 1981, all 59 community boards participated for the first time. OMB developed statistics showing that 53 percent of the boards' capital project recommendations were included in the city's Capital Budget/Community Development Program, and approximately 27 percent of their expense recommendations were included in the final expense budget.[12] With some minor variation, the funding approval rate has remained in the 40- to 50-percent range for capital items and 30- to 40-percent range for expense budget priorities. But what do these figures actually mean? Some would argue that all or most of these recommendations, especially in the capital/community development areas, would have been included in the budget anyway. A number of observers close to the operation of the budget consultation system estimate that the boards actually make a difference in only 5 percent or perhaps 10 percent of their capital proposals. But it is almost impossible to sort out whether agencies are coopting the boards to recommend agency agendas, or the boards are convincing the agencies to accept board priorities.

Some agencies actively use the community board budget involvement to push their own agendas. At the borough consultations, agency representatives openly solicit support and offer advice on strategies, often, it should be said, in response to board requests for such advice.[13] The Parks Department may be a leader in this, but Sanitation and Environmental Protection are also aggressive. What is the impact if different agencies put different amounts of energy into making their appeals in this forum? The boards tend to focus on "hard" services and rarely make requests for human or social services. This is true in both poor and middle-

12. *Profiles II: Public Participation in the Budget Process for Fiscal Year 1981 and CD Year VI*, (New York: City of New York, Office of Management and Budget, July 1980), pp. ii–iii.

13. Personal observation at the Borough Budget Consultations, John Jay High School, Brooklyn, 20 September 1982.

income neighborhoods. The overwhelming majority of projects, 73 percent in Fiscal Year 1982, involved public facilities (rehabilitation of parks, firehouses, police stations, schools) and the city's infrastructure (streets, highways, sewers, water mains, street lighting). "Community services" accounted for less than 6 percent of the total.[14] Does this reflect the priorities of all residents or the priorities of the people selected for the boards? It matches the city administration's capital budget priorities. But earlier experience would also suggest that this orientation continues to reflect the middle-class bias of the board members themselves.

There are further questions. The acceptance rate percentages count all projects included not only in the actual funding commitments for the current fiscal year but also those specified in the city's three-year capital improvement plan. The capital budget is a notorious political wish list. Which of the many community board projects "included" in the budget will actually be implemented, no one knows.

Expense budget recommendations (more police, more personnel to clean vacant lots, or shifting manpower from parks maintenance to tree pruning) are even more difficult to track. Because of the fiscal crisis, the city has consistently refused to accept board recommendations that require additional funds, but it tries to push agencies to fulfill requests within their existing resources. Many suspect that, at the district level, most agencies are just paying lip service to community board expense recommendations. However, in the ranking of citywide service priorities, the community boards may have made some significant difference. The fact that police patrol consistently tops the list as the most important service is not unexpected. But the fact that parks maintenance moved to the second spot in Fiscal Year 1983 (up from third place in Fiscal Year 1982 and seventh in Fiscal Year 1981) was noted by elected officials and administrators.[15] Many observers hold that the Parks Department

---

14. "Analysis of Community Board Service Program Priorities for Fiscal Year 1983," (New York: Office of Community Board Relations, 15 February 1982), p. 2.

15. *Profiles of Public Participation in the Budget Process for Fiscal Year 1982 and CD Year VII* (New York: City of New York, Office of Management and Budget, May 1981), p. ii.

received more maintenance funding, or was cut less than it might have been, because of the concern expressed by the community boards.

The budget consultation process is the most elaborate and time-consuming activity that the city administration asks of the community board members. It has been thoughtfully designed and carefully nurtured. But is it worth the effort, or is it perhaps an unintentional diversion of energy? What are the most obvious gaps and deficiencies? Some insiders say that the substance is not as great as the structure, which is another way of saying that the benefits do not justify the effort asked of the boards. Agencies differ in how seriously they take the process. Sanitation and Parks get high marks; Highways is often criticized for being unresponsive. And, in fact, this judgment seems to be borne out by the data. The Department of Transportation accepted proportionately fewer board highways projects (23 percent) than Parks included in its requested projects (79 percent) or Sanitation incorporated in its budget (82 percent).[16] The leadership at OMB has not been aggressive in calling agencies to account for such discrepancies.

Some community boards are becoming increasingly frustrated, impatient, and cynical about the budget consultations. As one outspoken chairperson has written:

> To be frank, the [budget] process as it now functions is a source of frustration to the Community Board. With a few notable exceptions, city agencies reduce the process to a sterile exercise in paperwork. Agencies fail to provide timely and accurate information . . . and they treat community boards as a bureaucratic inconvenience, to be ignored or minimized wherever possible. . . . Community Board #7 finds itself in an awkward position: the Board is asked by OMB to invest time, energy, and money—all in scarce supply—in a budget process which yields no demonstrable returns. . . . We ask, simply, whether any project initiated by the Community Board has ever been adopted in the form requested as a line item in the city budget. The answer appears to be no. In our district, the projects which are accepted

16. *Profiles II* (July 1980), p. xiii.

are invariably those initiated by city agencies, those substantially modified by city agencies, or those vigorously pursued by elected officials.[17]

This negative view is not universally shared. A successful former district manager sees the budget process as a "seismic change in how the city operates," since he feels that more and more of the agenda of city government is being set by the community boards every year.[18] Although this may eventually prove to be a valid judgment, the boards' current influence appears to be marginal. A recent study found that the community boards' top ten priority projects received only 7.4 percent of the entire city Fiscal Year 1983 capital budget (about $150 million out of a total $2 billion).[19] Affecting the expenditure of $150 million is not an insignificant achievement, but the figure does give some indication of the extent and limits of community board power under the current system.

There are still many other gaps in the existing approach to geographic budgeting. The consultations are functionally specialized. They occur in each individual agency, and the district service cabinet as a whole is not involved. This tends to structure out interagency budget coordination issues. The consultation process is also project-specific. Board members, staff, and agency representatives discuss one individual project after another. There is usually no attempt to look at how these specific items fit into an overall budget for the district. And finally, there is no consistent effort to tie budgeting to operational planning for service delivery. In some ways, budgeting has crowded out planning. The focus on individual capital projects diverts attention from the possibilities for redeployment of existing resources and service coordination. One analysis found that district consultations led to budget requests in 89 percent of the cases, but in

17. Sally Goodgold, "Statement of District Needs and Priorities for Fiscal Year 1983" in *Statement of Community District Needs, Fiscal Year 1983/CD Year VIII Manhattan* (New York: City of New York, January 1982), pp. 75–76.

18. Tom Cusic, interview, 23 June 1982.

19. "Community Board Top Ten Capital Budget Priorities: Their Current Status and Implications for the Budget Process" (New York: City of New York, Office of Management and Budget, Office of Community Board Relations, 1 October 1982), p. 22.

only 14 percent were there recommended changes in local service delivery operations.[20]

Overall, the community boards have had some impact on district capital budgets, particularly in raising the visibility of projects that might otherwise be lost—like the rehabilitation of a playground, resurfacing particular streets, reconstructing certain sewers, and so forth. Their recommendations helped modify citywide policy, for example, by raising the priority of funding for parks maintenance. And an important structure for community input has been put in place. But the city is at a turning point in developing the process. The boards have been deluged, some would say overwhelmed, by budget information and paperwork, and this could prove to be a diversion of energy, if it does not produce more results. There is the increasing danger of frustration and disillusionment among the participants. The consultation process needs to receive a more consistent response from all agencies, especially from OMB. And the budget recommendations need to be more closely tied to both service operations and long-term planning for the community districts. Service delivery and service coordination are generally the weak links in the community board system. An analysis of coterminality offers some insight into why this is so.

Coterminality and Management Decentralization

Coterminality was a centerpiece of the Charter Commission's decentralization strategy. The concept was loaded with a number of other objectives. As used by the Commission, coterminality did not simply mean the technical alignment of local agency service districts with community districts. It also included the decentralization of management authority to agency field officers for each district. This in turn was the basis for the planning and coordination of services through district service cabinets. The strategy has not been successfully fulfilled as yet. The ONG demonstration projects had suggested that coterminality without management decentralization would have little impact on service coordination. The subse-

20. Ernst and Whinney, *City-Wide: District-Level Consultation Evaluation, 1981* (New York: Ernst and Whinney, January 1982), sec. 2, p. 12.

quent history of the community board decentralization approach bears out this thesis. In addition, the seemingly technical issue of common boundaries unleashed some volatile political battles that undercut the whole effort to implement the decentralized system.

The 1975 charter amendments required the creation of community districts with populations between 100,000 and 250,000 (except for the Manhattan business area below 59th Street) by January 1, 1977. The reformers had anticipated that the city would be divided into 40 or 50 new districts, significantly larger than the existing 62 community planning districts.[21] In addition to the criterion that the areas coincide with historic communities, the amendments also required that they "be suitable for the efficient and effective delivery of services by municipal agencies."[22] But when the planners began to devise the new lines, they attempted not to change the existing community boundaries unless absolutely necessary for political or service delivery reasons. And when the public and politicians reviewed the proposals (Beame initially suggested 54 districts), there was even more resistance to change. As a consequence, the total number of districts was reduced merely from 62 to 59. In the process, few reforms were made and those that were often had starkly political overtones. Portions of the Maspeth community in Queens were reunited, but, under racial and religious pressure, Crown Heights was divided into two districts. Having completed the designation of the community boundaries at the last minute in December 1976, the Beame administration did almost nothing to plan for the required changes in agency field districts, which were to become coterminous by January 1, 1980. He left that management and political problem in the lap of the Koch administration.[23]

The strategy of conforming agency service districts with community districts was viewed as a crucial foundation for improving local planning and services. As one former district manager who worked without common districts stated: "Coterminality is of primary im-

21. See "Recommendations: City Government in the Community," p. 11.
22. New York City Charter, amended to June 1, 1977 (New York: City Record, Department of General Services, 1977), sec. 2701.
23. Jewelle W. Bickford, "On the Road to Coterminality," *New York Affairs* 6 no. 1 (1980): 36–38.

portance. The whole identity of a community is its boundaries. If the boundaries are not the same for the city officials that the community deals with, then they have conflicting interests."[24] The Charter specifically required that seventeen operating divisions in eleven agencies establish coterminous field districts. Ten of them had to develop common boundaries with each of the fifty-nine community districts. These included police patrol, parks maintenance, recreation, street cleaning, refuse collection, community social services, community development, youth services, child development, and special services for children. Seven of the agencies only had to conform their boundaries with aggregates of community districts. In this group were housing code enforcement, neighborhood preservation, housing rehabilitation services, street maintenance and repair, and health services, which eventually included the Department of Health and the Department of Mental Health, Mental Retardation, and Alcoholism Services. The Traffic Department was later involved at the borough level. Of the major city services, this exempted the Fire Department; those parts of Social Services which handled income maintenance payments (the local welfare centers), food stamps, and Medicaid certifications; and the Department of Employment, which sponsored the various training and public service jobs programs. Neither the semiautonomous Hospitals Corporation nor the independent Board of Education were included. But most of the core municipal service departments were incorporated in the coterminous system.

Initially Mayor Koch's Community Board Assistance Unit pushed ahead actively to meet the Charter requirement for service agency coterminality by January 1, 1980. With only minor exceptions all agencies essentially achieved their coterminality targets—except the Police Department.[25] In that case, the process proved to be not only technically difficult but bitterly political. As one inside ob-

24. Tom Cusic, interview, 23 June 1982.
25. Child development (day-care) and special services for children were also exempt. Neighborhood preservation and related housing rehabilitation programs continue to use their own catchment areas, which cut across community district lines. Recreation was given until 1983 to conform its lines but was able to institute coterminous districts in July 1981.

server of the battles stated confidentially, "People have a fixation on their local precincts," even though many seemingly local services, like patrol cars, are actually assigned through the central 911 dispatching system. There were major protests in a number of communities over proposed changes in police lines where citizens felt that shifting their districts would lower service levels, reduce land values, or worse. The Police Department had decided to implement coterminality in stages on a borough-by-borough basis. The Bronx precinct lines were shifted in January 1978. But in Manhattan, the coterminality proposals brought immediate strong protests from Little Italy, Soho, and Chinatown where organizations had fought for years to get Chinese-speaking staff into their local precinct. In addition, there was no satisfactory resolution for the Midtown business area where five precincts covered three community districts. In January 1979, the department went ahead and implemented coterminality in Queens, despite concerns in a number of communities about response time and the long distances they would be from their new precinct houses. Within three months, the Laurelton area of Queens errupted in demonstrations. Over 750 people took to the streets to publicize their claim that the administration had failed to keep its promise to provide a police substation for their community. "Pall bearers" carried a black-draped coffin labeled "The Corpse of Laurelton." Signs blared "Koch lies"; he was found guilty at a mock trial and hanged in effigy.[26] Simultaneously there was a loud outcry in the Bensonhurst area of Brooklyn. Here over 1,100 residents turned out for a rally to protest the inclusion of their area in the Coney Island community district. By May, newspaper headlines again showed "Koch hung in effigy." (Actually, this time his effigy was dunked from a bridge into Coney Island Creek in front of a 150-car motorcade.)[27] The political costs were too great. The Community Board Assistance Unit tried to proceed with the Charter mandate, but there was no strong constituency in favor of coterminality either in the affected communities or within the agency. The Police Department received a waiver from implement-

---

26. *Daily News*, Queens ed., 19 March 1979, p. 3.
27. Bruce Berent, "Koch Hung in Effigy on Coterminality," *Flatbush Life*, 7 May 1979, p. 2.

ing coterminality for the entire boroughs of Manhattan, Brooklyn, and Staten Island until January 1, 1983. Even with this three-year extension, the problems were not resolved. In November 1982, Mayor Koch announced that police conterminality would be put into effect for portions of Manhattan and Staten Island. But he called for another year's "delay" in shifting precincts in Brooklyn and an indefinite "deferral" for implementing coterminality in Midtown and Lower Manhattan as well as portions of Staten Island.[28]

These deficiencies are a hindrance to community government in some areas. But a much more important side effect of the political battles over district boundaries was the neglect and delay in implementing the whole management decentralization component of coterminality. This in turn played a major role in undercutting any significant effort to develop service planning and coordination at the local level.

MANAGEMENT DECENTRALIZATION
In addition to common boundaries, the Charter states that coterminality means:

> The head of each designated agency shall assign to each such local service district at least one official with managerial responsibilities involving the exercise of independent judgment in the scheduling, allocation and assignment of personnel and equipment and the evaluation of performance or the management and planning of programs. Each such official shall have operating or line authority over agency programs, personnel and facilities within the local service district.[29]

This has not been accomplished. As one participant commented, "The greatest failure in implementing [the charter amendments] was the complete failure to implement command or management decentralization within the agencies."[30] In general, the agencies

28. "Statement by Mayor Edward I. Koch," no. 284–82 (New York: City of New York, Office of the Mayor, 15 November 1982).
29. New York City Charter, Sec. 2704.
30. Tom Cusic, interview, 23 June 1982.

are less decentralized in terms of local decision making by district-level field officers in the early 1980s than they were when the ONG demonstration project was implemented.

After the bruising battles over coterminality in 1979, the Community Board Assistance Unit began to focus attention on management decentralization. But in January 1980, CBAU was merged with the mayor's unit for community political liaison and placed under new leadership in a combined entity called the Community Assistance Unit. CAU initially spent its time developing goals and a relatively elaborate process for defining and implementing management decentralization. Eight task forces were set up involving district managers and various levels of command within each operating agency, including the field officers whose jobs were to be redefined. The deputy mayor for operations was involved in meetings to kick off the planning process with agency leadership. In addition, there was an effort to move beyond a simple formal definition of power and authority to address the information and training needs of the district officers. But overall the results of this process have been disappointing. Parks revised its job description for maintenance supervisors and organized a formal training program for them at the Urban Academy. Similarly, Sanitation created a district manual for its superintendents and also had them participate in Urban Academy training. By the end of 1982, Highways was just nearing completion of its revised decentralization guidelines, but there was no longer any lump-sum, formula budgeting for street resurfacing at the district level. Other departments like Recreation and Traffic were still in the planning process, and there had been little progress in Housing, Human Resources, or Health. The Police Department was still recognized as the most decentralized agency, but this was primarily due to the nature of their work force (relatively large numbers of personnel with relatively senior field supervisors) and the residue of the administrative decentralization policies implemented under Commissioner Patrick V. Murphy. CAU had not dealt with Police on refining, expanding, or even formally defining management decentralization within the department.

There is little doubt that the city's deep fiscal crisis in the middle and late 1970s inhibited efforts to decentralize service operations.

When administrators were making drastic cutbacks in field forces, there was little to decentralize. Yet the widespread continuing deficiencies in management decentralization require an explanation that goes beyond these funding problems. Management decentralization that involves reorganization of internal agency procedures and major changes in supervisory attitudes is both complex and sensitive. It has not been made a priority by the Mayor's Office or CAU. Even where it is most developed, there have been important changes in emphasis. For example, neither CAU's official statement of its management decentralization goals nor the Parks Department job description for its maintenance supervisors specifically gives field officers responsibility for service planning and service coordination. This is the greatest gap in the community board decentralization system as it now operates.

Service Planning and Coordination

The Charter amendments made service coordination the responsibility of the district service cabinets. But service coordination did not occur. The few data that exist and the judgments of numerous participants and observers confirm a common theme. Service planning and coordination are the weakest links in the system.[31] Many district managers commented that the district service cabinets became primarily points of access to the agencies for dealing with individual service complaints. As one long-time participant said:

> The district service cabinet had little to do with service coordination but a lot to do with access. Individual complaints, like garbage on a particular block, could be handled because of this contact. But sitting down with Traffic to coordinate illegal parking summonses with Sanitation street cleaning schedules was worse than pulling teeth. They did not need to respond. And there was no push from the Administration.[32]

---

31. See, for example, Lebenstein, "A Report Card," p. 12.
32. Tom Cusic, interview, 23 June 1982.

This view is seconded by others who only noted a difference where cabinets had been exposed to the earlier demonstration projects. One district manager reported:

> The charter reforms reinforced and formalized the land use and capital budget experience of the older boards. Day-to-day complaint resolution became the sole responsibility of the district manager. Those district service cabinets with prior experience continued to be what they had been—mechanisms for service coordination with only a small portion of their time devoted to complaints. In areas where people didn't have that experience, the district managers and cabinets became complaint centers, like the old urban action task forces.[33]

Why did the decentralized system develop this way? Service coordination is difficult in the best of times. During a period of fiscal crisis it was even more difficult. There was little or no management decentralization in the agencies and, therefore, little or no flexibility for local cabinet members to work with each other in changing operational service patterns. In addition, earlier experience had shown that coordination requires a coordinator. As the appointee of the community board, the district manager was viewed by the agencies as a community advocate and not as the coordinator of mayoral service departments. The system became highly politicized. One survey showed that almost two-fifths of the initial managers had been administrative assistants to legislators and over 70 percent were involved in their local party clubhouses.[34] Without authority over the agencies or specialized training and experience in administration, the district managers needed time to learn about service operations and establish effective personal relationships with the district members. Yet turnover among the initial group of managers was very high—running at 40 percent citywide in the first year.

Moreover, district managers' salaries declined markedly in relation to those of the agency field officers on the cabinets, when

33. Lorraine Holtz, interview, 9 July 1982.
34. Madeleine W. Adler and Jewel Bellush, "A Look at the District Managers," in *New York Affairs* 6 no. 1 (1980): 50.

compared to the earlier demonstration projects. In 1972, district managers earned an average salary of $25,000—roughly equivalent to or somewhat above the salaries of most cabinet members. In 1977–78, under the new community board system, the District Manager salary had been drastically reduced to $13,600 with a maximum of $20,000. In many cases agency representatives were earning over twice as much as the district cabinet's presiding officer. These salary levels had an effect not only on the experience and competence of the people attracted to the position, but also on the respect and authority that cabinet members would give to district managers. In recent years there has been some improvement in the salary structure, but wages still lag. And, symbolically, the position is still not accorded managerial status by the city's personnel system. In 1983, the average salary was about $32,000. The earlier level in the 1970s demonstration projects would have translated to current salaries in the $40,000 to $45,000 range. Similarly, funding for each district manager's office, although it increased from a paltry $45,000 in 1977 to $85,000 in Fiscal Year 1983, would require at least $150,000 per year to match the levels set in the demonstration projects.[35] The reduction in the number and quality of district office personnel significantly hampered the district managers' ability to staff the development and implementation of interagency projects.

Earlier experience had also shown that decentralized service coordination requires central leadership. Such leadership has not been present. The Office of Community Board Relations at OMB gave detailed guidance and made extensive demands on the community boards and their staff to provide input into the budget consultation process. There was no comparably aggressive central pressure for local involvement in service planning and coordination, and little guidance was offered. As one former district manager explained: "The community board function is not service delivery. It is land use and budgeting—and reactive. There was no training in service delivery. It was lost. Service delivery is com-

35. See the estimate of the Nova Institute in *Funding Needs of New York City's Community Boards* (New York: Nova Institute, 1981), p. 25.

plaints, rather than coordinated planning. . . . Service coordination is a gap. There is not much interaction among the agencies."[36]

Many community boards not only lacked experience in working on service coordination issues, but they did not expect it of themselves or their staff. It was easier for the boards to grasp the individual land use or capital and community development budget issues that were thrust at them. In addition, agencies began to turn to the boards for advice and decisions on other specific matters: approval of priorities for building demolition, vacant lot cleaning, tree pruning, snow removal, and so forth. In these ways, the volunteer board members and their relatively small paid staff were inundated with details, decisions, and paperwork. They had little energy or ability to expand their roles in service coordination or planning. Yet, a number of boards began to recognize this as a deficiency. In one survey, many boards reported that they did not devote sufficient time to helping agencies revise current service delivery procedures and plan new programs, although they ranked service delivery as their highest priority activity.[37] The Mayor's Community Assistant Unit has started to work with district managers, agency representatives, and community board members to train them to move beyond using the cabinets as pothole complaint sessions to look at broader service coordination issues. Hundreds of participants have received orientation sessions, and this has begun to produce some results. Agency officers who have had the training appear to be more aggressive in using cabinet meetings to raise issues. A few cabinets are focusing coordinated attention on single issues like youth, or prostitution, or street peddlers. But generally, the citywide impact of this new attention has not yet overcome the earlier lack of leadership and guidance in coordinating service delivery.

In the absence of an overall drive for management decentralization and local service coordination, some agencies have initiated special projects in selected community districts. The Sanitation Department worked with the Flatbush-Midwood board in Brooklyn to develop a model for redesigning cleaning, collection, and street

36. Jane Planken, interview, 28 June 1982.
37. *Funding Needs of New York City's Community Boards*, pp. 11–13.

sweeping services within the existing allocation of men and equipment. Typical changes included shifting the frequency of collection from two to three times per week in some areas and from three to two in others to account for changing population density; increasing collection at public schools, especially ones that operated breakfast programs; working to increase the proportion of on-schedule pickups; and reducing the frequency of street sweeping in low-density residential areas in order to improve cleaning on commercial streets. After its success in Flatbush, the department commissioned the preparation of a guide to extend the approach to other communities.[38] But to date, only a disappointingly small number of boards have become involved in preparing sanitation service plans for their districts.

The Human Resources Administration established local Human Service Cabinets in five community districts.[39] These cabinets are chaired by the district managers and include representatives from all the major HRA units (child development, special services for children, general social services, income maintenance, food stamps, medical assistance, employment, and community development) as well as the Department for the Aging, the Youth Board, and in some cases the Department of Housing Preservation and Development (HPD). Aside from promoting the exchange of information among the various units, a number of innovative projects have been identified. Closer coordination has been encouraged between income maintenance and special services for children to assure the timely payment of welfare checks to families with children "at risk" or in foster care. In several cases, this has either speeded the release of children from placement or prevented the need for out-of-home care where children are living with their families. A number of cabinets have also tried to address the problem of housing abandonment by coordinating HRA income maintenance and HPD Neighborhood Preservation activities. Many areas face the serious

38. The Nova Institute, *Sanitation: A Guide to Community Board Participation in Planning the Delivery of Services* (New York: Department of Sanitation, October 1979).

39. The Nova Institute, *The Human Service Cabinet: An Assessment of the First Two Years of a Demonstration Project in Coordination of Service Delivery at the Community Level* (New York: Nova Institute, June 1982).

problem of buildings with multiple code violations and many tenants who are not paying rent. Such situations lead to serious deterioration and eventual abandonment unless some action is taken. By coordinating housing and welfare officials, it has been possible to negotiate arrangements to guarantee direct payment of rents to landlords, if the landlords in return agree to a schedule for removing the building code violations. Although the human service cabinets have been partially successful, implementation generally has not proceeded as rapidly or extensively as it might have with more forceful leadership. The cabinets do enable an assertive district manager or agency representative to get units within HRA to respond to issues in ways that would be highly unlikely if the system did not exist. But measurable results, in actual improved delivery of human services to clients and communities, have been minimal.

Aside from a few special projects, essentially the same judgment could be made about the work of the decentralized community board system overall. Success in improving service delivery planning and coordination among cabinet agencies has been minimal.

Options for the Future

The community board system has achieved a low-level equilibrium. The boards are woven into the fabric of city government, but they act at the margins. Some observers are concerned that these participants will become increasingly disillusioned and suspicious that they are caught in an elaborate process, especially in budget matters, which provides a structure for input but has little substantive impact on city government practice. Some see events at a turning point. One commented: "We are now at a fork in the road. We need to develop direction, or community government may fritter away into inaction."[40] But there is little indication of any dynamic demand for change either through pressure from the bottom in the communities or leadership from the top by the mayor or others in city government. Despite this, the gaps in implementing the current system present opportunities for action.

The boards are still not widely recognized in their own com-

40. Jane Planken, interview, 28 June 1982.

munities. One survey by the League of Women Voters in two active board districts in Queens found only 25 percent of the residents aware of their existence; and some observers who have had long experience working with boards throughout the city estimate that the public recognition of the boards would usually be in the 5 to 10 percent range.[41] Many boards have poor attendance and low levels of participation by their members. The boards are often badly organized with no functioning committee structure. And a number of boards are unrepresentative, especially of the poor, the minorities, or the young in their communities. Some analysts see the source of these problems in the politically motivated appointment of uncommitted or unqualified board members by the borough presidents. They call for the development of principles to govern the selection of board representatives, or the creation of a "blue ribbon" committee to monitor the quality of appointments.[42] Given the long history of the community boards' political dependence on the borough presidents, it is not clear that this kind of public suasion would have much impact. Some activists have been particularly concerned about the special disadvantages of community boards in poverty areas. They have tried to provide increased technical assistance to poverty area boards in order to help them develop special projects and compete for citywide resources.[43] These strategies continue to put the burden of change on the boards themselves. Judging by earlier experience, the efforts are not likely to achieve major results. The boards have neither the resources nor the authority to make much progress on their own. City government itself must lead. Even though the Charter Commission put the community boards at the center of its approach to community government, the mayor retained full responsibility for managing all the core city service agencies and, therefore, the mayor is still the key to any significant new development in the decentralized service delivery system. By giving the mayor no role in appointing the district

41. Lebenstein, "A Report Card," p. 17.
42. "The Community Board Improvement Project" (New York: Interface, May 1980).
43. See "Community Board Development Project, First Year Report" (New York: Community Services Society, 1982); and "Technical Assistance Needs for Poverty Area Community Boards" (New York: Interface, n.d.).

managers, the charter created a structure that does not provide incentives to improve service delivery and service coordination. Ironically, although community boards were the strategic focus for change, progress in decentralized management in New York still depends on the mayor having the political interest, vision, or commitment to make his office the center for strengthening the system.

The mayor has three broad options for developing community government *within* the current structure mandated by the 1975 charter reforms:

(1) Allow the current community board system to continue in its present course with no attempt to move it in any major new directions.
(2) Marginally improve pieces of the current approach, like insuring more consistent agency response to community board budget recommendations.
(3) Make a serious commitment to provide mayoral leadership to strengthen the system.

Decentralized mayoral management. The least developed aspects of the current approach, and those which offer the greatest potential payoff, are the various components of a decentralized mayoral management system. An aggressive strategy would involve implementation of management decentralization in the agencies; development of district-level service plans with an emphasis on service coordination projects; and efforts to tie together the district needs statements, land use decisions, service plans, and budget recommendations into a logically integrated process. All this would require more and better-coordinated training and technical assistance for all participants— the agency district officers, the district managers and their staff, and the community board members. It would demand a more consistent and vigorous commitment to the operation of a decentralized system by both the service departments and the overhead agencies. Most of all, it would require leadership and direction from the Mayor's Office.

What to implement. Three of the charter mandates dovetail with a mayoral management strategy and have not been fully implemented.

The Charter (Sec. 2707) requires each agency with service districts in the community to "prepare annually a statement of its service objectives, priorities, programs, and projected activities within each community district and each borough for the new fiscal year," if requested. This has never been done. Currently, agencies do provide information for a District Resource Statement. This provides information on current work force and equipment levels as well as some district-wide indicators of past performance. But it does *not* present an easily understood, future-oriented, descriptive plan for how these district resources will be used to deal with community priorities. How will the police and other agencies deal with after-hours clubs, or safety in particular parks, and so forth? In preparing such service plans, the charter directed the agencies to consult with the relevant district service cabinets and community boards. Thus the agencies were to take the initiative in preparing proposals, and the boards and cabinets would respond. This accurately reflects the essentially reactive posture of the boards. In practice, however, service improvement planning has been left to the boards to initiate. Leaving such a responsibility with the boards is unrealistic and systematic planning has not occurred. To move ahead on this front, the mayor would need to insure that the agencies assume the initiating role in the district planning process. The District Resource Statement was developed as a basis for moving toward joint agency and community planning and was not intended to be a substitute for it. During 1983, the resource statement was scheduled to include future performance indicators, but these would need to be accompanied by operational plans that are prepared by the agencies in consultation with the cabinets and boards. Such plans would not have to be elaborate. Several pages stating simply and clearly how resources would be used to deal with a few priority problems in each community would suffice.

The Charter (Sec. 21) calls for the Mayor's Management Report to indicate "agency service goals, performance measures and actual performance" for each community district "insofar as practicable." This offers the Mayor the opportunity to insure that agency service plans are effectively coordinated in each community district. This has never been done. It could be.

The charter mandates for coterminality (Sec. 2704) have not been completed. This not only involves conforming the service boundaries for Police. More important, it requires pressing forward to meet the management decentralization goals for each community service agency represented on the district service cabinets.

How to implement. This agenda would require strengthening both the central and the district levels of the current structure for community government. Given the technical orientation of this strategy and the link to the Mayor's Management Report, it would be appropriate to give the central role in guiding such an initiative to the management rather than the political side of the Mayor's Office. This would require shifting responsibility to the Deputy Mayor for Operations and his office, rather than leaving it with the more politically oriented Community Assistance Unit. The effort would depend on having sufficient authority with the agencies to move them to decentralize their field management and develop the capacity for district service and service coordination planning. This strategy would require a relatively small but sophisticated centrally-based field liaison staff to work with the cabinets, district managers, and community boards. To function effectively, these staff people would have to be perceived as technical service managers and not as political operatives. This liaison role would be extremely delicate. The staff would work with the agencies as the mayor's managers *and* as technical assistants to the community boards and their district managers. They would have to avoid the danger of undercutting the district managers and provoking the opposition, rather than the cooperation, of the boards.

While strengthening the center, it would also be important to strengthen the district managers and their staff. Both the maximum salary for the district managers, and the overall funding for the district offices would need to be increased. It will be difficult to insure that these increases result in more competence and quality in the managers and not just a windfall to existing employees. Perhaps there could be two different types of district manager position to be selected at the discretion of the local board. One would be a relatively highly qualified managerial appointee, and the other option would be a lower paid community advocate/administrative assistant. But the basic point is that developing effective district planning and service coordination requires more and higher-level staff in the communities. This has not been available. Without such assistance, few interagency projects can be planned or implemented.

A mayoral initiative to develop a decentralized management system could begin to compensate for the weakness of the charter-mandated community board approach. It could improve city service delivery. And, as a "bottom-up" strategy, it would complement the "top-down" productivity programs of the Mayor's Office of Operations and the agencies. But there would be inevitable tensions between the mayor's field representatives and the community boards and district managers. Other local elected officials, especially the borough presidents and council members, might also be suspicious of increased mayoral activity in their districts. Decentralized areal management is complicated and would require sustained support. Results would not be quick or easy, although over the long term they could be substantial.

The Achilles' heel of the New York strategy for community government is its dependence on the commitment and leadership of the mayor. In vesting only marginally increased advisory authority with community boards, the Charter Commission did not overcome this reality. Probably no attainable structure could.

A mayor and his staff could easily be skittish about embarking on a course of decentralization, viewing it essentially as giving up power to other groups like the community boards. Without an unusually strong commitment to citizen participation, this is not likely to happen. However, decentralization does not necessarily mean a reduction of central power. As the earlier district manager cabinet project showed, decentralized management can be a strategy to increase central control over agency field operations in order to improve services in local communities.

The Prospects for Decentralized Management

Although speculative, the signs point to the incremental strengthening of the existing community government system in New York City. There has been, and probably will continue to be, a gradual increase in funding for the community boards and in the salaries for the district managers. Agencies will be encouraged to decentralize, and the Mayor's Office of Operations will become increasingly involved in specific service coordination issues. But there will be no dramatic changes and little passion or deeper commitment to the decentralization process. The future of decentralization is a question that will no doubt surface in future mayoral elections. The community board system offers too obvious a citywide constituency to be ignored. However, the bidding for allegiance that does occur will take place within the present structure. There is little sentiment in the city for another round of charter reforms. Thus, although the 1975 amendments made the structure for community government independent of the mayor, the content of the structure will continue to depend greatly on whomever occupies that office.

The New York City Charter establishes a system that surpasses that of any other big city in providing a formal system for citizen and community advice on local land use and budget decisions. It also created the institutional facade for the decentralized management of service delivery through the district service cabinets. But it undercut the motivation for developing decentralized service planning and coordination by giving the mayor no power in appointing the district managers. The impact of the district manager cabinet as a mayoral management strategy to improve service coordination and responsiveness in New York communities was partially demonstrated a decade ago. Its potential for New York and other big cities, or other levels of government, has yet to be fully tested.

Decentralized areal administration introduces organizational and political alternatives to a national debate which focuses on the merits of categorical programs versus block grants and the New Federalism. Neither of these two current policy polarities deals directly with the many problems of community service coordination and responsiveness that have been described in this study. In contrast, decentralized management suggests organizational techniques that capture the benefits of program specialization (targeting resources, expertise, professionalism) while overcoming its major defects (fragmentation, lack of coordination, and self-serving unresponsiveness).

National, state, and local goals like economic revitalization, strengthening the family, or improving the neighborhood increasingly require the capacity to integrate resources and technical skills across large program units, to address the interconnected whole of a problem rather than its isolated parts. A child facing the risk of placement outside the family may need homemaker support, help with a physical handicap, and mental health assistance. A business considering investment in a neighborhood may be as concerned with safety (or employee training, traffic access, refuse disposal facilities, and community support) as with tax incentives. Yet, government organizational capabilities have not kept pace with these new needs. The district manager cabinet experience suggests that it is both possible and important to strengthen the administrative infrastructure at the community level, rather than limiting reform strategies to the creation of new central bureaucracies, or simply devolving the responsibility for solving problems on governors and mayors in the states and localities.

Federal and state policies could provide incentives to encourage the creation of decentralized institutional systems to manage the coordination of governmental agencies down to the level of the urban neighborhood (or county, subcounty, multicounty, even multi-state areas). Such a strategy assumes continuing a system of national, categorical programs but asserts the need and potential for blending these specialized parts into a comprehensive whole at the point of impact on citizens and communities. Middle-level field managers in the public bureaucracies often have a significant, untapped capacity to assume a more responsible role in this process.

The scope of an organizational policy to promote decentralized management must flow from substantive policy decisions. It could be applied to a relatively narrow sphere (support for the handicapped), to large functional groupings (human services), or to broad national purposes (economic development and full employment). The goals will determine the extent of the need to reshape both the central institutions that provide direction and the decentralized field systems that actually deliver services. It may be more effective at present to look less at grandiose organizational reforms and more at the opportunities for concrete improvements in coordinating services for specific target groups, like particular children and their families. What coordination devices could insure that the millions of children in Head Start and day-care programs actually receive the medical screening and treatment they are eligible for under Medicaid? How can we move the hundreds of thousands of children caught in the limbo of foster care or institutions into permanent homes or appropriate community placements? What coordination can make sure that handicapped young people receive the related services necessary for them to complete their education?[44] We now begin to have the understanding and capacity to address these issues, but we also need the commitment. Without clear policy objectives, organizational tinkering will solve few problems. But without the institutional capability to inform and implement, the policy-making process will too often remain a hollow, rhetorical exercise.

44. For an elaboration of this target group strategy, see John Mudd, "Coordinating Services for Children," *Human Services Coordination: A Panel Report and Accompanying Papers,* ed. Harold Orlans (New York: PICA Press in Association with the Council of State Governments and the National Academy of Public Administration, 1982), pp. 22–45.

INDEX

Addiction Services Agency, 85
Adler, Madeleine, 210*n*
Allee, Dennis, 153
Allison, Graham, 2*n*, 4*n*
Almond, Gabriel A., 6*n*
Alpert, Geraldine, 82*n*
Altschuler, Alan A., 32*n*
American Federation of State, County, and Municipal Employees, 98
Andrews, Kenneth H., 101*n*
Areal administration: and ONG, 68–69, 81–82, 93, 95–96; and specialization, 75–76, 82–83, 85; by district managers, 88–92; and future options, 219. *See also* Decentralized administration; District manager cabinets
Arnstein, Sherry, 41*n*

Banfield, Edward C., 13*n*
Barrett, Glen, 160
Barton, Allen H., 9*n*
Bay Ridge, 148; named demonstration district, 101; described, 121, 122–23; direct services in, 127
Beame, Abraham, 152–53, 154–55, 184, 204
Belliveau, Paul, 147*n*
Bellush, Jewel, 210*n*
Berent, Bruce, 206*n*
Bergunder, Ann F., 4*n*
Bickford, Jewelle W., 204*n*
Black, Guy, 88*n*
Blanc, Robert E., 180*n*
Blumenthal, Ralph, 107*n*

Board of Education, 49
Bock, Edwin A., 69*n*
Bombardier, Gary, 157*n*
Boyle, John M., 9*n*, 158*n*, 169*n*
Bronx River Shoelace Park, 124–26
Bruhn, Marsha S., 45*n*
Brumback, Ronald, 114*n*, 118*n*
Budgets, financing: and municipal unions, 18–19; for Model Neighborhoods, 43–44; for multiservice centers, 53, 54; of district manager system, 91, 165, 210–11; integration of, in Rockaways, 141–43; decentralization of, 146–50, 197–203; and New York's default crisis, 154, 155; city, under charter reform, 192
Bureaucracies: inattention to workings of, 4–5; and lack of coordination, 8–9, 11, 26–29, 53, 54, 167–70; and specialization, 14; and centralization, 15; and civil service system, 16–18; vs. citizen participation, 33, 39–40, 42–43, 48–51, 52; and ONG, 81, 82–83, 87, 95, 103, 106–07, 143–45
Bureau of the Budget, 149
Bushwick, 148; named demonstration district, 101; vacant-lots problem in, 113, 114; summer youth program in, 116; described, 128–29; lead paint poisoning problem in, 130–34; Highway funds in, 146
Butler, Bernard, 147*n*

Capital Budget/Community Development Program, 199
Centralization: of executive authority, 15; and problem of "distance," 16; of management, 26–32; administrative, 35, 41–42, 59, 61–64; attacked by Scott Commission, 93; as precondition for decentralization, 143, 181, 183–84, 188; dangers of over-, 168–69
Charter Commission, 153–56, 190–91, 203, 215
Child Development, Agency for, 27
Child Health Station, 147–48
Citizen participation, 32–52, 131, 184–88. *See also* Community boards
Citizens' Union, 45
City Planning Commission, 149, 194, 195
City Planning Department, 85, 192
Civil service, 16–18
Clark, Fran LaSpina, 158n
Colocation, 52–57
Command decentralization (police), 76–78
Community Action Program (CAP) Agencies (CAA), 25, 33, 34, 36–40
Community Assistance Unit (CAU), 192–93, 208–09, 212, 218
Community Board Assistance Unit (CBAU), 192, 206, 208
Community boards, 131, 155; history of, 44–48; under charter reform, 190–93, 209–14; and land use, 193–97; and geographic budgeting, 197–203; future prospects of, 214–22
Community control, 32–52, 184–88
Community Development Agency, 27
Community Planning Districts (CPD), 70–71, 73–74
Community Service Officer programs (CSOs), 42, 43, 130

Compartmentalization, problems of, 14–15
Coordination, of service delivery: defined, 2, 7; theories aout, 3–4; overview of problem, 6–11, 13–22; centralization to promote, 26–32; and CAAs, 38–39; and Model Cities programs, 41–44; and mayoral outreach programs, 52–57, 59, 63–64; and ONG, 67–68, 79–82, 89, 95, 104–08, 187; through district manager projects, 108–20, 125–26, 131–34, 136–39, 141–43; analysis of problem in big cities, 166–84; affected by budgeting process, 202–03; and coterminality issue, 203–04, 207; under charter reform, 209–14
Costikyan, Edward N., 18n, 34n
Coterminality, 181–83, 203–09, 217–18
Council Against Poverty, 36, 37
Crown Heights: named demonstration district, 101; tests social service information system, 119–20; described, 134–35; neighborhood preservation program in, 136–39; and coterminality problem, 182, 183, 204
Crozier, Michel, 17n, 22n

Dahl, Robert A., 22n, 71n
Darnton, John, 152n
Davidson, Joseph, 96n
Decentralization: political, 32–53, 65–67, 153, 155; school, 48–51; and multiservice centers, 57; command (police), 76–78; of budgeting, 146–50, 197–203; management, 177–84, 207–09, 216–22. *See also* Decentralized administration
Decentralized administration: need for, seen, 63–64; planning for,

through ONG, 64–75; and areal administration, 75–76; police model for, 76–78; and city agencies, 78–85; problems in ONG plan, 85–87; district managers' role in, 88–92; costs of program for, 91, 165, 210–11; and politics, 92–100; demonstration districts for, 100–01; operation of cabinets in, 102–08; projects undertaken by cabinets under, 108–43; central leadership needed in, 143, 181, 183–84, 188; ONG's central role in, 143–46; in budgeting, 146–50, 197–203; institutionalizing program of, 150–56; and successes of program, 158–63, 164–66; and limitations of program, 163–64; problem of coordination under, 166–76, 209–14; and decentralization of authority, 178–81; and coterminality, 181–83, 203–09; and community groups, 186–88; through community boards, 190–203; future of, 214–22
Decentralized management, 177–84, 207–09, 216–22
Derthick, Marths, 4n
DeWitt, John, 56n
District manager cabinets: formation of, 67–70; composition of, 80 (table); and incentives, 87; budgeting of, 91, 165, 210–11; politics of, 92–100; demonstration districts for, 100–01; first months in operation, 102–08; coordination projects of, 108–20; and projects to increase responsiveness, 120–43; and ONG's role, 143–50; institutionalizing, 150–56; lesson of experiment, 158–66; coordination problems illuminated by experiment, 167–84; and neighborhood responsiveness, 184–89; under

charter reform, 190–93, 209–14; and future options, 218–19. See also Community boards; Office of Neighborhood Government
District managers: role of, 88–92; first months in job, 102–03, 104–05, 106–08; as "brokers," 121–28; role in poverty areas, 128–34; as "entrepreneurs," 134–43; problems of, 143–44; usefulness as coordinators, 167–75; under charter reform, 190, 210–11; and future options, 218–19
District Resource Statement, 198, 217
Downs, Anthony, 175n
DuBrul, Paul, 21n
Duhan, Dick, 136, 175n

Eidsvold, Gary, 83n
Elazar, Daniel, 72n
Elections: and responsiveness, 35, 36; turnouts for, in New York City, 40 and n, 49–50; and charter revision, 155. See also Political parties; Politics
Elish, Herbert, 97n
Environmental Protection Administration, 27, 78, 177

Fainstein, Norman I., 13n, 187n
Fainstein, Susan S., 13n, 157n, 158n, 161n, 187n
Fantini, Mario, 50n
Farr, Walter G., Jr., 66n
Feldstein, Lewis, 62n, 67n, 94n
Fesler, James W., 17n, 65n, 68n
Field administration: and civil service system, 17–18; and productivity programs, 31–32; overcentralization of, 63; ONG strategies for, 67–101; defining units for, 70–74; and police reorganization, 76–78; and problems encountered by ONG, 85–88; and district managers,

88–92; usefulness of district
cabinet system in, 103–07, 158–60,
168–69, 178–81; and
management decentralization,
207–09
Fitch, Lyle C., 25*n*
Flatbush, 212–13
Frederickson, George, 69*n*
Friedman, Nathalie S., 12*n*, 109*n*,
122*n*, 186*n*

Gans, Sheldon P., 29*n*
Gardner, Sid, 67*n*
Geographic budgeting, 197–203. *See
also* Budgets, financing
Gifford, Kilvert Dun, 25*n*
Ginsberg, Sigmund G., 17*n*
Gittell, Marilyn, 50*n*
Golding, Naomi, 122*n*, 186*n*
Goodgold, Sally, 202*n*
Goodman, Roy, 153, 154–55
Gordon, Diana R., 24*n*
Gotterher, Barry, 60*n*
Grollman, Judith E., 53*n*
Grosenick, Leigh E., 21*n*
Grossman, David A., 149*n*
Gulick, Luther, 3*n*

Hallman, Howard, 34*n*
Hamilton, Edward, 30*n*, 97–98
Haney, Paul, 1*n*
Head Start, 37
Health Department, 82–83, 96, 114,
132, 133, 147–48
Hearn, Robert W., 178*n*
Heclo, Hugh, 5*n*
Heginbotham, Stanley J., 76*n*, 101*n*,
134*n*, 169*n*
Heilbron, Susan, 159*n*
Highways Department, 87, 96,
146–47, 179, 208
Hiltbrand, Ed., 122–23
Hirsch, Eloise, 55*n*
Holtz, Lorraine, 190
Horton, Gerald T., 29*n*

Hotel Task Force, 24
House, Robert, 108*n*, 122
Housing: problems of public project,
105–06; lead paint poisoning
problem in, 131–34; in Rockaways,
135; new construction vs. lost units,
figures on, 136*n*; preservation of,
in Crown Heights, 136–39; and
ONG's problems with HDA,
179–80; and land use issues,
193–97; and abandonment
problem, 213–14
Housing and Development
Administration (HDA), 96, 132,
179–80
Housing and Urban Development,
Department of (HUD), 53–54
Human Resources Administration
(HRA), 177; created, 27;
specialization within, 79–82; plans
to decentralize, 95, 96; provides
direct services, 126–27; and lead
paint poisoning problem, 133;
ONG's problems with, 179–80;
establishes Human Service Cabinets,
213
Human Service Cabinets, 213–14
Hunts Point, 54–55

Jacobs, Jane, 68*n*
Jones, Sidney E., 116*n*, 130–31
Josephson, Bill, 67*n*

Kahn, Alfred J., 8*n*
Kaiser, John A., 60*n*
Kamerman, Sheila B., 8*n*
Katz, Howard G., 134*n*
Kaufman, Herbert, 2*n*, 5*n*, 14*n*, 69*n*
Keller, Suzanne, 72*n*
Kelly, Thomas V., 77*n*
Kerr, Andrew, 94*n*
Knott, Jack, 3*n*
Koblentz, Joel D., 118*n*
Koch, Edward, 156, 192–93, 204,
206–07

Kolberg, William H., 21n
Kotler, Milton, 34n
Krauskopf, James A., 37n
Kriegel, Jay, 97−98, 150

Landau, Martin, 3n
Land use, 193−97
Lane, Robert, 147n
Langsam, Janet, 105n, 141
La Noue, George R., 34n
LaSpina, Fran, 157n
Lawrence, Paul R., 88n, 92n
Lead paint poisoning, in Bushwick,
    130−34
Lebenstein, David, 195n
Lee, Elwyn C., 77n
Lehman, Maxwell, 34n
Leone, Sebastian, 66n
Liebman, Lance, 66n
Lindblom, Charles E., 4n, 22n
Lindsay, John, 1n, 16 and n, 26, 66n;
    and outreach strategies, 57, 59−60;
    and ONG, 65−66, 70, 92−94,
    97−100, 144−45, 151; retires as
    mayor, 150
Lipsky, Michael, 5n
Little city halls, 57−59
Lorsch, Jay W., 88n, 92n
Lubavitcher Rebe, 135
Lynn, Frank 155n

Maas, Arthur, 68n
Maas, Robin, 76n, 96n, 165n, 181n
McDowell, Chuck, 159
Management decentralizaion, 177−84,
    207−09, 216−22
Manes, Donald R., 66n
Manpower and Career Development
    Agency, 27
Marrero, Victor, 103n, 107n, 129−30
Marris, Peter, 4n
Martin, L. John, 19n
Mason, Bryant, 62n
Maspeth-Ridgewood, 148, 204; named
    demonstration district, 101;

described, 121, 123; environmental
    monitoring in, 123−24; "one-
    step service" developed in, 126−27
Mayor, office of: and increased
    centralization, 15−16; and CAPs,
    39−40; and Model Cities programs,
    41−42; and community boards, 45;
    and multiservice centers, 54;
    outreach programs of, 57−64; and
    ONG, 65−66, 88−89, 90, 92−94,
    97−100, 144−45; instability of,
    183−84; authority undercut by
    charter reform, 190−91; and
    geographic budgeting, 197; and
    management decentralization,
    208−09; and future of decentralized
    management, 215−20
Mayor's Management Report, 217, 218
Meade, Curt, 114n
Media: impact on neighborhood
    concerns, 19−21; and charter
    reforms, 155, 206
Merit system, and civil service, 16−18
Mezzardi, Joseph, 159
Middleton, Donald J., 112n, 139−41,
    179n
Milton, Catherine H., 77n
Mitchell, Robert, 123n
Model Cities program, 33, 34, 41−44,
    115, 129−30
Morris, Charles R., 154n
Mott, Basil J. F., 5n
Moynihan, Daniel P., 157n
Mudd, John, 149n, 222n
Multiservice centers, 52−57, 177
Murphy, Patrick V., 208
Mustalish, Anthony C., 83n, 114n, 159

Neighborhood Action Program, 136
Neighborhood city halls, 57−59
Neighborhood councils, 44−48. See
    also Community boards
Neighborhood government, 33−34,
    184−88
Neighborhood Police Teams, 77n

Neighborhoods: and responsiveness issue, 11–13; shift of power from, 18; media's impact on concerns of, 20–21; and productivity programs, 30–32; citizen participation in, 32–52; and outreach programs, 57–64; defined, 70–74; coordination projects in, 108–20; projects to improve service delivery in, 120–43; responses to district cabinets, 184–89. *See also* Community boards; District manager cabinets; specific neighborhoods

Neighborhood Youth Corps, 115

Newfield, Jack, 21n

New York City Charter: revision of, 150, 153–56; reform provisions, implementation, 190–93, 204, 205, 207; and land use, 193–97; and coterminality issue, 203–09; and future of decentralized management, 215–20

New York Times, 155

Nie, Norman H., 6n

Niskanen, William A., 3n

Nolan, Patricia, 114n

Nolting, Orin F., 68n

Nordlinger, Eric A., 18n

Novick, Lloyd F., 83n

Ocean Hill–Brownsville, 49

Office of Community Board Relations (OCBR), 198, 211

Office of Management and Budget (OMB), 197–98, 201

Office of Neighborhood Government (ONG): formation of, 65–70; defines neighborhoods, 70–74; areal administration as objective, 75–76; police decentralization as model for, 76–78, 79; organization of agencies under, 78–82; problems encountered by, 82–88; role of district managers in,

88–92; politics of, 92–100; demonstration districts for, 100–01; role of, in decentralization, 143–50; and institutionalizing cabinet system, 150–56; reactions to program, 159–66; and coterminality, 181–83. *See also* District manager cabinets

Office of Neighborhood Services, 152

Office of Special Housing Services, 24

Ostrom, Vincent, 3n

Otey, Charles F., 162n

Parks Department, 73–74, 84–85, 112–13, 179, 208

Parks Vandalism Task Force, 112–13

Patrolmen's Benevolent Association, 98

Petrocik, John R., 6n

Plunkitt, George W., 23

Police Department, 73, 87, 179; and Model Cities program, 42, 43; command decentralization in, 76–78, 95, 208; and park safety, 112–13; and coterminality issue, 205–07

Political decentralization: through citizen participation, 32–53; and district manager cabinets, 93; and city charter revision, 153, 155

Political parties, 93 and n; decline of traditional role, 5–6, 13, 15–16, 19–21; and municipal unions, 18, 19

Politics: of ONG, 92–100; in Bushwick, South Bronx, 128–29, 131; in Crown Heights, 134–35; and institutionalizing cabinet system, 151, 152, 154–56; and community boards, 191, 210, 215; and coterminality issue, 204, 205–07. *See also* Elections; Political parties

PPB (planning-programming-budgeting) systems, 25, 26, 30

Pressman, Jeffrey L., 8n
Productivity programs, 30–32
Professionalism, growth of, 22

Quick Response Citizen Complaint
Service, 117

Rabinow, Barney, 73n
Rebe, Lubavitcher, 135
Recreation Department, 95, 96, 113
Rein, Martin, 4n, 7n
Reorganizaion, governmental:
overview of, 2–6; through
centralization of management,
26–32; through citizen participation,
32–52; through colocation,
52–57; through neighborhood
outreach programs, 57–64. See also
Decentralized administration
Responsiveness, of service delivery:
defined, 2, 11; overview of
problem of, 11–13, 14–22; and
elections, 35; and community
boards, 47–48; and little city halls,
59; and ONG, 67–68, 89,
184–89; district manager projects to
improve, 120–43
Richardson, Elliot, 67n
Ridley, Clarence E., 68n
Riordan, William L., 23n
Rockaways, 148; named demonstration
district, 101; cabinet officers
cooperate in 104; described,
135–36; budgets integrated in,
141–43
Rogers, Theresa F., 12n
Roggeman, Peter, 108n
Rose, Stephen M., 4n
Rosenbloom, David L., 19n
Rucigay, Emil, 122–23

Sanderson, John, 105n, 116n, 122
Sanitation Department, 73, 87, 179,
208; problems of, 27, 86; and Model
Cities, 42; opposes decentralization,

96–97; and coordination problems,
109–10, 111–12, 114; and
redesign of services, 212–213
Savas, E. S., 17n
Sawyer, Susan G., 140n
Sayre, Wallace, 5n, 93n
Schools: and CAP, 37; decentralization
of, 48–51, 173; safety of, in
South Bronx, 129–30
Schultze, Charles L., 5n
Scott Commission, 93
Seidman, Harold, 5n
Service delivery: and the "rat
problem," 8–9; citizens'
perceptions of, 12–13; impact of
municipal unions on, 18–19;
impact of the media on, 19–21; for
emergencies, 23–24; and
productivity programs, 30–32; and
CAP, 36–40; and Model Cities
program, 42–44; and community
boards, 46–48; through multiservice
centers, 52–57; through Urban
Action Task Force, 59–64; effect
of district cabinets on, 163–64;
effect of district cabinets on,
163–64, 165–66; and
decentralization, 177, 211–12; and
HRA, 213–14. See also
Coordination, of service delivery;
District manager cabinets;
Responsiveness, of service delivery
Severo, Richard, 9
Shapiro, Paul Meinetz, 178n
Sherman, Lawrence W., 77n
Shoelack Park project, 124–26
Smith, Bruce L. R., 34n
South Bronx, 103, 146–47; named
demonstration district, 101;
park-cleaning problem in, 112;
parking problem in, 114–15;
service monitoring in, 118;
described, 128–29; school safety in,
129–30
Specialization: of programs, 8–11,

14–15, 21–22; reinforced by civil service, 17; and coordination problem, 43, 63; and citizen participation, 51–52; as problem in areal administration, 75–76, 82–83, 85
Stanley, David T., 19n
Stein, Andrew, 66n
Sugarman, Jule, 96n
Sundquist, James L., 3n, 38n
Superagencies, 26–29, 179–81
Sutton, Percy E., 66n
Szanton, Peter, 2n

Task Force on Reorganization, 26
Thomas, Robert McG., Jr., 152n
Traffic Department, 74, 85, 109–10
Truman, David Bicknell, 69n

Uniform Land Use Review Procedures (ULURP), 193–97
Unions: municipal, 18–19; teachers', 48, 49, 50; and ONG, 98
United Federation of Teachers, 49, 50
Urban Academy, 208
Urban Action Task Force, 59–64, 115, 150

Verba, Sidney, 6n
Voting. See Elections
Votreflich, Max, 159

Wakefield-Edenwald, 103, 148; named demonstration district, 101;

examples of coordination of services in, 105–6, 110, 116; Citizen Complaint Service in, 117; described, 121–22; Shoelace Park developed in, 124–26; employment program in, 127–28; Highway funds in, 146
Walsh, Annamarie Hauck, 25n, 32n
Walsh, David, 159
Walton, Richard E., 56n
Warren, Roland L., 4n
Washington Heights, 31, 148; named demonstration district, 101; street-cleaning problems in, 110–11; park safety in, 112–13; described, 135; public employment jobs in, 139–41
Washnis, George J., 44n
Water Resources Department, 85
Weisman, Steven R., 152n
Wellington, Harry H., 19n
White, Kevin, 57
Wildavsky, Aaron B., 3n, 8n
Wilson, James Q., 5n, 13n
Winter, Ralph K., Jr., 19n
Wood, Jeffrey S., 66n
Work Relief Employment Program (WREP), 140–41

Yates, Douglas, 11n, 13n
Yin, Robert K., 13n
Youth Services Agency, 27, 116

Zimmerman, Joseph F., 34n